*Planning and Growth in Rich
and Poor Countries*

Contributors:

WALTER BIRMINGHAM, B.SC. (*Econ.*)
FREDA CONWAY, B.SC., M.A. (*Com.*)
A. G. FORD, M.A., D.PHIL.
P. S. GROVES, B.SC. (*Econ.*), PH.D.
S. K. NATH, B.A., B.SC. (*Econ.*), PH.D.
M. J. PULLEN, B.A., M.A. (*Econ.*)
HOWARD REES, M.A.
J. W. WILLIAMS, M.COMM., PH.D.

Planning and Growth
in Rich and Poor Countries

Edited by
W. BIRMINGHAM and A. G. FORD

Foreword by
PROFESSOR R. L. MEEK

FREDERICK A. PRAEGER · *Publishers*
New York · Washington

BOOKS THAT MATTER

*Published in the United States of America in
1966 by Frederick A. Praeger, Inc., Publishers
111 Fourth Avenue, New York 3, N.Y.*

© *George Allen & Unwin Ltd., 1965*

Library of Congress Catalog Card Number: 66-16834

PRINTED IN GREAT BRITAIN

FOREWORD
by
Professor R. L. Meek

The preparation of this book was begun at Leicester University in 1963, on the initiative of Mr Walter Birmingham and with the active encouragement of the late Professor A. G. Pool. Under Professor Pool's guidance, the Department of Economics at Leicester had made something of a specialty of the subject of Economic Development, and Mr Birmingham's suggestion that a collective textbook should be written was enthusiastically received by the staff.

At that time all the contributors to the present volume (with one exception) were working at Leicester University and taking part in a course on Economic Development designed primarily for second and third year economics students. Mr Birmingham and Dr Ford lectured on the more general and theoretical aspects of growth, and Miss Conway on the demographic aspects; Dr Groves and Mr Pullen dealt with a number of questions relating to growth in Great Britain; and Dr Nath, Mr Rees and Mr Birmingham discussed problems of development in three countries of which they had extensive personal knowledge—India, Sierra Leone and Ghana respectively. The essays in the present book—with the exception of Professor Williams's very welcome piece on New Zealand—have grown from the contributions made by each of the authors to this lecture course.

Mr Birmingham and Dr Ford, as editors of the volume, have aimed at much the same audience as called forth the original lecture course—namely, second and third year students of economics. The theoretical sections have been kept fairly simple, however, in the hope that others besides students of economics may find the book useful.

Although only two of the contributors now remain at Leicester, the Department of Economics is still carrying on and extending the tradition of specialized teaching in the field of Economic Development which was built up in Professor Pool's time. The present book is one which I know we shall wish to use as a textbook at Leicester for many years to come, and I venture to hope that students and teachers in other universities may also find it a worth-while addition to the literature on this fascinating and vastly important topic.

Department of Economics
Leicester University
March 1965

NOTES ON THE AUTHORS

Walter Birmingham, B.Sc. (Econ.)—At one time or another on the faculties of economics in the Universities of Wales, Ghana and Leicester, and Roosevelt University, Chicago. Now Warden of Toynbee Hall, London.

Freda Conway, B.Sc., M.A. (Com.)—A graduate of London and Manchester Universities. Lecturer in Statistics at Leicester University and now at Salford Royal College of Advanced Technology. Author of *Descriptive Statistics*.

A. G. Ford, M.A., D.Phil.—Graduated at the University of Oxford 1951 and awarded the D.Phil. in 1956. Lecturer and Senior Lecturer in Economics at the University of Leicester in 1953–65. Now Reader in Economics at the University of Warwick. Author of *The Gold Standard 1880 to 1914: Britain and Argentina*.

Paul S. Groves, B.Sc. (Econ.), Ph.D.—Took his first degree at the University College of Hull in 1942, though he spent his final year at the London School of Economics. He held a Rouse-Ball Studentship at Trinity College, Cambridge from 1945 to 1948. Lecturer in Economics at the University of Leicester until 1964.

S. K. Nath, B.A., B.Sc. (Econ.), Ph.D.—A graduate of the Universities of Delhi and London where he was awarded his Ph.D. for a thesis on Welfare Economics. Author of articles in *Oxford Economic Papers* and *Economic Journal*.

M. J. Pullen, B.A., M.A. (Econ.)—Graduate of the Universities of Keele and Manchester. Taught economics in a grammar school for a year. Now Lecturer in Economics at the University of Leicester.

Howard Rees, M.A.—A graduate of the University in Wales. He has held academic appointments at Fourah Bay College, Sierra Leone, and at the Universities of Belfast and Durham. He is now Lecturer in Economic Statistics at the University of Leicester.

J. W. Williams, M.Comm., Ph.D.—A graduate of the Universities of Otago and London, Professor of Economics at the University College of Ghana until 1961 and now Professor of Economics at the University of Otago.

CONTENTS

TABLES

DIAGRAMS

INTRODUCTION

When economics was still a young science the growth of the wealth of nations was a vital aspect of the subject. Increasing sophistication brought pre-occupations with other aspects which so fascinated the theoreticians that economic growth was left almost entirely to the applied economist and the economic historian. But in the last three decades the analytical economists have turned their attention increasingly to the theoretical problems of economic growth. Growth models have become ever more complex. The stagnation of the 1930's with their mass unemployment has passed into the province of the economic historian while we watch the rate of growth of the gross national product and assess it critically. No longer do we set the merits of private enterprise and *laissez faire* against those of the planned economy because with economic growth as an economic objective of high priority in every nation, planning has become an essential exercise for every government whether it be of a country with an advanced economy or of one which is the least developed of the underdeveloped. Anyone with any pretensions to understanding the present world economic situation or the present state of economic science has to know something about economic growth and how it can be planned.

The purpose of this book is in the first place to provide students of current affairs, both inside and outside the universities, with a theoretical framework for an intelligent appreciation of the problems of economic growth which face the nations of the West now that they have embarked upon the planning of their economies. No attempt has been made to examine specifically any of the economies of the Soviet bloc because the political and social system of those countries creates such great differences from the Western economies as to vitiate comparison. But the influence of Soviet thinking does of course permeate all current discussion of the theory of economic growth and the Western practice of planning is also beginning to be influenced, particularly in the less developed countries of the neutral world.

The second objective is to furnish case studies of economies with widely differing circumstances in order to display the peculiar problems of economic growth and planning in different economic contexts. In particular the contrast between the high-income countries and the low-income countries is underlined. But since density of population is also such a significant factor in planning, the case studies have been chosen to bring out this contrast also.

Of the high-income densely populated countries, an extensive analysis of the United Kingdom has been made both in its general and in its regional aspects since it is becoming increasingly obvious that planning has to be intimately concerned with regional development if national objectives are to be realized. New Zealand has been chosen to illustrate the economic development of a high-income sparsely populated country.

Among the poorer regions of the world, India has been taken to illustrate the problems of the densely populated countries and West Africa those of the sparsely populated. West Africa has other characteristics which make it particularly attractive as a special area of study. It has many small nations newly come to independence which may possibly not be economically viable except as parts of larger units; Sierra Leone is one such and is included in these case studies. But also within West Africa is Ghana which has already developed her economy to provide a national income per head some three times as great as that of India.

An appendix has been added which discusses population trends as background material for the more specifically economic body of the book.

CHAPTER I

Economic Growth: A Theoretical Outline

by A. G. FORD

1. *Introduction*

By economic growth and economic development we shall mean in
this study sustained increases in output per head, for it is only by this
that a community's living standards can rise over the long period. It
is not sufficient to look at output growth in absolute terms, for this
could be obtained by disproportionate use of factor inputs with
diminishing returns prevailing such that output per head might actually fall. Indeed, this definition carries with it the implications of
better methods, changed methods, the acceptance and adoption of
technical progress, which are so necessary to provide growth in output per head once the spectacular economies of scale relating to given
productive techniques have been exhausted and the Malthusian
demon of diminishing returns to labour begins to appear.

This notion of change—basically 'non-marginal' change—is an
essential ingredient of economic growth; not only is economic change
important, but also social, political and religious changes can be
vitally conducive to economic growth. In economic matters the process of economic growth has to be examined with respect to both the
supply of goods and services and the demand for them. Supply requires us to consider changes in productive methods, industrial
structure and geographical location; innovations, inventions, the
application of existing techniques in new territories and the many un-
spectacular minor improvements all contributing to raise output per
head. These changes may well be different in degree depending on the
'stage' the economy concerned has attained. When considering the
demand for goods and services we must remember that as real output
and incomes per head increase demands for individual goods will not
expand proportionately to preserve the old pattern of demands—
increases in incomes will be directed more and more towards the
purchase of new goods, not previously enjoyed. Part of the problem
of attaining smooth economic growth lies in matching the increases

in outputs of individual goods with the increases in demands for them and this has to be embraced within the aggregative problem of matching the increase in total output with the increase in total demand. The importance of this will vary from country to country, the former being perhaps more important for a rich than for a poor country.

The rapidity or otherwise of changes in social attitudes, in the political framework, in aspirations and in comprehension, will have a vital bearing on the economic process of economic growth. Environmental factors will be crucial in determining the responses of a society to economic stimuli and the extent to which they are translated into economic growth.

Before examining these issues in detail one important question must be raised: why seek to grow? Many motives can be adduced: on the 'respectable' side, growth can increase a poor country's economic well-being by the relief of abject poverty and famine, together with the associated discontent, while a richer country can be enabled to enjoy a fuller life with the masses enjoying consumption patterns previously only for the few. Yet other less reputable, but equally important motives exist—to satisfy greed or pride, and to augment power. Growth involves change of all kinds, while the case for growth is often treated as self-evident by many, but it is important to ask further whether a happy, stable, and not always primitive, society should be broken up by growth plans and whether what these offer is a real improvement in social as well as economic terms. The economist, as the 'new missionary', must ponder these questions.

Of course, many members of a society will actively want to enjoy higher living standards, but are they aware of, and are they prepared to accept, the price which growth demands—namely, changes of all kinds, social and political upheavals, the miseries of the displaced, the victims of progress? The price is demanded not only of underdeveloped territories in Africa, say, but also of mature economies such as Britain. As human beings we all want the fruits of growth without the pangs. Hence there is need for greater awareness of all that is implied by rapid economic growth, when framing policies and making choices or providing incentives to help 'win over' people to changed methods.

Assuming, then, that growth is desired, how might growth be encouraged and guided? Although this survey concerns itself mainly with economies having a growing monetary sector, a few words are needed first on the subsistence type of economy with few, if any, monetary transactions. Here, needs are simple—food, clothing, fuel and shelter. Material wealth is less prized than other goals such as athletic or procreative prowess. For growth in output per head to take place, political and social changes are necessary and in particular changes in objects desired—people must become materially acquisitive—while greater output per head may be coaxed out by taxes on such peasants to induce them to produce a surplus. Such social processes may be initiated by 'alien' interests—the missionary, the teacher, the plantation or mine owner, the foreign entrepreneur. With greater awareness of other and better consumption and production possibilities, the intrusive spread of the monetary economy, and the educative process, the change in values and the acceptance of new methods may be facilitated. Comprehension of these changes and the significance of the development process will strongly influence the pace of the growth in output per head and the expansion of the monetary sector.

To revert to our main concern—growth in output per head in economies with considerable and growing monetary sectors—let us recall one basic Keynesian principle: expenditure generates income, output and employment. In more detail:

Private consumption expenditure + private investment expenditure + governmental current and capital expenditure + exports of goods and services, all valued at market prices − taxes on expenditure − imports of goods and services = National Product at factor cost.

At first sight, it would appear that to achieve economic growth all a country need do is to ensure by suitable fiscal and monetary policies that aggregate expenditure grows annually by the desired percentage. Two obstacles immediately arise. First and of the utmost importance, supply of output, which this naïve approach ignores, may be unresponsive, so that all that growing expenditure produces is rising prices and real output per head does not increase. Secondly, even if supply is responsive to growing domestic expenditure, purchases from abroad may increase rapidly while export sales, not within one's immediate policy control, may fail to expand sufficiently. A balance of payments deficit then emerges and any rises in prices would aggravate this. Indeed some see economic growth as the expansion of the supply of products, with little attention paid to the market for these products, but over-concentration on the supply side has obscured one important aspect of economic development, that markets need to be there and to be expanding to absorb increasing output; it is not enough to produce a growing volume of candles when the population want electric light bulbs. Furthermore, it must constantly be remembered that markets cover not only home demand

B

but also world demand. It is not enough to produce more output, important though this is, attention must be paid to the composition, quality and marketability—the economic worth—of the increased output.

2. *Growth without change*

After such warnings, we can consider how output per head may be expanded; the discussion will be in real terms which eliminate price changes, while the further problems posed by rising prices will be considered later.

Basically, whether we consider output of goods from a firm, an industry, or a country, we assert that the volume of output per unit of time has a precise relationship to the quantity and quality of the inputs of factors of production. This we call the production function. Moreover, it is not enough for our purposes to consider how the flow of output can be increased; we are concerned with growth in output per head, which is the measure of improvement in living standards and material well-being. If the labour force forms a constant proportion of total population, this means we have to focus attention on ways and means of increasing the productivity of labour, or output per worker, and of maintaining the rate of increase, a more severe task than increasing output in absolute terms, especially if we recall the bogy of diminishing returns.

What are the possibilities of achieving such increases in productivity of labour assuming given techniques and unchanged factor qualities? More output can be obtained from the firm or farm by adding more of any one input, although eventually marginal returns diminish and total output may ultimately decline, so that this method holds out little hope. More promising is the expansion of all inputs especially if there is scope for achieving internal economies of scale; the downward sloping part of the long-run average cost curve indicates that greater output can be produced at lower real costs per unit so that output per head expands. Experience indicates that this process is not continual: in some cases there is little scope for such economies, in others there are initially spectacular economies of scale, which are not succeeded by further economies, so that factors secure only constant returns to scale or even diminishing returns once the optimum size of unit is exceeded. (We can, at this stage of our analysis, neglect the problem of the source of the increased inputs.)

The growth of an industry may be seen as the expansion of production of the individual member firms and subject to the same rather gloomy long-run view of the drift into constant returns to scale, with one important proviso. As an industry expands, an extra stimulus to growth in output per head will be provided for the industry if it can secure external economies. For instance the expansion of an industry may enable a firm supplying it with components to achieve internal economies of scale, and the lower cost of the components, if passed on to the customers, will appear as an external economy for the firms in the component-using industry. Other examples are found in a lowering of the cost of transport, or of capital goods. Such gains are distinctly limited and furthermore, it is probable that the expansion of one industry may be achieved at the expense of another which gives up its factors to the former.

Let us consider the sources of the additional input of factors of production. Population growth effectively limits the rate at which the labour supply can be expanded, unless it is feasible to increase either the average number of hours worked or the proportion of total population actually working and these are both subject to an upper limit. It is worth remembering that the economic organization of the country, the productive techniques in use and the supplies of other inputs might be of such a nature that they impose a limit to the numbers of workers who can be employed in co-operation with these other factors. Unemployment, actual and disguised, arises if this limit is lower than that imposed by the population.

The stock of capital inputs (in the sense of machines, roads, spades, railways, ports . . .) can only be expanded if some portion of factors producing current output are diverted from the production of consumption goods to producing investment goods (assuming no borrowing from abroad). Additions to capital stock (net investment) are only possible to the extent that the society concerned is prepared to refrain from consuming the whole of its output. With given resources and techniques, an acceleration in the rate of capital formation means less immediate consumption and more savings, either public or private, or both. The potential for more production in the future requires the sacrifice of some consumption now, a truth which becomes more unpalatable the poorer the country concerned, since the need is greatest for extra capital formation just when the need for more current consumption is most urgent.

Assuming elastic supplies of other inputs to co-operate with increases in capital, with its slow growth in size through limited net investment capital becomes the main limiting factor on the expansion of output in absolute terms and of output per head. A crude analytical device, which stresses this, is the *Capital-Output Ratio*. This is defined as the value of actual capital stock divided by the value of actual output in any time-period. If the values in different time-periods are computed at constant prices, comparisons through time can be made. The capital-output ratio can be computed either as the average for the whole economy or in terms of marginal increments. More precisely, the marginal version is the ratio between an increase in the value of the capital stock and an increase in the value of net output thus facilitated. It can be employed to suggest how much extra capital is needed to produce a £1 increase in net output per time-period at constant prices. Such a measure is helpful in estimating likely investment needs, if a certain increase in output is desired. With given techniques, the size of these ratios will depend on the length of time-period over which the flow of output is computed, and much current discussion is on an *annual* basis in terms thus of annual marginal capital-output ratios. It is often tacitly assumed that the supply of co-operating factors is highly elastic so that if the extra capital goods are introduced the extra output will be forthcoming. These annual ratios, it is clear, are aggregative measures, the size of which will depend on the industrial structure of the economy and its stage of development.

In summary, then, assuming given techniques, unchanged factor qualities, and full employment of a growing labour force, the hopes for increasing output per head depend on the realization of internal and external economies of scale, with the rate of growth of output per head declining as these are gradually exhausted. Once constant returns to scale prevail, if the labour force and population increases match the increase in capital, then the growth in output will be proportionate to population growth and, in our terminology, economic growth (output per head) ceases. As a special case, but with important applications in practice, if disguised or actual unemployment due to lack of co-operating factors prevails, additions of capital in *new* industries can produce an increase in aggregate output, and hence in output per head if people are found employment or transferred from occupations where the marginal productivity of labour is zero to those where it is positive. This rise in aggregate output per head will continue though at a diminished pace where diminishing marginal productivity of labour prevails in the new occupations, so long as there exists a reserve army of unemployed. Once high levels of employment are attained undisguisedly, and economies of scale exhausted, we must look elsewhere for ways in which increases in output per head can be obtained and maintained over time.

3. *Growth with change*

Economic analysis and historical evidence join hands in suggesting that to obtain sustained economic growth it is crucial to look to improved factor qualities and to improvements in techniques actually employed as the main interconnected propulsive forces. One has but to cast one's mind back over the past 200 years of European progress in production to see this. Improved techniques appear in several so-called industrial revolutions, while the spread of literacy and mass education are an essential aspect of improved factor qualities.

Although the introduction of wider educational facilities must be regarded as highly desirable in themselves, we shall concentrate on one particular aspect—their role in improving the quality of the factors of production. In this respect their key importance lies in improving the qualities and skills of the labour input. Labour productivity may be increased by improving the quality of the labour input by more education, which is interpreted broadly, ranging from the acquiring of literacy and simple skills to far more complex technological and university training. Furthermore, the role of education can be seen not only in this context, but also in a broader sense as a weapon for changing ingrained traditional social attitudes, for promoting understanding of the growth process and recognition of the need for change, if growth is to take place or to be accelerated, and these points are equally applicable whether the society is developed and mature, or under-developed and backward. More specifically, attitudes and responses to change, with greater understanding of the growth process, can be altered in a manner favourable to growth, whether it is a matter of broadening entre-preneurial horizons or persuading labour to work regular hours instead of celebrating the feasts of Saint Monday and Saint Tuesday and repenting on hangover Wednesday. Furthermore, it may well be necessary for a government to direct the course of education in its higher reaches—for example, by insisting that more doctors, engin-eers, and economists be produced, and fewer lawyers and historians —though the need for such direction may decline the richer a country is.

It may be possible to improve the quality of land with the use of fertilizers and crop rotation, or to improve in many ways the design and quality of capital goods, and all this will be facilitated by the greater awareness of the growth process which education has fos-tered. These improvements merge into the second category of propulsive forces, changes in productive techniques. They are per-haps more conveniently discussed under this heading.

Improved productive techniques which bring changes in the production functions currently in use in a country are best viewed as lowering the unit costs of production in real terms, a downward displacement of the *long-run* average cost curve of an enterprise. In some cases we see freshly invented techniques being utilized immediately upon discovery, in others there is the application of existing knowledge of techniques to areas where these techniques are new in the sense that they have never been used previously, although known. In all cases changes occur and displacement problems may arise, but an additional difficulty arises with the fresh application of existing knowledge. What has worked well in one environment will not necessarily work well in another without perhaps a substantial lapse of time for the learning process to operate. It must be remembered constantly, when dealing with the application of existing techniques to new areas, that a wide gap may well exist between actual and potential performance, and its size will depend on environmental factors and responses, which are frequently non-economic. It is the business of those concerned in the growth process, governments, entrepreneurs, officials and workers, to seek to minimize this gap. Here, again, the role of education at all levels is crucial to induce ready acceptance of new methods and to achieve the potential which new methods promise.

A second type of improved technique is the innovation or invention which uses new techniques to produce new goods to satisfy consumers' wants more adequately than those established products they displace. It may be impossible to record any rise in an index of output per head in aggregate when there is a switch of £x million from gas to electricity for lighting purposes, although those making the switch feel better off or believe their economic welfare has increased. We can note that such improvements do represent a real advance in economic growth even though the calculations of output per head fail to record it. Many improvements utilize this type of technique and also the type discussed earlier so that classification is difficult. For example, the nineteenth century transport innovations of the railway and the steam ship brought new methods to provide transport services by displacing stage-coaches and sail, but also there was a wide difference between travelling on a stage-coach and in a railway carriage: other examples were the new sources of power, electricity and oil, which superseded coal, and the twentieth century transport innovations of the mass-produced motor-car and the aeroplane.

Enough has been said to indicate the crucial roles of improved factor qualities and techniques and the provision of wider education in achieving lower real unit costs of production, greater output per head, and hence a more rapid rate of economic growth. The implication of change and of a society's responses to change is also vital—whether society is forward-looking or bound by traditions. For on these attitudes and responses, as well as on the quality of the real natural resources available, will depend the progress of a country in hard, materialistic, economic terms.

4. *Underdeveloped Countries*

It has been tacitly implied in the above discussion that these broad notions of the sources of economic growth can be applied to a variety of economies regardless of level of attainment. It is high time that this was questioned. Are the problems confronting an economically mature country different in character from those of a poor or underdeveloped economy in their quest for economic growth? Doubts are reinforced if we bear in mind Rostow's famous view of an economy evolving through five stages—the traditional society, the preconditions for take-off, the take-off, the drive to maturity, and the age of mass-consumption. When viewed broadly, the problems involved in increasing factor supplies and qualities, in coping with and adapting to change, or in ensuring growing effective demand, appear common to all stages despite their having to be tackled at widely different levels. Nevertheless, when broken down into specific adjustments in particular cases, these involve very different structural changes. For example, a shift of labour from agriculture to manufacture in an underdeveloped country will require different methods as compared with a shift of labour from one manufacturing industry to another in a developed economy, policies will vary as regards desired savings' ratios, the capital-output ratio will vary through these stages as the direction and character of required investment changes, and so on. Hence it seems desirable in the rest of our analysis and recommendations to make an explicit division of economies into two categories, poor, underdeveloped, backward economies and mature, developed, rich economies.

There is some degree of arbitrariness associated with such relative divisions and definitions for there is in fact no single indicator upon which to rely in making such classifications. Nevertheless, in practice it is easy to place most countries into one category or the other by paying attention to several crucial characteristics which are frequently found together.

First, a country may be called poor if its real income per head is low relatively to those prevailing in Western Europe, North America,

and Australasia. Whether it is also underdeveloped or not, backward
or not, does not follow automatically. This will depend partly on the
existence of unused resources, as for example hidden talents of the
population or mineral resources, for it might be the case that such is
the dearth of resources in a poor country that they are fully developed
already, and partly on the ways in which existing resources are
deployed. But, in general, we find poverty, underdevelopment and
technical backwardness coinciding. Just how good a criterion of
well-being real income per head is, has been questioned, but it is
generally accepted as significant when comparing societies of similar
aspirations and roughly similar productive structures. On the other
hand when comparing widely differing types of society, the coverage
of the statistics of national incomes will vary considerably depending
on how many transactions enter into the national income accounts.
In a peasant society which is producing largely for consumption on
its own farms, the farmers only selling the *surplus* of their output
over consumption, real income per head will appear unduly depressed if only monetary transactions are included. Real output
per head would appear a more suitable measure, but in such economies the estimation of the true output of productive units which
consume most of their own output has proved difficult. Nevertheless,
making use of the former criterion of real income per head the
United Nations found that in 1949 the average of the high income
group of countries was seventeen times greater than that of the low
income group of countries. It is very dubious whether varying
statistical practice and coverage can be responsible for such differences, over-estimated though they may well be. From a western
standpoint low-income countries are poor and, with some qualifications, underdeveloped as well.

Poor countries are usually under-equipped with real capital as
compared with the rich western countries. That their real capital per
head is low is reflected in low consumption of electrical power per
head, in few railways and roads, small ports, and inadequate schools.
Closely allied to this aspect is the use of primitive methods both in
agriculture and in industry with an unskilled, often illiterate labour
force and highly labour-intensive conditions of production. Furthermore, in such poor countries a high proportion of the labour force
is employed in agriculture to provide the population's basic dietary
needs with the corollary of a high proportion of national income
being spent on foodstuffs. Other features which help as a check on the
correctness of classification are provided by estimates of the expectation of life of the indigenous people and the protein content of
the typical diet. A final crucial characteristic of a poor, under-

developed and backward country is found in the tendency for output per head, or still worse, aggregate output to stagnate at a low-level static equilibrium.

Why are some countries 'poor'? Why have some countries made rapid progress while others are stuck in a static equilibrium of abject poverty? We shall leave on one side the many social, political, institutional, and religious hindrances to economic growth which can have vital importance and in our answer pay attention to the strictly economic reasons. Assuming that any sustained increase in output per head can only come if net investment takes place, a basic economic factor impeding growth in output per head is a country's lack of capital which involves a number of 'vicious circles of poverty'. The problem of extra capital formation is accentuated if the rate of growth of the population is high.

The first vicious circle is concerned with the supply of capital. People have low real incomes per head because of their low productivity, due largely to the lack of capital, which results from a small capacity to save. To build up the capital stock, resources have to be released from producing for current consumption and this can only be done by current saving. The pace at which capital is accumulated will depend on the amount of such savings. This small capacity to save is the direct result of low real incomes per head so the circle is closed. Poverty restricts the supply of capital, thus perpetuating poverty.

The second vicious circle is concerned with the demand for capital. At first sight this might seem virtually boundless in an underdeveloped country and it would appear ludicrous to suggest that poverty could be perpetuated because of an insufficiency in demand for capital, but if we consider a private enterprise type of economy in which private investment is governed by the profit motive, then it becomes quite feasible to regard the inducement to invest for private entrepreneurs as low and limited because of the low purchasing power of the people which is a direct consequence of low real income per head. This has resulted from low productivity which in its turn has been caused by a shortage of capital due to the lack of incentive to invest. In a publicly controlled and planned economy, however, this circle loses much, if not all, of its effect, although the supply of capital circle remains as restrictive as ever.

If shortage of capital is reinforced by lack of natural resources and by market imperfections the problem of inducing economic growth is aggravated. The simple answer to the first problem—and perhaps the answer is too simple—lies in increasing, on a sufficiently large scale, the society's stock of real capital by investment, both in material goods, and in human beings through improved education and training.[1] Investment, in the short run, can only be increased above inadequate current levels either by extra savings if current resources are fully employed, or by assistance from abroad to enable extra resources to be purchased.

Ways of breaking the second vicious circle might be provided partly by increasing real incomes as a result of increased productive capacity from a greater supply of capital, and partly, since the inducement to invest for a private entrepreneur is limited by the size of the market, by measures designed to widen the market for particular products. (These measures will be discussed later; they include the provision of better transport facilities, monetary expansion, export promotion, and the balanced development of a range of complementary industries under state guidance.)

Let us revert to the more serious problem of increasing the supply of real capital. The need for increased savings from a given real income to accelerate the growth of output is emphasized by the crucial interrelationships between the fraction of income saved, the productivity of new investment (here defined as the marginal output-capital ratio or the reciprocal of the marginal capital-output ratio), and the growth rate in productive capacity.[2] If the fraction of net real income saved is s, and current annual net real income is Y, then sY is the value of the real resources currently released and available for real capital formation or for net investment, assuming current income is at the maximum figure permitted by the factor supplies. If all the resources released are used for capital formation, and if on average at this stage of development of the economy an extra £1's worth of real capital stock will enable £x's worth of extra net real output to be produced per year,[3] then the extra annual output (forthcoming once the projects have matured) can be expressed as xsY. The annual growth *rate* can be expressed as $xsY \div Y$

---

[1] In a situation where labour is fully employed and productivity unchanged the transfer of a man from production for current consumption to university or technical college training will involve some loss of consumption output, and some extra savings or cut in consumption will be required on someone's part if he is to be fed and clothed, just as much as if he had been transferred to road-building. This does not apply in cases of disguised unemployment where the man's marginal productivity in consumption good (i.e. food) production is zero. The problem here may be the redistribution of a given food output. See below.

[2] This assumes a simple economy with no governmental or international transactions to complicate matters.

[3] Assuming an elastic supply of co-operating factors. If labour had to be moved from existing occupations, the increment in output as a result of investment must be net of the foregone output in these occupations.

or xs. This would be in percentage terms if s was expressed initially as a percentage.

Thus if the annual marginal capital-output ratio is 4, so that the net increase in output per year is $\frac{1}{4}$ of the net investment, and if savings is 5 per cent of national income, then the annual growth rate will be $1\frac{1}{4}$ per cent of national income. If the country concerned wishes to increase its growth rate to $2\frac{1}{2}$ per cent, and if the marginal capital-output ratio remains unchanged, the implication of this formula is that the fraction of income saved must be doubled—no small undertaking in a poor country at or near subsistence level. Such a requirement could be mitigated if the productivity of investment could be raised by the adoption of better methods, or changed attitudes, so that x were larger. Hence these simple interrelationships emphasize that an acceleration in the rate of growth of an under-developed economy requires an increase in the fraction of income saved or an increase in the productivity of capital.[1] Whether economic growth, in our sense of a rise in output per head, takes place will depend on the race between growth in output and growth in population. The possible 'feed-back' effect from a rise in output per head might be an acceleration in the population growth rate, thus slowing down the rate of economic growth, or it might reduce the rate of population increase thus accelerating the rate of economic growth.

Of course such a model is far too simple, particularly in its assumed constancy of the marginal capital-output ratio and in its aggregative treatment of the problem in a closed economy with no governmental transactions. Yet it does provide some guidance to governments in assessing the likelihood of success once a growth rate has been selected as the minimum desirable and politically feasible. If a rough estimate can be formed of the likely magnitude of the marginal capital-output ratio, then an estimate can be made of the fraction of national income which must be saved to conform to these estimates. Comparison of this fraction with estimates of the actual fraction saved in the immediate past will give some indication of the feasibility of these plans, and indeed the need for outside aid and assistance. Alternatively the government might estimate how much saving might reasonably be expected, and then calculate the increment in annual output forthcoming once such savings had been transformed into completed capital projects. Thus it could arrive at

[1] If the increase in productivity of capital is not devoted to *new* projects as in this example, but is used to improve the *existing* capital stock, there will be a once and for all rise in the output of the economy as a result of the better utilization of existing resources. This could prove a powerful force in some circumstances.

its likely growth rate. Such calculations undoubtedly have a sobering effect on ambitious plans and extravagant hopes; the main fear is then of dampening aspirations, of killing initiative, and of magnifying despair.

In the illustrative example above, a marginal capital-output ratio of 4 was used, as falling in the middle of the range of various *ex post* estimates of such ratios from $2\frac{1}{2}$ to 7. The large variability of estimates of this key ratio partly reflects the well-known truism that there is a marked difference between what capital can do and what it actually does. The size of the difference depends on environment and the qualities of co-operating factors, and also depends on different investment projects with differing individual capital-output ratios. The selection of projects within the aggregate of capital formation will strongly influence the annual capacity-creating effect of new investment.[1] Experience has indicated, first, the crucial role of the learning process in narrowing this discrepancy between actual and potential performance, and secondly that the capital-output ratio might be expected to vary considerably, but predictably, through the stages of economic development. As the pre-conditions of economic progress are fulfilled by the building-up of the country's social overhead capital, such as in transport services, electrical power and other public utilities, education, and hospitals, the ratio can be expected to be much more than 4 since such investment typically is long-lived with, on an annual basis, a low marginal output-capital ratio. Once these pre-conditions are established, the ratio will then improve and the development of rapidly-growing sectors with high output-capital ratios should help the country to take off into self-sustained economic growth.

Without wanting to detract from the importance of many other economic factors and of the non-economic forces which shape the environment within which the economic system operates this discussion has emphasized the shortage of capital, both material and human, as the basic reason for poor underdeveloped countries remaining in that state and experiencing little or no economic growth. However favourable other factors may be for promoting economic growth, little will be achieved unless capital formation and the development of skills proceed at a sufficient pace. In the absence of any overseas aid this will depend on the willingness and ability

---

[1] For example, the marginal capital-output ratio involved in increasing the supply of electricity or railway traction would be much higher than that involved in light manufacturing or agricultural improvements so that the aggregate marginal capital-output ratio would depend on the relative importance of each of these categories of investment within the aggregate investment programme.

of the population to save from current incomes and thus release scarce resources from producing consumption goods. Although this analysis is useful in setting out the problems and indicating their possible solution, it is couched in aggregative terms and raises further questions: What sort of investment is required? What direction do we wish the economy to take? What sort of goods do we want to produce in the future? Do we want more investment in manufacturing, or in irrigation, in export industries or in import-substitute industries?

The future course of the economy will depend on the various investment projects adopted which when added together form total investment. The following discussion will examine criteria for the selection of appropriate investment projects and will seek to clarify the basic issues facing governments.

In considering the question of what to produce, what investment projects to undertake, it might seem best to concentrate on the scarcest resource, capital, and adopt investment projects for the production of those goods with the lowest annual marginal capital-output ratios or the highest marginal output-capital ratios, (the increment in output in these ratios being net of any depreciation attributable to the project). If the length of life of the projects were the same and the times of availability of the increased outputs in the future were the same then this conclusion would prove satisfactory. However, if the times of availability of the returns differ, the marginal capital-output would prove an unsatisfactory guide to choosing the more worth-while projects. Furthermore, this method would perhaps lead to a wrong choice between two projects, each costing the same, if project A had high annual yields over, say, a 5-year period, while project B had lower annual yields spread over, say, a 20-year period. Although the former would have the higher marginal output-capital ratio, the more appropriate comparison of the relative worth of A and B is obtained from examining the present values of each of these future streams of output. (The present values are arrived at by discounting the future stream of output at the ruling rate of interest.) The higher the rate of interest prevailing, the more importance is attached to returns in the near future; the lower the rate, the more importance is attached to returns in the distant future.[1] Such a calculation might indicate the adoption of the 20-year 'pay-off' project, but, quite apart from the difficulty of

---

[1] The present value of £1,000 worth of output receivable in three years' time is $\frac{£1,000}{(1+r)^3}$ where r is the ruling rate of interest expressed as a fraction. The higher is r, the lower will be the present value.

deciding what is the prevailing interest rate, the decision determined by the current rate of interest might seriously underestimate the people's time preferences for more output all enjoyed now or next year, rather than spread out over more years. Moreover, it might be thought wise at whatever cost to supply some immediate incentives in the form of more goods to secure the ready co-operation and understanding of the population in the development process. These considerations would lead us to employ a higher discount rate than the current rate of interest. Thus, on its own and unqualified, the marginal capital-output ratio is insufficient and the later argument points the way to a more satisfactory criterion, which we shall develop in terms of rates of return.

In the nineteenth and early twentieth century, with free enterprise and the British practice of free international trade, the answer to such questions was clear: produce what is anticipated to be the most profitable by the firms and individuals concerned. This very often meant that the underdeveloped countries would specialize in the increased production of primary products for export. The implicit criterion was the anticipated private profitability of the venture, or the private marginal productivity of the capital embodied in the venture, when this is interpreted as a rate of return, and not a physical increment per unit of capital (i.e. Keynes's marginal efficiency of capital). Hence this would suggest that, if the aggregate amount of investment was fixed, then its composition should be determined with reference to the private marginal productivity of the investment projects, by adopting those with the highest profit rates from amongst the possible investment projects. Alternatively, if the overall total for investment is not fixed, then all those projects should be adopted, of which the private marginal productivity exceeds the ruling rate of interest, the marginal project being the one the productivity of which just equals the rate of interest. The rate of profit, rate of return, or private marginal productivity of capital is to be calculated by estimating the future earnings of the project (anticipated receipts, net of payments to co-operating factors) in each of the years of its expected lifetime, and by then computing what rate of discount would make the present value of this stream of earnings just equal to the present cost of the project.[1]

[1] Discounting is necessary because £1,000 *receivable in one year's time* has not the same value as £1,000 *now*; for £1,000 *now* could for instance be employed in purchasing one-year risk-free bonds to earn interest, and, if the rate of interest were, say, 6 per cent would amount to £1,060 in one year's time. £1,000 would then be the *present* value of £1,060 receivable in one year's time. More generally when r is the rate of interest expressed as a fraction (6 per cent is expressed as

However, this approach based on private marginal productivity, or private profitability is open to severe criticism.[1] Profitability is derived from private estimates of gains and losses as they affect the individual entrepreneur or manager of the project and completely

$r = \frac{6}{100}$), then £1,000 is the present value of £1,000 $(1 + r)$ receivable in one year's time. The present value of £1,000 receivable in one year's time is found by asking 'what sum of money will amount to £1,000 in one year's time, if the rate of interest is 6 per cent?' If £x is the sum of money, then in one year's time

$£x + £\frac{6x}{100} = 1,000$

$$\text{whence } x\left(1 + \frac{6}{100}\right) = 1,000$$

$$x = \frac{1,000}{\left(1 + \frac{6}{100}\right)} = £943 \cdot 4$$

More generally, when r is the rate of interest, $\frac{1,000}{(1 + r)}$ is the present value of £1,000 receivable in one year's time; $\frac{1,000}{(1 + r)^2}$ is the present value of £1,000 receivable in two year's time; $\frac{1,000}{(1 + r)^n}$ is the present value of £1,000 receivable in n years' time. The longer the period before a sum is receivable, the more it has to be reduced or 'discounted' to arrive at its present value. Furthermore, the higher the rate of interest, the greater is the reduction in the present value of a given sum receivable n years hence.

The next step is to ask what discount rate will make the present value of, say, £1,000 receivable in two years' time just equal to, say, £800 now. If d is the discount rate expressed as a fraction, then the value of d is provided by solving the equation

$$800 = \frac{1,000}{(1 + d)^2} \text{ , whence } d = 0 \cdot 106 \text{—or } 10 \cdot 6 \text{ per cent.}$$

If this were an investment project with a current cost of £800 and with expected earnings of £1,000 receivable two years hence, then d would give its profit rate or private marginal productivity of $10 \cdot 6$ per cent. If a project's current cost were £10,000 and its expected earnings were £3,000 in the first year, £3,000 in the second year, £3,000 in the third year, £2,000 in the fourth year, £1,000 in the fifth year, £1,000 in the sixth year, and £0 in the seventh year, then its marginal productivity could be calculated from

$$10,000 = \frac{3,000}{(1 + d)} + \frac{3,000}{(1 + d)^2} + \frac{3,000}{(1 + d)^3} + \frac{2,000}{(1 + d)^4} + \frac{1,000}{(1 + d)^5} + \frac{1,000}{(1 + d)^6}$$

$$\text{whence } d = 0 \cdot 10 \text{—or } 10 \text{ per cent.}$$

---

[1] If two projects are *mutually exclusive*, this criterion will indicate the more profitable in terms of the return on capital, but the one thus selected need not necessarily have the lower average cost, when abnormal profits are being earned.

fails to take account of the social benefits or gains and social losses or costs which do not accrue to, or bear on, the private entrepreneurs, but which have important effects particularly in underdeveloped societies. Marked divergences can appear therefore between social and private valuations.

The most familiar source of such divergence is provided by the various external economies and diseconomies arising from a project or group of projects both in respect to production and to consumption. A new road, for example, has beneficial effects in that it reduces congestion on other alternative routes and so reduces costs of transport for users of those routes; on the other hand, if it leads to the growth of extra traffic it may increase congestion and costs of transport for users of feeder routes. These effects would be ignored if the calculations included only the gains accruing to users of this new road, and the annual capital and maintenance costs of the road itself. Furthermore, the new road might mar the scenic beauty of the countryside, or alternatively enable more people to enjoy an attractive route as compared with a dreary one.

The state might indeed assess the future earnings and costs of a project very differently, taking a different view from the private entrepreneur's about the influence of technological change on price and cost ratios in the future. It might for example take note of the effects of the introduction of such privately-valued projects on income distribution, on population growth, on industrial concentration, or on dependence on foreign trade. In so far as such a project had effects which ran counter to the state's social objectives, the state would value it less highly than the entrepreneur. If a group of projects which seemed most profitable on private grounds would serve to increase the country's dependence on exports of primary products as the basis of economic growth, then these projects would be down-graded by a state whose social and political objectives were to avoid 'colonial' dependence on international trade, to escape from the stigma of 'primary producer', or to justify the claim to be 'industrializing'. Such a government would look with more favour in its social valuations on 'import-saving', rather than 'export-promoting', projects, quite apart from any economic arguments in favour of the former.

It is clear that we should look for our criterion for the selection of investment projects to social marginal productivity, which redefines profitability to include such social benefits, valuations, and costs as would not enter into private calculations. It is possible to adjust private estimates of future earnings and costs of projects to allow for external economies and diseconomies, to allow for the

government's doubts about the suitability of export-biassed development, and its preference for domestic industrialization. With this
criterion, specific investment decisions cannot be made without a
previously determined set of social and political objectives, which will
shape the estimates of the social profitability of investment projects
and thus influence their ranking and desirability. Indeed, there is a
distinct danger that this approach which seeks, without providing
any ready-made solutions, to clarify the issues involved in the broad
choices facing an undeveloped country may prove too subjective to
be helpful. For a country's social and political aims and policy
might be so far removed from the realities of its situation that the
resultant, socially determined pattern of investment would further
economic growth to a very limited extent compared with alternative
patterns based on private profitability or on other social aims. For
example, a country which shapes its new capital formation to take
account of its social and political desire for greater self-sufficiency,
may find that it is paying too heavy an economic price in losing the
benefits of international specialization and failing to realize internal
economies of scale because of an inadequate domestic market. The
government of a country needs to take stock of its plans so that it
may realize the possible price of its social and political policies by
looking at those divergences between social and private marginal
productivities which cannot be explained by external economies
and diseconomies. Governments seeking to improve the material lot
of their subjects owe it to them not to divorce their social and
political aims and the resultant investment pattern too much from
the reality of their economic position if their plans for economic
development are to become self-sustaining. Some sort of balance
must therefore be struck between social objectives and economic
realities, where great divergences occur, so that the sacrifice of
economic growth is not too great.

Although it is true that specific investment decisions wait upon a
set of social objectives, nevertheless it is possible to outline a general
approach, much of which may be glaringly obvious to the countries
concerned. Priority must be allocated first to investment in social
overhead capital whose social net product is high (educational
facilities, transport services, power generation, hospitals, and irrigation might well come into this category). Once the infrastructure of
the economy has been built up, the key factors influencing social
profitability—and thus highly relevant to the choice of investment
pattern—are provided by market potentialities on the demand side
and the probability of the creation of external economies on the
supply side. The former would suggest the adoption of investments

C

the products of which had obvious markets; examples are building and construction industries, import-competing industries, export industries, food production for domestic markets and complementary manufacturing industries which would provide additional markets for each other's output. When this is coupled with the requirement that the investments should create external economies such as a better division of labour, greater skills, or further utilization of social overhead capital, the conclusion follows that investment should be directed to 'growing points' in the economy, rather than scattered haphazardly over the face of the country. Thus an underdeveloped country should concentrate its various investments in mutually dependent clusters in certain favoured areas which seem to have the promise of most rapid growth, bearing in mind that such areas must previously have attracted such social overhead capital as power, transport, schools and housing facilities. Often such areas will be in the vicinity of ports, large towns and junctions of natural transport routes and should be chosen with economic considerations upper-most, since it is from these that a chain reaction of economic growth may be started to spread throughout the economy.

Since poor countries frequently have a precarious balance of pay-ments they might well, when considering the social productivity of projects, give weight to their export-creating, import-requiring, and import-saving characteristics, and should favour those projects with greater export-creating or import-saving potentialities. It is impossible to assess these potentialities without forming some view on the future course of the world prices of exports (frequently primary products) and the prices of imports (frequently manufac-tures) and hence the likely terms of trade (often the crucial ratio of primary product prices to manufactured goods prices). Moreover, current comparative cost ratios may afford a poor guide to future ratios when technical progress and rising productivity should have awakened a backward economy, and when infant industries might have grown into giants.

In the typical case an underdeveloped country currently exporting primary products must review critically the future world markets for them. These market demands are probably inelastic both with respect to price changes and to changes in world incomes so that any growth in supply which exceeds the growth in world demand over time is likely to bring a secular fall in the prices of such commodities. Furthermore, such a fall will lead to a deterioration in the ratio of primary product prices to the prices of manufactured goods, for experience since 1945 has indicated that with full employment in the major manufacturing countries no fall can be expected in the prices of manufactured goods despite steady increases in labour productivity. Rather, the processes of free collective bargaining have given rise to pay increases equalling or more usually exceeding the increases in productivity, so that prices have tended to rise as manufacturers have passed on increases in average labour costs to maintain their profit margins. Assuming that the future is going to be like the more immediate past, many underdeveloped countries have come to the socially acceptable conclusion that they should industrialize behind a substantial tariff barrier. It is not enough, however, to look at the behaviour of the terms of trade in making such decisions: attention must also be paid to the future course of comparative cost ratios, which would still support an expansion of the output of primary products for export if productivity were to grow so rapidly in this sector as to outweigh the deterioration in the terms of trade. On the other hand, it is conceivable that the future course of comparative cost ratios would move in favour of manufactured products and thus further support the case for industrialization. No general rules can be laid down here; much will depend on the particular circumstances of a country. What is of vital importance is the realization that a country should seek some balance between home and foreign-trade projects. For there will be a growing need for imports associated with domestic industrialization and rising real incomes, and if projects designed to expand the production of primary goods for export are neglected it might not be easy to find the foreign exchange necessary to pay for the growing volume of imports. A country in formulating its development plans should recognize explicitly that the balance of payments may prove a limiting factor.

These international considerations are but one example of the familiar proposition that the various sectors of the economy are interdependent. Since investment in one part of the economy has effects on other parts of the economy, it is not enough to look at growth points. These have to be expanded into balanced growth for the whole economy. Such interdependence underlies the view which we have adopted that the relevant investment criterion is social marginal productivity rather than private marginal productivity, and that external economies should be sought not only in specific areas but also in the economy as a whole. Furthermore, when viewed nationally, the success of certain investment projects may depend crucially on expansion of supplies from other sectors. Investment will thus have to expand on a broad front, in appropriate proportions in various sectors, so that these can move forward in balance, without growth in production being impaired by shortages of inputs or of foreign exchange. Internal consistency in the pattern of growth in production and investment is thus a characteristic of the balanced growth of the whole economy,[1] and to achieve such consistency it may be necessary to adopt some state direction of investment projects.

Besides stressing the need for consistent individual plans within an overall expansion plan for the economy and the need to look for external economies or diseconomies at a national level, the balanced growth of an economy also helps to provide the domestic markets for the increased output, without which private entrepreneurs may be so inhibited from expanding that the earlier-quoted vicious circle connected with the demand for capital might strangle the economy. The creation of extra capacity by investment in a wide range of industries including agriculture will bring an overall enlargement of the market as people working with more capital and better methods become each other's customers.

Two further points must be made about this approach. First, where the balanced growth doctrine involves the turning away from expanding production and foreign trade in those lines with most advantageous comparative cost ratios it should be realized that by its commercial policy the country is foregoing immediate gains. It receives as compensation in the future the external economies arising out of the process and further compensation will accrue if future comparative cost ratios and terms of trade move in the anticipated way.[2] Our adoption of the balanced growth doctrine involves the subjective assessment that the future compensations will substantially outweigh the present losses incurred through not adopting a development policy based upon the prescript 'produce more of what you can produce well *already* and import those goods which *at present* you produce expensively if at all'. Furthermore, this does not mean that self-sufficiency is the aim at the other end of the scale from free trade, but a compromise is struck between the gains from external economies and technological improvement and the losses arising from an incomplete adoption of 'free trade' production patterns. This compromise is of course based on subjective elements and may *ex post* be found ill-judged, but it is perhaps a less risky course than a pattern of economic development based on unfettered free trade, or one based on complete self-sufficiency.

[1] Balanced growth is not achieved by expanding each sector by say 5 per cent. If a particular pattern of output as a whole is to expand by 5 per cent, this will usually necessitate unequal rates of expansion in various sectors of the economy, indications of which will be provided by input-output tables, if available, for the economy.

[2] There is an ultimate gain if they move in such a way as to diminish the future gains from present comparative cost ratios—for example, if the prices of the indicated exports fall in the long run relatively to import prices.

Secondly, it must be emphasized that balanced growth does not mean concentration on industrial and manufactured products alone. The expansion of food production should have an important place in any balanced growth programme and will play an essential role in facilitating economic advance in manufacturing sectors. Not only does an increase in food production for the home market have immediate importance in the relief of hunger and the enhanced economic efficiency of the labour force, but it also means a growing market in the agricultural sector for the new manufactures of the nascent manufacturing sector, as the farmers' incomes rise. Indeed, an increase in the incomes of the agricultural sector might form the chief market for light industrial products in an underdeveloped country, and so prove to be a pre-requisite for the expansion of manufacture, while an increase in agricultural productivity may be needed in order to release labour for capital formation or for working in new factories without any fall in food output occurring as a result of the transfer of human resources. In addition, the industrial sector may thrive better if it concentrates on meeting this growing demand from the agricultural sector rather than on producing substitutes for luxury imports. Agricultural and industrial development must then be regarded as complementary and interdependent, and not competitive: an underdeveloped country which deprives domestic food production of capital to improve techniques and expand output risks not only the dislocation of its growth programme but also actual starvation. This presents in a dramatic way the interdependence of sectors which it is vitally necessary to recognize in formulating consistent plans for economic growth.[1]

The actual choice of techniques and methods for producing extra output of a particular good should take account of several comparisons, of which perhaps the most important is the factor price ratio of capital and labour. If capital is relatively dear as compared with labour, then labour-intensive methods should be adopted in preference to capital-intensive methods. Men, wheelbarrows and

[1] A considerable school of thought would stress the differing viewpoint that more rapid economic growth may be attained by a 'big push' on a limited front. Deliberately created bottlenecks and shortages can provide an incentive for private entrepreneurs to undertake fresh investment designed to alleviate such shortages. Furthermore, the demonstration effect of a successful big push on a limited front, by realizing internal economies of scale, may stimulate entrepreneurs to emulate such success in other sectors, and may fire the enthusiasm of the population for the 'development plan', making them more willing to accept sacrifice and change. Many economists are sceptical on these points and believe that balanced growth with its more immediate aims of extra food and simple manufactures will provide sharper incentives for the population.

shovels for instance should be used to build an irrigation dam, rather than bulldozers and excavators, in a country where capital is extremely expensive as compared with labour, for in this manner construction will be cheapest. This rule needs qualifying, as with the investment criterion earlier, to take account of the state's broad economic and social objectives, for the choice of techniques will largely be settled by adopting that method for which the social marginal productivity is highest, the relative factor prices being an important consideration. It is, however, dangerous to lay down hard and fast rules based on this ratio alone for the adoption of labour-intensive or capital-intensive methods, since it does neglect other factors such as the possibility of external economies, the length of gestation periods, the effects on the distribution of income, subsequent population growth, and hence income per head, and the balance of payments aspects.

Let us assume that suitable investment programmes have been formulated. The bigger the programme the more rapid will economic growth be. Hence it will benefit a country most to choose the largest programme that its savings will permit. But savings may be so low that only a very small programme can be adopted, and with it a low growth rate. Is it possible, then, to increase the fraction of income saved in order that the growth rate may be accelerated?

At first sight there would appear to be limited possibilities in poor democratically-run countries for such self-help to accelerate the rate of growth. In poor countries even small extra savings represent great sacrifices in terms of consumption goods foregone. However, in over-populated countries where disguised unemployment prevails, not as a result of any deficiency in demand but through lack of co-operating factors such as land or capital, this disguised unemployment does represent a possible savings potential in the form of underemployed human resources which might be transferred from ineffective work on the land to projects for simple capital formation such as rural roads, school construction, and irrigation schemes.[1] Under conditions of disguised unemployment where the marginal product of labour is zero on the farms but output is shared out on an average basis, any transfer of labour from agricultural pursuits would not affect farm output so that anything extra this labour could produce would be sheer gain; no-one's real consumption need fall at all. While this is perfectly sound in theory, the practical problems may prove fearsome. First, one has to ensure that farm output does not fall as fewer mouths to feed immediately may diminish the incentive for those

---

[1] Another example would be the transfer of children from the land to schools where their skills and aptitudes could be cultivated.

remaining on the farms to work as hard as previously; secondly, those who remain on the farm must not consume any more but must channel the 'surplus' food to those who have been transferred to simple capital formation projects and to new factories in the primitive manufacturing sector; thirdly, one has to move the labour from farms to other projects without undue coercion. If the 'surplus' labour can live on the farm and march off to road-building as their brothers journey to the fields, then these problems will be of easy solution. But such handy projects may soon be exhausted, and further projects require migration, thus posing serious problems in the distribution of food even assuming that the labour has moved voluntarily.

While these problems might be solved under certain forms of political organization, utilizing state direction of labour and large communal farms to enable the state to get hold of the food and prevent those remaining on the land from eating 'too much' and the disguised capital formation potential might thus be realized, their solution in largely traditional societies with western democratic methods prevailing and without coercion seems less likely. An increase in agricultural productivity and food production by those remaining on the farms as a result of better methods and increased capital formation in this sector may well be the prerequisite to the realization of this disguised 'saving-and-capital formation' potential, although it may be difficult to persuade peasant farmers to accept such changes while the surplus labour remains on the land, and on the other hand increased food supplies may be required to bring about the migration of this labour.[1]

In poor under-populated countries where the main occupation is frequently subsistence farming, agricultural improvements can be seen more explicitly as the crucial factor which will permit an increase in the fraction of income saved, an increase in the rate of capital formation, and rising economic growth. For here the urgent requirement is improved agricultural methods to raise agricultural productivity so that fewer men can produce at least the same amount of food in total, while others are released for capital formation projects and eventually light manufacturing. In these circumstances the consumption of food per head will not fall, and each individual's consumption need not fall. Those who remain on the land must by a conscious act of new saving not consume any more from their increased output but channel their extra production to the market. If the farmers save the proceeds from the sale of this extra output

---

[1] Increased food supplies from abroad as part of economic aid from richer countries could solve this transitional problem.

they will not bid the newly released human resources away from new capital formation projects. Alternatively the agricultural sector might be taxed by the government to prevent agricultural consumption from rising. As in the overpopulated countries the problems of the voluntary migration of labour, the redistribution of food, and the willingness to make the savings needed to permit an increased rate of capital formation must be recognized as very real difficulties which are more easy of solution the more rapid is the growth of labour productivity in food production.

Indeed, the importance to poor countries of increasing the productivity of labour in food production cannot be overstressed, whether they are over- or under-populated, whether seeking to industrialize on a massive scale or seeking to establish light industries. It will enable the fraction of income saved to rise and thus capital formation to be accelerated without increased malnutrition or actual starvation. It will solve the major problem created when men are transferred to simple capital projects—namely, how to feed them. If on the other hand food production, or more widely agriculture, is neglected as an 'inferior' pursuit in favour of the more 'dignified' manufacturing, when labour is moved to new projects away from the land then the country will court disaster through inadequate production of food and failure to realize any extra savings except at the cost of starvation for some. It may, indeed, be concluded that the poorer the country the more important it is for it to concentrate initially on increasing food production and agricultural productivity as the first step to the acceleration of economic growth.

The state need not stand idle; it too can play an important part in raising the fraction of income saved, with its potentiality for achieving such an increase rising as the economic development of the country proceeds. If individuals and firms are unwilling to increase private savings, then the government can supplement them by public savings through budgeting for a surplus. This would almost certainly have to be attained by an increase in taxation designed to diminish private consumption spending and thus release scarce real resources for capital formation. This, of course, assumes that the increase in taxation will not be matched by a fall in private saving, a danger which all too frequently may have to be faced, but which can be minimized by imposing extra taxation on those who make no savings. Such a course might seem morally, politically and socially repugnant to many and might have to be reinforced by another policy, equally unpalatable, that of minimizing the taxation bearing on those groups with high marginal propensities to save. These will include the wealthier business sections of the community who might be allowed to pay only low profits taxes in order to make it possible for them to save out of profits. The propensity to save out of profits is higher than for other categories of income, as businessmen seek to amass from undistributed profits reserves for future expansion. The state can also encourage savings by raising most of its revenue from taxes on expenditure and keeping income taxes low so that incentives to risk-takers and the ambitious are not damped too much. That policies such as these to increase the fraction of income saved are likely to be unacceptable to electorates because of their regressive bias merely underlines the fact that there is no easy way to increase saving in a poor country.

There would seem to be small initial scope for deliberate fiscal policy to increase savings in a poor democracy, but once real incomes have started to rise substantially as early development plans meet with success, fiscal policy can assume the important task of preventing the fraction of income saved from falling. For as educational facilities are expanded and economic growth proceeds, people come into contact with better goods or with superior patterns of consumption which previously had been unrecognized. New aspirations are created. The so-called 'demonstration' effect of rich countries' consumption standards encourages imitation with a concomitant rise in the propensity to consume and a fall in the propensity to save. Unless checked, this must cause deceleration in the rate of economic growth. As incomes per head rise the ability to save expands, but because of growing awareness of new possibilities the willingness to save declines. It is easier to adopt new consumption patterns than new production techniques so that the demonstration effect can create serious difficulties. However unpopular they may be, some restrictive fiscal policies will be essential if the pace of growth is to be maintained.

Governments fearful of the unpopularity of increased taxation may adopt the time-dishonoured expedient of recourse to the printing press to enable them to claim extra real resources for their development programmes and to use the subsequent inflation to create extra 'forced' savings. Alternatively, they may provide a cheap money environment so that banks are willing to supply funds for capital projects very freely and likewise an inflationary situation will be produced. This inflationary process, it must be emphasized, will not produce extra real resources in total, but will initially bring a redistribution of their use. Some will have to cut their consumption in real terms and it may well be those weakest and least able to look after their own interests who bear the burden. The state or would-be investors might succeed in getting control of extra real resources for their capital formation projects, but it is also possible that the inflation will so distort values that less socially desirable but more immediately profitable ventures will be carried out. Quite apart from the ethical and political difficulties of the inflationary process and the fact that an economy does not function efficiently when overstrained, it does seem that inflation as a device for increasing the fraction of income saved is both less predictable and perhaps less equitable than a budget surplus. Nevertheless, inflation may be the only way open to a government with a poor administrative system unable to collect taxes from a population which has a tradition of tax avoidance.

We may, then, conclude that there is no painless way of extracting more savings from a given real income, and that there is little scope for any dramatic increase in the fraction of income saved in many poor countries. Yet large sums are needed, usually in foreign exchange, to acquire the real resources needed for the large investment projects which establish the infra-structure of the economy, the precondition for economic growth. We must, therefore, turn from reliance on self-help alone to assistance in the form of grants or loans from other, richer countries as a vital supplementary source of capital.

Generally external help, whether in the form of immigration of capital or of labour, is needed to increase the real resources available to the underdeveloped country over and above its immediate current stocks so that capital formation, the acquiring of skills and economic growth may be accelerated. The immigration, temporary or permanent, of labour will help to open bottlenecks caused by scarcity of particular kinds—for example, teachers, engineers, technicians, or other 'experts'—or, indeed, the general shortage of labour in certain underpopulated areas of high potentiality. Important though the 'loan' of labour is, in the following discussion we shall concern ourselves only with external loans and grants of capital.

The receipt of a loan or grant from abroad increases the amount of foreign currency accruing to an underdeveloped country and hence its ability to acquire imports.[1] As the foreign exchange bottleneck is broken, so the various import requirements associated with economic development can be more easily met and capital formation can be accelerated, although it must be remembered that this is not a

[1] When it is not used up immediately and entirely for this purpose, it will provide finance for projects if the country is reluctant to find this by the sometimes inflationary methods of cheap money or the printing of notes. Without any change in the severity of trade barriers such increased spending will eventually lead to more import purchases.

necessary consequence following from the receipt of help from abroad. If the increased supplies of foreign exchange are spent on, for instance, armaments or luxury imports economic development is not likely to benefit. Increased supplies of foreign exchange will permit the import of capital goods on a larger scale and more especially will be helpful in meeting the requirements for indivisible social overhead capital as the infrastructure of the economy is built up. Indeed, borrowing abroad, or the receipt of grants from abroad, may be the only way to finance some large indivisible projects and their import requirements. Alternatively, the increased supplies of foreign exchange may be used to purchase extra consumer goods from abroad, thereby releasing factors of production currently employed in producing these. This might be particularly helpful in the case of an underpopulated country where domestic labour was urgently needed for capital formation but without overseas aid a transfer to this use would mean a severe fall in food production, whilst in an overpopulated country also where wage-goods are scarce it would facilitate the transfer of surplus labour. In both these cases, if full use is to be made of the assistance from abroad, domestic consumption must not rise; foreign loans and grants have to be a supplement to permit domestic real capital formation in excess of domestic savings. If the loans or grants are used to permit an expansion of home consumption and to serve as a substitute for domestic savings, then capital formation will not be accelerated; nor will it be if the loans are used to increase foreign exchange holdings or to permit increased hoarding of gold.

The form of the external loans or capital imports is an important factor influencing the degree to which they supplement home savings. In the earliest stage of development the type most likely to bring increased capital formation is direct business investment by overseas companies. This has tended to flow, in underdeveloped countries, into the existing export industries or into transport under-takings designed to facilitate increased primary product exports, rather than into new industrial or manufacturing undertakings. While this directly increases capital formation and may well create external economies, nevertheless its acceptability must not be taken for granted. For such a flow has been held responsible for the creation of 'dual' economies with technologically advanced export sectors owned and operated by foreigners, growing up alongside backward domestic sectors which have barely been influenced by growth in the other sector. It is of great importance nowadays to see that growth promoted by such methods in export sectors does influence the whole economy to a much greater extent. Such investment may not fit in with the underdeveloped country's own economic plans, if expansion in the export sector is given a low social priority as compared with domestic industrial expansion so that the social marginal productivity in export production is much lower than its private marginal productivity to the foreign companies.

Loans to public authorities whether made by foreign private citizens or government or by international bodies such as the World Bank or the International Development Agency have in the past helped particularly in the building up of social overhead capital thus establishing the preconditions of economic progress. Since these loans are controlled in their use by the receiving country's public authorities, there is a danger that they may not accelerate the pace of capital formation, for they may be used to cover an existing budget deficit, and merely act as a substitute for domestic savings; whilst relieving the shortage of foreign exchange, they may well not relieve the shortage of capital, but just increase current consumption. A second problem arises for the government striving to use such loans to supplement home savings in the process of capital formation: how quickly can the economy absorb such inflows and translate them into capital formation, when considerable movements of people as well as goods may be necessary for the successful completion of capital projects, particularly those designed to lay the social foundations of the economy?

Foreign loans (and grants, *a fortiori*), when not privately handled and geared to a market, may not hasten the pace of capital accumulation, but just permit extra consumption. Loans may increase the country's overseas debt-service burden without increasing the productivity of the country. On the other hand if properly used by the recipient public authorities to create the pre-conditions of economic advance, such loans and grants are invaluable. Aid in the form of goods, as when rich countries build as a gift a steel-works or electricity generating plant has the double advantage that capital formation is achieved with certainty and that no burden of debt-service is imposed upon the poor recipient country.

As the flow of loans proceeds, the recipient country will incur a mounting interest charge payable abroad which will bear more and more heavily on the balance of payments and lessen the amount of foreign currency available for the purchase of imports at least until the projects financed by the loans have matured. If they have made no export-creating or import-saving contributions to the balance of payments, the burden is a permanent one. The service charge will in any case involve the transfer of some portion of the increased output abroad so that real incomes will be lower than if the projects had been domestically financed. This is, of course, the price of borrowing capital, and may well be worth it if the projects make a significant contribution to the economy. It is an additional reason why borrowed capital should be used as wisely and as productively as possible, while it should be recognized by lenders that the payment of service charges provides an emotional factor in underdeveloped countries leading to xenophobia and an inclination to 'bite the hand that fed them'.

Bearing in mind that it is highly likely that the private rate of return on marginal investment projects in rich, developed countries will be higher than on investment projects in poor, underdeveloped countries and certainly higher than the rate of interest which a rich country dare charge without attracting criticism, the argument of the preceding paragraph may be used to reinforce the humanitarian argument that assistance from rich countries should not only be provided free of any interest charges but also free of any amortization payments—in other words as free gifts of aid. The general principle of taxing the rich and subsidizing the poor, or of using the budget to lessen inequalities of incomes before tax, has been accepted for fiscal policy within a nation; let it now be extended to lessen the international inequalities of incomes per head by rich countries making grants and gifts of capital to poor countries to further their economic growth, trusting them to use this assistance wisely without the discipline imposed by the service charges on loans.

It would be difficult for the richer countries to argue that they were too poor to afford to give 2 per cent of their national income to underdeveloped countries, and many underdeveloped countries might think that the problem of aid would be solved if the social conscience of rich societies were suitably affected. But a rich country such as Britain could reply that the donor's problem is not one of poverty or social blindness but of inadequate international reserves inhibiting the gift of funds on such a scale. For Britain would be committed to gifts to the tune of £550–£600 million a year when her balance of payments on current account shows a surplus on average of less than £200 million a year, her international reserves of gold and foreign exchange are only £1,000 million, and her quick international liabilities (£ balances) as high as £4,000 million. Britain, it is said, could not lend abroad, let alone make free gifts, on such a scale, because it would provoke a balance of payments crisis which would denude her already inadequate reserves. In general international illiquidity appears the major barrier which is preventing the flow of aid from rich to poor on a worthwhile scale, and thus retarding the rates of growth of underdeveloped countries. To indicate the magnitude of the problem it has been estimated that if real income per head for underdeveloped primary producers is to grow at 3 per cent from 1961 to 1975, the size of loans and grants needed to offset the associated debits in their balances of payments will rise from 9 billion US dollars to 19 billion.[1]

However, is it really true that lack of international liquidity is such a daunting problem? It is clear that any underdeveloped country receiving loans or grants from richer countries would promptly spend them on the products of the richer countries so that any loss of reserves by the richer countries would only be temporary. No underdeveloped country is likely to use aid to bolster its official international reserves. Although underdeveloped countries would probably use such overseas financial assistance to buy the goods of developed countries, the natural fear of a rich country looking at the problem in isolation would be that if for example Britain were to lend or grant capital to 'X' and if 'X' were to use the funds to buy say West German capital goods, then a transfer of gold and convertible currency would take place from the scanty British official reserves to the more ample West German reserves.[2] Apprehensive of such an outcome, a rich country, looking at its own lending alone, might be unduly careful and make only very limited assistance available.

Possible solutions to such difficulties may be outlined. First, a rich country can link its aid or loans to underdeveloped countries to specific projects and specific purchases by the latter from the former to minimize the danger of loss of foreign exchange or of possible unemployment. While it may be found that this 'tying' of aid may be more difficult in practice than would appear at first sight, it is also open to the serious theoretical objection that it prevents the recipient from buying where it chooses and forces it to purchase in what may well not be the cheapest market. Indeed, the donor country may not be able to provide the sort of products the recipient needs most. That something is better than nothing is the consolation.

Secondly, the above argument has assumed that the donor or lender is committed to a fixed exchange-rate system in which balance of payments' deficits and losses of international reserves assume crucial importance. A second possible solution would be provided if the country, or indeed the world, adopted a flexible exchange-rate system. Then any tendency for foreign currency receipts to fall short

---

[1] A. Maizels, *Industrial Growth and World Trade*, N.I.E.S.R., 1963.

[2] In the unlikely event that these funds had been raised at the expense of domestic British spending, and the resultant unemployment tolerated, then declining activity in Britain would lessen imports and diminish the loss of reserves caused through this triangular use of funds by the underdeveloped country.

of foreign currency payments after loans or aid had been granted and used by the recipient country would be automatically corrected by a depreciation in the donor's exchange-rate. The underdeveloped country would be free to buy in the cheapest market and enjoy the multilateral use of funds from abroad. But in the present international monetary environment the very mention of flexible exchange-rates, let alone their advocacy, by any rich country's authorities is virtually impossible.

Nevertheless, it should be possible for rich countries to lend or grant aid to poor countries on the scale of 2 per cent of national income per annum on an untied or multilateral basis within a fixed exchange-rate system if all developed countries participated in a concerted programme of financial assistance. This would require contributions from richer countries on some agreed scale,[1] and to avoid charges of neocolonialism and interference they would probably have to be channelled through some United Nations or other 'official' agency. Some part of British aid would stimulate purchases from France and the USA, some part of French or American assistance would stimulate British exports and so on, so that balance of payments' difficulties would be mutually alleviated. Furthermore, if the contributions of each were made at the expense of home expenditure, the fears of inflationary pressures which might arise in a full employment environment could be laid: if the richer countries were in slump conditions, the contributions could be made from newly created money and when used would provide a useful stimulus to the increase of spending and employment. Unfortunately this 'ideal' scheme would seem at present almost as unacceptable in practice as the adoption of flexible exchange-rates. Underdeveloped countries must expect most loans and gifts in the near future to be tied with their attendant disadvantages.

It is not enough for richer countries to lend or make gifts. To recall the example of Britain in the years 1870–1914, not only did she make loans on an unprecedented scale, sometimes as much as 8 per cent of her national income, but she also imported on a growing scale the products of the developing countries, dealing at the same time a severe blow to British agriculture as she switched her purchases towards the cheaper imported foodstuffs under a regime of

[1] Factors influencing the size of contributions would embrace not only size of the national income, but also real income per head as indicative of ability to contribute, the ratio of trade to national income which would influence the ability to transfer any given sum without balance of payments' disruption and the level of the country's international reserves or perhaps the ratio of them to its annual trade. It would be easy to devise some such formula but to get it accepted by all is another matter.

free trade. Richer countries have to be prepared to buy on a growing scale the products, both primary and manufactured, of the underdeveloped countries, and not shut them out of their markets by protective tariffs, or by forming customs unions, common markets, or free trade areas amongst themselves. Most valuable assistance to underdeveloped countries could result if richer countries were prepared to make tariff cuts on products imported from underdeveloped areas without expecting any reciprocal treatment for their own exports to these areas. It is true that certain sections of the developed countries' economies would be adversely affected as their productive structures 'moved over' to more sophisticated products, but they are wealthy enough and skilled enough to compensate for such changes by retraining schemes, industrial location policies and so on. There is, indeed, some justification for the underdeveloped countries' plea for 'Trade, not aid'.

Ignoring the social and political environments which can cramp or encourage growth, the underdeveloped countries' problem has been stressed as one of capital shortage, both in material form and in human skills. This is the basic economic factor limiting economic growth. Capital shortage, it has been argued, can be relieved only to a limited extent by domestic endeavours to increase the fraction of income saved and the proportion of resources devoted to real capital formation. For the acceleration of already inadequate, or even nonexistent, growth rates, without too much misery and starvation, aid in the form of capital and labour from rich countries is absolutely essential, and that for preference in the form of outright gifts channelled through an official United Nations organization rather than in the form of interest-bearing loans. Such overseas aid can be particularly important for the building up of the social overhead capital and infrastructure of underdeveloped countries as a precondition for take-off into more rapid and sustained growth. In what direction the economy will move depends on a blend of its economic resources, its social objectives and its views about the future, which will influence calculations of the social marginal productivities of various investment projects, but it is important that the country should seek consistency in its various plans to ensure smooth balanced growth. Furthermore, it has been argued that since the market mechanism and reliance on decisions of private individuals would prove inadequate to achieve external economies and socially desirable economic growth, these would need supplementation by active state participation and guidance—planning in a broad sense, rather than detailed control of every aspect—to attain those objectives.

5. *Developed Countries*

Let us now assume that an underdeveloped country has established its social overhead capital and has taken off successfully into more substantial economic growth with rising living standards, an adequate fraction of income saved and its industrial sector (perhaps privately owned) growing steadily. To achieve continued growth will present further problems which we must now examine.

In a developed, mature, or rich country the problems of achieving growth in the supply of goods and in the stock of capital are less serious than in an underdeveloped country though they are not to be ignored; but the problems of growth in demand for goods both in aggregate and for particular items become more important. Indeed, it may well be asked whether after take-off a predominantly private enterprise type of economy can achieve in theory, let alone in practice, regular growth by matching growing demands against growing supplies.

This problem may be presented in its simplest aggregative form by considering the dual aspect of net investment. On the one hand investment spending serves to create incomes while the projects are under construction, and on the other, once completed they add to capital stock and to productive capacity, assuming a positive marginal physical productivity of capital. Hence growth in demand for output is necessary to keep the economy working at full capacity in the future, when productive net investment is taking place. If we assume a simple economy with constant prices and a given marginal capital-output ratio, in which consumption and investment expenditures generate incomes, disposed of in a definite way on consumption expenditure and saving according to a given consumption function, the possibilities of achieving a full-capacity growth rate and economic stability can be illustrated.

Let us first suppose that at full capacity income (OB_1 in Diagram 1) net savings (A_1C_1) are being made; these must be offset by an equivalent amount of investment expenditure (I_1) in order to preserve full-capacity operation in time period 1. But this investment will add to capacity in period 2, the additional capacity being determined by dividing the investment undertaken by the marginal capital-output ratio to get the increased flow of output possible. This increases the size of the full-capacity income in period 2 by B_1B_2 ($= A_1C_1 \div \Delta K/\Delta Y$) to OB_2, from which increased income net savings rise to A_2C_2. In order to maintain full capacity operation in period 2, investment must rise to I_2. In its turn this investment will produce a bigger capacity effect (B_2B_3) than the previous investment, so that

D

investment in period 3 must be yet larger to ensure full-capacity operation of OB_3. Thus to achieve full capacity operation over time, when productive net investment is taking place, investment has to increase to provide a growing demand to absorb the greater capacity, and in its turn likewise produces further growth in full-capacity income.[1]

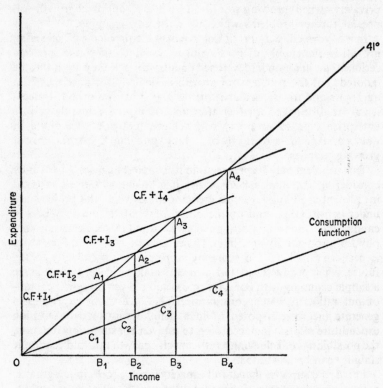

Diagram 1. A Simple Economic Model

A numerical example may help to clarify these matters and pave the way for the calculation of a formula determining growth rates. Let us suppose that $C_t = 9/10\ Y_t$:

The Marginal Capital-Output ratio $= \Delta K/\Delta Y = 2$

Full-Capacity Income in period $1 = Y_1 = 1,000$.

[1] The usual 'Keynesian' equilibrium position with income constant per time period and *ex ante* $I = ex\ ante\ S$ (depicted by the intersection of the Consumption Function + Investment line with the 45° line) is thus shown to be of short-run value.

Since consumption equal 900, full-capacity savings will be 100, so that investment in period 1 must be 100 in order that full-capacity working may be attained. The capacity-creating effect of this investment in period 2 will be $100 \div 2 = 50$, so that full capacity income in period 2 will rise to 1,050 and full capacity savings to 105. Hence in period 2 investment must rise to 105, whose capacity effect of $52 \cdot 5$ will cause period 3's full capacity income to rise to $1,102 \cdot 5$ and required investment to $110 \cdot 25$ . . . and so on. It will be noticed in this example that Y_2 is 5 per cent greater than Y_1, and Y_3 is 5 per cent greater than Y_2—a growth rate of 5 per cent has emerged for income, and likewise for investment.

More generally we can derive a formula by writing 'v' to stand for the desired marginal capital-output ratio and 's' to stand for the marginal propensity to save so that the multiplier is 1/s. To absorb the extra capacity of I_1/v in period 2, I_2 must exceed I_1 sufficiently for this increase in investment $(\Delta I = I_2 - I_1)$, when 'multiplied up', to generate enough extra income to achieve this. That is

$$\frac{I_2 - I_1}{s} = \frac{I_1}{v}$$

$$\frac{I_2 - I_1}{I_1} = \frac{s}{v}$$

or more generally $$\frac{\Delta I}{I} = \frac{s}{v}$$

The required growth rate in investment will be equal to the marginal propensity to save divided by the marginal capital-output ratio. So long as the average propensity to save equals the marginal propensity to save, this formula will also give the required full capacity growth rate in income.[1]

We have now to ask whether it is possible for businessmen to be induced to undertake investment outlays at such a growth rate, for we have ignored the motivation of investment decisions, and have asserted that investment must grow at such and such a rate to ensure

---

[1] From the multiplier $\left(\dfrac{\Delta I}{s} = \Delta Y\right): \Delta I = s\Delta Y$ (1)

Also $I = S = aY$ (where a = average propensity to save)   (2)

Divide (2) into (1) to get $\dfrac{\Delta I}{I} = \dfrac{s}{a}\dfrac{\Delta Y}{Y}$

Thus where $s = a, \dfrac{\Delta I}{I} = \dfrac{\Delta Y}{Y}$

the maintenance of full-capacity working over time. Businessmen must believe that growth at x per cent is a permanent feature of their economic environment in the future if they are to be willing to instal extra capital, the income generative powers of which assure current full capacity operation, to enable them to meet without strain the anticipated growing demand for their output.[1] Repetition of this each time-period ensures a continuance of growth: income has been growing steadily at x per cent in the past which makes businessmen believe it will continue to grow in the future at this rate. Thus these investment outlays can be induced on the requisite scale by the prospect of future growth at the approximate full capacity rate which has indeed obtained in the past. There is much truth in the saying that in a private enterprise economy growth takes place because businessmen believe in growth; once they cease to believe in growth, growth ceases. This is so important a lesson that these models cannot be regarded as mere conjuring tricks.

In the context of the real world it would seem highly unlikely that an economy could grow at such an 'equilibrium' full capacity rate continually, for many chance occurrences could cause divergence between required and actual investment outlays. In our earlier numerical example, required investment of period 2 was 105 to ensure that income of 1,050 would be generated to absorb fully the productive capacity of 1,050. If, now, actual investment were 104, then expenditure and income of 1,040 in total would be generated in period 2 so that excess capacity of 10 would appear. The normal entrepreneurial reaction to this excess capacity will be to cut investment in period 3 to say 100, so that income generated in 3 is 1,000, while full capacity income is $1,050 + 104/2 = 1,102$. Even more excess capacity has appeared and normal business reactions will aggravate this situation in the future, so that a divergent movement away from the full capacity path has resulted from the initial discrepancy.

---

[1] In effect this is a 'forward-looking' accelerator, with investment in time-period t being governed by the difference between anticipated output in periods $t + 1$ and $t : I_t = v(Y_{t+1} - Yt)$. Past behaviour of the system may be expected to govern anticipated outputs.

Similar growth formulae and models can be obtained by using an accelerator which is influenced explicitly by past behaviour of income and output. For example if $I_t = v(Y_t - Y_{t-1})$ and $S_t = sY_t$ (ex ante relationships), then if ex ante $I_t = $ ex ante S we have: $v(Y_t - Y_{t-1}) = sY_t$ from which we get

$$\frac{Y_t - Y_{t-1}}{Y_t} = \frac{s}{v}$$

Income must grow at this rate to induce sufficient investment to offset planned savings and so preserve equilibrium growth.

Again, if in period 2 actual investment had been 106, expenditure and incomes of 1,060 would have been generated as compared with a full capacity output of 1,050, bringing overtime working, strain on plant and a distinct feeling of shortage of capacity. Normal business reactions to this in period 3 would be to increase investment outlays yet more to say 115, so that demand for output would rise to 1,150 while full capacity output would be $1,050 + 106/2 = 1,103$, and thus the initial shortage of capital would be aggravated.

Hence, in the strict terms of this model, any divergence from the equilibrium growth path will set in motion self-aggravating tendencies, if entrepreneurial reactions, such as underlie an 'accelerator' theory of investment decisions, are assumed to govern private investment. This model provides some insight into the way growth and instability are inextricably linked in a private enterprise economy and enables us to recognize sources of instability. Further it explains the curious paradox that to cure a capital shortage less should be invested and to cure an excess more investment is required because the multiplier effects exceed the capacity effects of the normal entrepreneurial reactions.

Can, indeed, these full capacity or equilibrium growth rates be attained in practice, for we have been assuming tacitly that there were no shortages in the supply of co-operating factors to go with increasing capital stock? Whether an economy can consistently attain such rates in the supply of output depends, first, on an adequate growth in labour supply from the growing population, and secondly on the increase in labour productivity from technical progress and innovation. Combining these two it is possible to achieve a growth rate in the supply of output which the economy could sustain with full employment of labour. However, there is no *a priori* reason why this growth rate should match the required full capacity growth rate. Indeed, if the full capacity growth rate cannot be sustained because of bottlenecks and shortages of particular types of labour so that the actual growth rate of the economy slackens, businessmen may diminish their estimates of future growth and cut their planned investment so that it falls below planned savings; the economy will then tend to move into depression. Further, if the achievable growth rate exceeds the full capacity growth rate, any temporary divergence upwards will not be stopped initially by shortage of co-operating factors and thus a runaway boom may develop until eventually factor shortages check it—the so-called full employment ceiling. Thus the introduction of supply considerations into this model enhances the likelihood of economic fluctuations and instability.

Yet care must be exercised, for in the real world no vast instabilities, such as might be suggested by this model, have emerged in the growth of the richer economies. Upward divergent movements, as we have noted already, are checked by the existence of a 'full-employment' ceiling of output, after which they will dissipate themselves into the price increases of 'excess demand', inflation with real growth slackening and eventually declining. Downward movements can be checked and even reversed by the existence of a floor provided by those components of effective demand more stable than induced investment. To judge from empirical research, net saving becomes zero at some positive level of income when all income is spent on consumption, while governmental expenditure is usually stable in the short-run, unless misguided notions of balanced budgets and fiscal purity hold sway. Furthermore, the simplification that all investment is induced must be abandoned. Long-range autonomous investment and innovational investment, which does not rely on income growth to justify it, are forms of investment which are not geared closely to short-term changes in demand and must be recognized as of value in providing a floor. Again, in the downward movement, induced disinvestment is limited to replacement orders insofar as its depressive income effects are concerned, since orders for capital goods cannot be cut by more than a figure which reduces them to zero—gross investment orders cannot be less than zero. All these features help to provide limits between which the economy may oscillate uncomfortably, but rarely getting out of hand as it did in Britain in 1931.

Additional stabilizing features may be present if there is a tendency in a boom for the share of profits in national income to rise at the expense of wages and if the marginal propensity to save out of profits exceeds the marginal propensity to save out of wages. A shift in income distribution in favour of profits will raise the fraction of income saved and lower the fraction consumed, thereby diminishing the severity of the upward pressure of demand on the economy. Likewise in a slump if the share of wages rises at the expense of profits, the fraction of income saved will fall and the fraction consumed will rise, thus mitigating the severity of the decline in spending. In the post-Keynesian world, positive anticyclical governmental policy operating through fiscal and monetary measures has also further reduced the tendency to severe fluctuations. Indeed, business confidence may remain high in the face of destabilizing pressures, simply because businessmen are convinced that the government will take reflationary measures, and so lessen the need for such measures! On the other hand, should business confidence once falter and autonomous investment decline as well, then severe deflation could easily ensue as it did in 1931.

Thus a mature, developed private enterprise economy may well be expected to experience economic fluctuations as it continues to grow but with fluctuations kept within bounds by the stabilizing influences mentioned earlier. These limits must not be viewed as constant but as growing: the ceiling is continually being raised by population growth which raises the size of the labour force and by technical progress and innovation which raises its productivity. The floor is being raised by growing autonomous investment of a more regular character than induced investment, by growing public spending which is often the result of the acceptance of 'welfare state' policies and their execution and by the upward shift of the consumption function as people are tempted through emulation, the appearance of new goods, and high-pressure advertising, to spend a greater fraction of any given real income on consumption goods. Whether economic growth, in the sense of rising real incomes per head, is being achieved, will depend, as in underdeveloped countries, on maintenance of full employment and improvement in labour productivity. Technical progress and innovation, and the ready acceptance of change by the society, are the crucial factors influencing the growth in labour productivity, whether the society is rich or poor, privately operated by the 'hidden hand', paternalistically guided or rigidly state-controlled.

For a rich developed economy there are two main dangers to face in attempting to attain smooth expansion; first, the danger of cyclical fluctuations—most frequently associated with privately operated economies—and secondly, the danger of long-run stagnation—not necessarily absent from 'socialist' economies. In meeting these dangers emphasis must be placed on public economic policies designed to create a stable, confident environment favourable to growth. As an overall objective of economic policy, full employment is not enough; rapidly rising productivity of labour and increasing economic efficiency are equally essential, and policy should be framed with these ends in view.[1]

In so far as it is possible, taxes should be avoided which reduce incentives severely, discourage saving and the provision of risk capital, impede the adoption of modern methods of production, or bear heavily on those 'new' products which have considerable growth potential and scope for sizable economies of scale. A tax system designed first and foremost to foster economic growth may, however, run counter to other cherished social objectives which might be

[1] The timing and size of policy measures are all-important: in certain circumstances these might produce fluctuations of their own, if applied tardily or excessively.

partly achieved by alternative fiscal policies. For example, a tax system with a low rate of progression in income tax, low profits tax, and low purchase tax on so-called 'luxuries', which have the potential of becoming everyone's necessities, would foster economic growth but it is hardly one which would commend itself to a society wishing to achieve a more equal distribution of income after tax, wishing to tax 'unearned' incomes more heavily, or generally wishing to 'soak the rich'. Obviously some balance has to be struck between 'ability to pay' and 'influence on economic growth' as guiding principles of taxation policy, in much the same way as organized labour might have to compromise between policies designed to get a bigger share of a given real income or to maintain a given share of a bigger real income.

Besides fostering confidence that growth and full employment will be maintained, the state must also try to produce an environment in which change is welcomed, in which new methods are speedily adopted, in which cosy inefficiency and a quiet life for industrialists are ostracized, and yet in which the victims of economic progress are not thrown on the scrapheap but treated with compassion and provided with fresh opportunities and hope. To achieve these ends, expenditure on education and industrial training, on research and development, on generous re-training facilities to increase the industrial mobility of the labour force, on housing to increase its geographical mobility, and on encouragement to industry to move to depressed areas, all have high priorities. On the other hand the state should seek to avoid protecting the inefficient industries by subsidies or tariffs or by countenancing restrictive practices: better to let a dying industry pass away quickly, providing at the same time alternative employment opportunities and re-training, than to cosset it with subsidies.

Furthermore, in its influence over the pattern of investment decisions, the state is wise to secure the highest social marginal productivity of capital, thus taking into account external economies and diseconomies, rather than to allow private profitability to be the determinant. Many of the considerations which were discussed earlier for underdeveloped countries apply also to a more developed country in computing social marginal productivities, although other countries may be less tolerant of a mature, developed country pursuing, for instance, a protective policy in a world climate favourable to free trade. Stress must be laid too on the need for overall guidance from the state towards achieving consistency in the pattern of future investment, so that growth plans are not frustrated through the appearance of bottlenecks which might arise from a series of unco-ordinated private investment decisions. Input-output analysis for the economy concerned forms a most valuable tool for lessening the likelihood of such shortages and for providing the basis of a coherent growth plan.

Given the adoption of such policies by the government, what further obstacles to smooth growth might be encountered? One crucial difficulty lies in estimating how people will wish to spend the increments to their real incomes. The available evidence suggests that the existing pattern of expenditure is no clear guide to the pattern of their marginal expenditure, since they are inclined to spend much of their additional income on goods previously beyond their financial reach. Will the decision-makers in the system (whether socialist or private enterprise) gauge more or less correctly the direction of new demands and have installed productive capacity in the appropriate places? If not, and if capital has been directed wrongly, then apart from the waste involved, there is a distinct danger of excess capacity in some industries adversely affecting business confidence so that depression follows.

The need for technical progress and change to achieve economic growth has been emphasized repeatedly, and it has been suggested that the state should endeavour to create an atmosphere and in- stitutional arrangements conducive to mobility of all kinds. Yet in a society in which democracy and the rights of the individual are respected, the problem still remains that change is accepted reluct- antly by labour and management: the plans and hopes of a rich society can be thwarted by conservative attitudes, by traditions, and by the social system just as much as in a poor, underdeveloped society. Unwillingness to move either geographically or industrially, un- willingness to change to new methods, stylings, materials and products can be effective brakes on economic growth in any society.

Even if an economy has achieved a steady rate of economic growth based on growing domestic markets, how will international economic relations and repercussions affect the possibilities in the future? Imports of merchandise and services may be expected with con- fidence to show a rising trend, for 'import-saving' growth is un- likely to extend over the whole range of a country's imports and in any case growth of mutual trade in manufactures is a characteristic of advanced countries. Increasing imports can cause balance of payments' difficulties unless exports of goods and services rise sufficiently, for a rich country cannot expect an influx of capital as a permanent feature to enable it to continue to grow regardless of its export performance.

If a country's export performance falls short of the growing import requirements associated with its growth rate, what can it do to remedy the growing balance of payments deficit? It has four choices: it can devalue its exchange-rate; or it can adopt a flexible exchange-rate system; or it can impose trade controls and restrictions and exchange controls while maintaining a fixed exchange rate; or it can deflate aggregate spending by restrictive fiscal and monetary policy. Each of these regrettably will go against some one or other desired policy objectives. For example, changing the exchange-rate offends against the world-wide desire of treasuries, central bankers, and orthodox financiers for a fixed exchange-rate system and the widely adopted governmental policies for 'maintaining the exchange-rate'. Trade and payments restriction flies in the face of a general world movement towards the freeing of trade, payments, and capital movements with its stimulus to efficient international specialization, and in addition denies the underdeveloped countries the extra markets they so badly need for their exports and for the furtherance of their growth plans. In this context it might be noted that what is internationally acceptable behaviour in an underdeveloped country as regards the imposition of restrictions on international transactions, will certainly not be acceptable in the case of rich countries, especially if they have a large share of world trade. Deflationary policies, designed to damp down home expenditure and force manufacturers to sell more abroad to maintain the growth in output, in practice have resulted in stagnation, no growth in exports, and even unemployment. While checking the growth in imports, such policies have not solved the long-run problem of growth without balance of payments difficulties, nor have they necessarily made the economy more competitive or more ready to modernize.

Which of the above policies is adopted, and which social objective is given preference and which abandoned, depend very much on the size, structure, and international commitments of the country concerned. Given the current world opinion in favour of a convertible fixed exchange-rate system (the 'new' gold exchange standard, underpinned by the International Monetary Fund), for any large country of the western group, especially if possessing international banking connections, the only possible course of action is apparently deflation. This is to eliminate the deficit in the balance of payments by reducing the actual growth rate in incomes and imports to a more realistic figure consonant with the growth rate of export earnings.

But why should one accept the current growth rate in exports as given and mould economic policy around this? Why is it inadequate to sustain domestic growth without deflationary policies? It is especially important to ask these questions if the resultant 'realistic' growth rate in incomes, when adjusted for population growth, is less than in other comparable countries. In seeking explanations of the inadequacy of export performance in such an environment, one key factor is provided by the behaviour of one country's export prices relatively to other major exporters' prices. Cost inflation, if more rapid than elsewhere, may have gradually made its exports less competitive. Other factors might be the country's lack of adaptability and slowness to move over to new products more in demand in the world.

If these are the explanations for inadequate exports, it would seem unlikely, to judge from recent European experience, that the remedy lies in orthodox deflationary policies. Cost inflation in the form of either price-wage-cost or wage-cost-price spirals has seemed un-amenable to deflationary policies, even when pressed far enough to slow down income growth to stagnation, if they have avoided pro-voking a politically intolerable level of unemployment. For, under the pressures of the doctrine of comparability and the zeal to maintain traditional differentials regardless of economic circum-stance, 'wage-wage' inflation has appeared and the labour market has shown a built-in tendency to push pay in general up quite irrespective of the behaviour of productivity, so long as the un-employment percentage remains reasonably low. Because in these mildly deflationary circumstances output has stagnated and employ-ment remained virtually unchanged there has been little or no increase in labour productivity so that the increases in pay have increased labour costs per unit and these have been passed on in the form of increased prices of products. The generalized increases in pay have increased purchasing power so that much the same output has been sold at higher prices, and cost inflation has appeared to gain a momentum of its own and to perpetuate itself. To remedy this state of affairs one way would be to attain rapid growth in labour productivity so that pay increases can be offered which do not look ludicrously small and which also do not cause unit costs of produc-tion, and hence prices, to rise. Now the most likely environment in which this might be achieved with the preservation of full employ-ment is one of rapid growth in total output. If this has had to be checked for balance of payments reasons, cost inflation will continue apace, exports will become less competitive, and we have the in-gredients of another vicious circle.[1]

Clearly there is an *impasse* here in a society with a freely organized labour market. An escape can be found if the state is prepared to

[1] The argument assumes that rivals' export prices remain unchanged. There is less need for concern if they were to rise at the same rate.

interfere in the labour market to prevent a wage-wage inflation by means of an incomes policy designed to prevent pay increases in aggregate from exceeding the improvement in labour productivity in aggregate. For this is required to keep the price level stable with unchanged profit margins. In a democratic society such an incomes policy would have to be understood and accepted by its citizens if it were to prove effective; only in a totalitarian society could it be made effective by imposition. Alternatively, of course, full employment could be abandoned so that enough unemployment was generated to impose the necessary discipline on the labour market to eliminate tendencies to cost inflation. This, however, is not likely to engender an atmosphere conducive to growth.

Faced with such difficulties, a developed country seeking to maintain rapid economic growth despite a sluggish export performance, will be severely tempted to break the current rules of international good-neighbourliness and adopt a flexible exchange-rate system in an endeavour to remain competitive although at the expense of a steady depreciation in its domestic currency as a store of value. Provided that the country is reasonably small and has no international banking business, such a policy may be tolerated by its neighbours, but it does contain dangerous elements if the progressive depreciation gets out of hand and inordinately large domestic price increases occur. Alternatively, the sluggish export performance might be treated as a hard fact of economic life to which imports must be trimmed by a policy of selective controls, so that domestic expansion might continue at the desired rate without balance of payments deficits. Once again this policy is more suited to a small country, which has less to fear from retaliation than a large country, and which has more chance of being allowed to deviate.

In such a world environment what can a large country, faced with domestic demands for high employment and sustained growth, do to meet these demands? First, there emerges the crucial role of the state to ensure that it both remains competitive in export markets and that it continues to grow. The need to introduce an effective incomes policy to prevent the appearance of cost inflation is of paramount importance. Secondly, the state can do much to encourage domestic industry rapidly to adopt technically advanced methods of production and to move over so that productive efforts are directed to new products in growing international demand. Furthermore, as stressed earlier, this process of moving over from easier industries (and agriculture too) is one important way in which rich countries can help poorer countries to develop their own exports and economies. Rapidly growing exports, providing motive power for growth, may then emerge from an internationally competitive and technically progressive economy, providing a more favourable balance of payments and thus enabling domestic investment to expand and untied overseas aid to be increased also without balance of payments fears.

6. *Conclusion*

As in the case of the poor, underdeveloped country, the general drift of the arguments has indicated the need for some measure of state planning or guidance in an endeavour to achieve smooth sustained growth. Certainly this intervention is necessary at the aggregative level, while at the micro-economic level the market mechanism must not be despised, for it can fulfil its tasks of allocation and promoting competitive efficiency well, once sustained growth is being achieved and various social objectives have been laid down. Yet, aggregative state guidance and emphasis on consistency in planning future projects will by no means guarantee steady growth, for uneven technical progress or sporadic innovation or the fickleness of consumers at home and abroad can throw into confusion the best laid plans. What state intervention can do is stabilize these disturbing features and lessen the fluctuations arising from such irregularities and from the fact that the state is not omniscient.

No magic all-embracing prescription for growth has revealed itself either for developed or underdeveloped countries. Many of the policies advocated have to be modified according to the responses of the society concerned and its resources. But there has emerged a general presumption that in all countries some form of general guidance from governments will be more successful than undiluted private enterprise in achieving socially desirable economic growth. How much planning, how much intervention, on what scale and degree of complexity, are questions which cannot be settled *a priori*; they must be discussed in the context of the differing political and social backgrounds, the varying resource endowments, and the past performances and the future prospects of individual countries. This chapter, then, has paved the way for the more practical analyses and recommendations which relate to the several countries reviewed.

CHAPTER II

Planning for the Growth of an Advanced Industrial Economy: the United Kingdom

by P. S. GROVES

1. *Introduction*

Planning for the growth of an advanced industrial economy is complicated, but in another sense basically easier than for an economy a an early stage in its development. There are cumulative mechanisms already in existence which may need only energizing or reinforcing and there is the inheritance from the past of equipment and installations, even though some of this inheritance may be the result of past errors. One of the interesting questions for any particular economy which is already advanced is how high a rate of growth can be maintained. Experiences have differed but whether this is due to different potentialities is not clear.

The National Economic Development Council (NEDC), established as a planning organization for the United Kingdom, held its first meeting in March 1962. As this chapter includes a commentary on the first report of the NEDC,[1] it is of interest to examine the setting in which this organization emerged.

Perhaps the most surprising feature of this attempt at planning economic development in the United Kingdom is that the idea was adopted by a government which for so long had abhorred the very term planning. The planning envisaged, however, was different from that of wartime which was still the public image of planning at the time of the 1951 General Election.

The objectives of government economic policy during the 1950's were to maintain full employment, to maintain stable prices (in the sense of a constant level of prices rather than a steady rate of price increase), to maintain a favourable balance of payments, to maintain and extend sterling as an international currency, and to increase the real income per head of the population. This order does not indicate the priorities given to the various objectives. Government policy during the 1950's attempted to reconcile these objectives in the

[1] NEDC, *Growth of the United Kingdom Economy to 1966* (HMSO, 1963).

face of recurring balance of payments difficulties and domestic inflation.

Table 2.1 shows that economic policy was successful in maintaining full employment—in no year did the overall rate of unemployment rise above 2·2 per cent. The retail prices index, however, shows that the government was less successful in preventing prices from rising— retail prices rose by almost 50 per cent between 1950 and 1960. Table 2.1 illustrates another feature of post-war Britain which has been of increasing concern, the rapid rise of money wages and the widening gap between wages and earnings. This rise in money wages has been greater than the rise in output per man, but, allowing for rising prices, the rise in real weekly earnings has moved very much in step with output per man.

Table 2.2 shows that the annual rate of growth of the gross domestic product at factor cost was rather disappointing. Perhaps of greater significance, however, is the variation in the annual rate of

TABLE 2.1

Indices of Wages, Earnings and Productivity, 1950–1960

	1950	1951	1952	1953	1954	1955	1956	1957	1958	1959	1960
Average weekly wage rate	100	108	117	122	128	137	147	154	159	164	168
Average weekly earnings	100	110	119	127	136	149	160	167	172	180	193
Retail prices	100	110	119	123	125	131	137	142	147	147	149
Real weekly earnings	100	100	100	103	109	114	117	118	117	123	130
Output per man	100	97	100	103	106	109	109	111	112	118	122
Percentage unemployed	1·5	1·2	2·0	1·6	1·3	1·1	1·2	1·4	2·1	2·2	1·6

Sources: Worswick and Ady, *The British Economy in the 1950's*, pp. 292 and 536, London and Cambridge Economic Service, *Key Statistics of the British Economy 1900–1962*.

growth to be found between 1950 and 1960—ranging from 4·6 per cent in 1954 and 1960 to the stagnation of 0·4 per cent in 1952 and 0·3 per cent in 1958. The 1950's were a period of what has come to be called stop–go economic policy. Demand in the economy had been cut back whenever a domestic boom looked like becoming out of hand and was causing balance of payments difficulties. This was done in 1955 and again in 1960. Moreover, investment programmes in a number of key public sector industries, critical for the long-run growth of the economy, were frequently cut as part of the short-term stabilization policy; the fluctuations in public fixed investment are

TABLE 2.2

Gross Domestic Product, Investment and Trade, 1950–1960

(Percentage change from previous year, at constant prices)

	1950	1951	1952	1953	1954	1955	1956	1957	1958	1959	1960	1950–60 Average annual rate of growth
Gross domestic product at factor cost	3·8	3·2	0·4	4·0	4·6	3·4	1·6	1·8	0·3	2·4	4·6	2·6
Private fixed investment	4·2	−6·3	−6·8	9·5	20·1	14·8	7·9	4·6	4·3	4·3	12·6	6·1
Public fixed investment	5·7	7·5	7·5	11·8	−0·1	−4·9	1·2	3·7	−2·5	8·5	5·0	3·7
Exports	15·2	1·6	−0·9	−0·3	7·3	7·4	5·3	2·1	−3·2	3·1	5·1	3·2
Imports	1·5	11·8	−8·4	6·4	3·9	10·8	5·0	0·9	−1·4	8·1	11·1	5·4
Current account balance (£ million)	+306	−365	+168	+148	+125	−156	+207	+216	+342	+140	−272	
Current account and long-term capital account balance (£ million)	n.a.	n.a.	+34	−46	−66	−278	+20	+110	+149	−347	−459	

Sources: As for Table 2.1.

shown in Table 2.2. Restrictionist monetary policy has also been applied to prevent an undesirable outflow of short-term foreign capital from the London money market; the 7 per cent Bank Rate of the autumn of 1957 was an example of this. These policies have hardly been conducive to a steady rate of growth of the Gross National Product.

The pay pause of 1961 may be regarded as the watershed in the government's thinking on the long-run achievement of its major economic objectives, the prevention of inflation, a healthy balance of payments and a higher rate of growth. It was in the period after the pay pause that government thinking turned to increasing output, productivity and exports as the more lasting solution to many of Britain's economic difficulties, rather than continuing to rely solely upon short-term reduction of demand. In this economic setting the government took tentative steps towards increasing the degree of planning in the economy by creating the NEDC and the National Incomes Commission (NIC).

The functions of the NEDC have been to examine the performance of the country's economy with special reference to future plans, to consider what are the obstacles to securing a faster rate of growth and to find ways of increasing it. The Council is independent of any government department and is composed of representatives of both sides of industry, employers and trade unions, supported by a technical staff of economists and statisticians. The Council's first report is in effect an answer to the question put to it by the government of the feasibility of a 4 per cent per annum rate of growth of output from 1961 to 1966. The page and paragraph references given in this chapter refer to the Council's first report.

2. *Definitions*

The quantity the growth of which is under discussion is the 'gross domestic product'. The words product and output may be taken as synonomous. The prices used to value and to add up the items of output are market prices. The total output equals gross domestic incomes generated in producing this output, plus indirect taxes, less subsidies. The growth rate is reckoned by comparing the gross domestic product for successive years using the same set of prices to value the items in each year; the set of prices used are the market prices for 1961, the base year. Thus, the growth rate is of gross domestic product at constant prices. This method of comparison is, of course, chosen in order to eliminate changes in the size of the total due to price fluctuations alone. It follows that the actual

E

domestic incomes generated in the successive years may differ from the gross domestic product at constant prices, since the equivalence between value of output and total of incomes only holds if the prices actually current in the year in question are used in valuing the output. The significance of 'gross' is that no deduction for the depreciation in value of buildings and capital equipment is made. The significance of 'domestic' is that incomes derived from property held abroad, and incomes going abroad from property held in the United Kingdom by foreigners, are all excluded. The 'product' is the product which is produced in the United Kingdom, the value of which accrues to residents in the United Kingdom.

Although the means of adding together the different commodities which form 'output at constant prices' are prices which only have significance in relation, among other things, to the final tastes of consumers, it should be noted that the 'growth' we are considering is not solely the increase in output of commodities for final consumption in a pattern determined by the wishes of consumers. This is so, even if we take it that the government (local and national) as purchaser is acting as a politically directed agent for the consumers as a whole. In an advanced economy a large part of output during any time-period consists of capital goods and goods in process, designed for the production of final consumable output although the fruit may not appear as such until some time ahead. Broadly speaking, the amount of this sort of output is controlled by firms (and the government), and is not immediately under the direction of final consumers as to type and quantity, though at one or more removes there are important connections between the quantity and composition of final output for consumption and of current investment, which have to be taken into account by any planning body.

So investment goods form a large block of output which could grow and be counted in calculating the rate of growth in total output even though currently consumed output were growing little or not at all. If the amount of saving which final consumers, firms or the government make out of currently distributed income does not match the value of output not designed for immediate consumption then serious problems of stability arise for a private enterprise economy or, for that matter, for a more socialist one. This issue is one which must bulk large on a planning body's agenda.

There is another similar issue. Out of incomes distributed in a free enterprise economy, final consumers can choose within limits what mixture of home-produced and foreign commodities they wish. If the tastes of consumers lie in the direction of maintaining or increasing the proportion of imported commodities consumed then one implication of a given rate of growth of output (and, therefore, of income) is the provision of greater export receipts to avoid balance of payments difficulties. Exports, at constant prices, form a part of the 'gross domestic product' the growth of which is our subject. In any planning for a given rate of growth of total output (which involves a similar rate of growth of total incomes) one requirement is that there be an equivalent or greater increase in this export component, even though, like capital formation, it does not enter into current consumption. This is another component of gross domestic product which may grow and count towards the general growth of 'gross domestic product' without, and perhaps at the expense of, any growth in current final consumption.

On the other hand since it is not directly controlled by final demand in this country, it would be perfectly possible for the export component to grow out of proportion to what was needed for the finance of current imports, although of course, the multiplied repercussion of increased exports would itself result in some increase in imports.

3. The Activation and Stability of Growth

While it may be easier to start growth in a highly developed rather than in a less developed economy, there are certain ill-effects which may follow with greater speed from this facility than they would if the whole process were slower.

To cut into the circular flow of income, output and expenditure, let us as a point of departure take it that the growth programme is started domestically by an increase in expenditure of consumers on final output, of firms on capital formation, or of government on either. The last is directly under government control and in an advanced economy there are a number of techniques by which the first two may be influenced. Let us assume that the start is not being made from deep depression but at or near full employment. Increased expenditure from any or all of these sources will generate increased incomes which will themselves be spent, and a cumulative rise in incomes and expenditure will spread through a system which is already almost completely a money economy, and which has a developed banking system to speed the velocity of circulation of money with fair rapidity. What is to be hoped is that output for domestic sale will grow at a parallel rate, taking into account the 'leaks' from the circulation of saving and of expenditure abroad. If it does not, then a general rise in prices will follow, and the economy will have missed its aim of growth with price stability. Some price increases for particular items are inevitable, and there are those who would argue that even a general rise, so long as it is kept within narrow limits, is a fair price to pay for a growing economy. Clearly these are elements of flexibility though they should not be abused, one important consideration being the trend of prices in the world outside.

Prices include those of the factors of production, and particularly of labour. In this country the discussion of policies for growth has come to be associated with discussion of policies for the control of wages as part of a general incomes policy; and some confusion even existed between the two bodies set up by the Macmillan government to deal with each, NEDC for growth and NIC for incomes policy. In the context of the recent history of attempts to control inflation, there is of course a close connection between the two. It should be noted, however, that the problem of wage-push inflation is one of full employment, and not of growth as such. While the growth target of 4 per cent a year that the government had in mind would certainly demand full employment with the removal of restraint on trade unions that this entails, it has been consistently argued by the Trades Union Congress and now appears to have been accepted by the government, that trade union pressure is more likely to be contained when there is something to give each year which can be balanced by rises in output per worker, and so will not be inflationary. A consistent rise in output per worker is one feature of growth and is also stimulated by growth (for example, the more speedy replacement of older machinery which is likely when demand and output is rising).

A policy for growth may therefore aid the solution of the wage-push problem and therefore the successful maintenance of full employment. It is none the less true that growth must be carefully planned by so regulating its rate as not to allow demand-induced inflation, which would itself destroy any attempt at an incomes policy. Further, as part of the policy of securing successful growth, some sort of incomes policy must ensure that the balance of payments issues which will arise with growth are not prejudiced. A rise in wages may have a direct effect on export costs, and too high a rate of increase in any incomes may make the home market unduly attractive.

The balance then is somewhat delicate. To secure an incomes policy, growth may be necessary while to achieve growth without running into difficulties, an incomes policy may be necessary: the parts are interlocking. This is not to say that there may not be some elements of flexibility in the situation. Much depends on the state of trade and the trend of prices externally.

4. *Planning the Capacity for Output*

A highly capitalistic economy implies that the production of any commodity requires many other commodities, some of which may be indivisible blocks of equipment or buildings, and be highly expensive. To see at what rate the output of each commodity and, therefore, total output can grow is like fitting together a complex puzzle. The output of industries are more inter-related in a developed than in an undeveloped economy (though inter-relations are important there also), and any plan for a developed economy which attempts adequately to assess productive possibilities is necessarily a complicated one.

In a developed economy, however, the network of industries producing output for each other as well as for the final consumer is already there; much fixed equipment and some stocks of goods in process already exist. There need be no lengthy period of waiting while the capacity to produce some essential component is built up. A great deal of the necessary waiting has been done in the past, some a considerable time ago. It is true that additional capacity has to be created to meet the needs of a steady rate of growth at all stages but it is possible for this to be achieved if at least the same proportion as before is saved out of the growing incomes. Indeed, some additional foregoing of immediate consumption is to be expected as incomes rise; and this in itself can provide, if the magnitudes concerned are appropriate, the means by which output and incomes grow. The two processes of creating more capacity and foregoing some potential increase in consumption can go on together and can match. This is not to say that they necessarily will match; examining this issue is one of the tasks of a body such as NEDC in any assessment of the implications of suggested rate of growth.

Even if the willingness of companies or final consumers to forego present consumption exists, there are limits to the rate at which balanced development of capacities can take place. These are physically set by the time restrictions involved. However generously resources are released for building up some particular installation, a certain time will be required before it is ready to produce. Crash programmes may abbreviate this, but they are usually economically undesirable. The limits are likely to be set by building and civil engineering, in which heavy overtime working to meet completion dates has already become a common feature.

Starting from some point in time, but not, as said before, one of deep depression, there may be idle capacity in some or all industries. Where this is so the initial problem is minimized since capacity may then be more fully worked. Firms may also have plans for future expansion at a greater or lesser degree of maturity, and perhaps schemes already under construction. It should be noted that the planning of expansion, even before work starts, is to an important degree time-consuming; later productivity may be sacrificed if preparatory thought is over-hasty. Preliminary research or pilot experiments may be necessary.

If a start to the growth programme is made at or near full employment, what rate can be achieved within the next few years will depend very largely on the existing state of plans and projects under way in a number of the more important industries; it will depend on something which is given at the moment and is capable of only marginal influence in the immediate future. The NEDC's first inquiry, therefore, was into the existing plans and expectations of selected industries and what difference would be made to them if a rate of growth of 4 per cent per annum in gross domestic product took place over the next five years.

The industries investigated were, in the public sector, coal, gas, electricity, and the Post Office, and in the private sector, agriculture, chemicals, chocolate and sugar confectionery, building, civil engineering and building materials, heavy electrical machinery, electronics, iron and steel, machine tools, motor vehicles, paper and board, petroleum and wool textiles.

'In the selection of the industries to be approached, weight was given to importance in the economy (contribution to national product and to exports, and investment and labour requirements); the need to cover a reasonable cross-section of British industry (consumer goods, capital goods and service industries and both public and private sectors); and the need to include industries representing growing points in the economy as well as those for which there is not the same opportunity for expansion of output.'[1]

In their comments on the implications for them of the 4 per cent per annum rate the industries were asked to take into account only their own capacities and needs, and not to attempt to assess the effect on the supply of factors (equipment, materials and manpower) in the economy as a whole, though this would be very much the concern of the NEDC itself. Development plans were sufficiently well advanced for the reassuring conclusion to be reached 'that from the viewpoint of physical capacity there appeared to be no insuperable obstacles to its (the 4 per cent rate's) achievement'.[2] Table 2.3 shows the estimated percentage increase in output for the seventeen

[1] NEDC: *Growth of the United Kingdom Economy to 1966*, p. 1.
[2] Op. cit., p. 19.

industries in relation to a 4 per cent a year growth in gross domestic product between 1961 and 1966.

At the beginning of a programme, physical limits, or time limits, are out of the control of the government, any planning body or even the firms concerned. They will still exist as the programme goes forward through time, but then, equally the plans and projects of a date a few years ahead come within the control of firms and there-

TABLE 2.3

Growth in Output, 1956–1966

ESTIMATED GROWTH IN OUTPUT IN SEVENTEEN INDUSTRIES, RELATED TO
4 PER CENT PER ANNUM GROWTH IN GROSS DOMESTIC PRODUCT 1961–1966

Industry	Increase percent per annum	
	1956–61	1961–66
Heavy electrical machinery	n.a.	13·0
Motor vehicles	8·1	11·0
Electricity	8·6	10·0
Electronics	5·9	10·0
Machine tools	3·0	8·0
Petroleum	11·6	7·6
Chemicals	5·9	7·6
Crude steel	1·3	5·5
Building and civil engineering	3·5	3·9
Distribution	2·6	3·8
Agriculture	3·3	3·4
Gas	1·4	2·8
Paper and board	4·2	2·6
Iron castings	−0·4	2·5
Wool textiles (woven fabrics)	−2·4	2·0
Coal	−3·0	0·9
Wool textiles (yarn)	−0·1	0·8
Chocolate and sugar confectionery	0·0	0·7

Source: NEDC, *Growth of the UK Economy to 1966* (Table 1, p. 5).

fore to some degree of the government or its planning body a few years earlier. At any future date the planning body and the firms will be committing themselves but decisions taken will determine what the commitment is to be. The importance of the sort of calculation needed is clear.

The form it would take is obviously very complex, since it would involve forming some estimate of final demands for all sorts of output for any given rate of growth, and so deriving estimates of the fixed capacity needed in each industry which are themselves, of course,

estimates of the output of industries producing the fixed construction
and equipment. To do this the output of industries producing goods
at intermediate stages needs to be known, since their capacities are
also at issue. However to think of the matter solely as a series of
stages, ranging from the final consumable article to the factories,
roads and bridges, is itself a simplification. To take one example,
motor-cars are an item of final consumable output. But some cars,
such as those for salesmen and executives, are also needed in the
production of other goods and services. So to know the final demand
for motor-cars one needs to know the rate of production in most
other industries, as well as the future preferences of consumers
between motor-car and other final output. To estimate accurately
the rate of output of motor-cars needed for any given general rate of
growth we have to know the output of most other industries. Moreover, we must know the output of the motor-car industry itself since
its own salesmen and executives need its own products. The output
of the motor-car industry is an input not only to most other industries
but to itself as well. So that to determine the size of the motor-car
industry we need to know its own size.

The solution to the sort of problem and paradox here put verbally
will be familiar to those used to a neat algebraic device whereby we
assume we already know the size of the motor-car industry and
assign a letter, say a, to it. Then if the size of the motor-industry is a
its own requirement of motor-cars will be say 1/100,000th of a.
Similar symbols can be assigned to the outputs of all other industries,
and an equation relating them to their need for motor-cars formed.

The collection of statements in equation form thus built up will
express the aggregate relationship between the size of all industries
(including the motor-car industry) and their need for motor-cars.
This collection can then be added on to some statement, in equation
form, relating a particular size of output, and therefore of income in
the economy as a whole, to the predicted final consumer demand for
motor-cars. This statement itself will be a relationship between the
aggregate of the symbols expressing the output of other industries
(including the motor industry) and the final consumer demand for
motor-cars, since the aggregate of the otuputs of all industries will
determine aggregate income, on which the prediction of the demand
for motor-cars is based. When this particular equation is added to
all the rest previously mentioned the result will be a collection of
equations expressing the relation between the output of all industries
and the demand for motor-cars.

The same process of forming equivalent collections of equations
can be gone through for each industry in turn. For each industry the

sum of the relationships between the output of all other industries and the demand for its own output will be brought together. Some collections will be simpler, some may be more complicated than the particular example chosen. For example the collection would be simpler for an industry, such as machine tools, though in this case the direct relationships with other industries would be more important, and perhaps even more widespread. In other cases, such as pottery, the direct relationships might be much less widespread, both as input to other industries, and as need for the output of other industries; the need by final consumers would be relatively more important.

We may take it then that in order to find out the needed capacity of any one industry for any given size of total output of the economy as a whole there are three main things that it is necessary to know: (*a*) the demand from other industries for its product, (*b*) its own demand for its product, and (*c*) the demand of final consumers for its product. Symbols have been assigned to each industry representing its output; there are the same number of symbols as there are industries, and these are the 'unknowns' which are to be found. The number of relationships in equation form which have been presented or predicted may be added up as follows: (*a*) as far as direct demands from other industries for the product of any specified industry is concerned there are as many equational relationships as there are industries, less one (the industry specified itself), (*b*) as far as the demand of the specified industry for its own product is concerned there is one, (*c*) as far as final demands by consumers are concerned there is one, linking income to the amount demanded of the output of that particular industry. However, we may take it that income equals the aggregate value of output of all industries (this is a slight simplification to which the qualifications which should and could be made were noted in the first section). Let us also take it that we predict prices of output for the years concerned. Then income resolves itself into all the symbols for the unknown outputs for each industry times their respective predicted prices, added together.

It would seem then that the number of equations is the same as the number of industries whose output we have to determine, plus one linking total income to final consumption demand. The quantities we had to find out in order to determine the required size of any particular industry for any size of output as a whole were also the same as the number of industries, plus one. In algebraic terms the number of simultaneous equations is the same as the number of unknowns; we have the number of relationships we require to solve the problem for each industry.

It is clear from the way in which the argument is put that if we solved the problem for one industry (its required size for any given rate of growth) we should be solving it for all industries. To go through the process suggested we should have to build up information about the relationships between the output of each industry and the inputs required from any other industry, as well as about the relationship between total income and final consumer demand for those products which entered into final demand (an export of anything, even if not a consumption good, would count as a final demand). This is known as building up a social accounting matrix, and the whole process as input-output analysis. Since the number of simultaneous equations so formed would be extremely large it is most convenient to set them out in a two-way table known as a matrix and the special techniques of matrix algebra utilized for their solution.

The NEDC hopes to draw on work of this kind when it has progressed sufficiently. Meanwhile, it has made use of simpler estimated relationships as an aid in the assessment of the important issue with which the foregoing discussion started, namely, estimating the relation between fixed capacity in manufacturing industry and the output it can produce, with a view to determining likely rates of investment required if growth is not to be limited for the physical or time reasons referred to earlier. The resulting NEDC estimates of the gross fixed investment required in 1966 assuming a 4 per cent per annum growth rate between 1961 and 1966 are shown in Table 2.4. For purposes of comparison the figures for 1961 are also included.

5. *Prices and Productivity*

To assume fixed relationships between outputs of one kind and inputs of another while likely to be reasonable in many cases, may be a simplification in others. There may be certain flexibilities which complicate prediction although they make it less important that prediction should be completely accurate. In the problem of the physical limits on output a few years ahead, the possibility of varying stocks of non-perishable commodities is another source of flexibility, and therefore stock-holding is an important item in the capital formation required for any given level of output. For some important industries, such as electricity supply, there is no possibility of holding stocks of the product and this is one reason why planning this particular industry's rate of growth is troublesome. Another source of flexibility is importing, which has at times been used as, for instance, in the supply of coal. Prudent planners might as a form of insurance make some provision for this in their balance of payments calculations.

Any flexibility of relationships raises another important issue. Prices did not enter into the foregoing discussion except incidentally as a means of totalling final output to translate it into terms of

TABLE 2.4

Fixed Investment, 1961 and 1966

GROSS FIXED INVESTMENT IN 1961 AND 1966 ESTIMATED ON THE BASIS OF A 4 PER CENT PER ANNUM GROWTH

Industry	£ million at 1961 prices	
	1961	1966
Oil refining	19	29
General chemicals	185	205
Iron and steel	227	92
Motor vehicles	85	90
Heavy electrical machinery	4	6
Electronics	21	29
Wool textiles	10	11
Paper and board	14	15
Chocolate and sugar confectionery	10	11
All manufacturing industry	1,276	1,500
Agriculture	155	171
Coal mining	87	69
Construction	77	100
Gas	40	32
Electricity	360	681
Water	47	59
Postal services and telecommunications	116	201
Transport	399	445
Distribution	281	412
Social services	239	340

Source: NEDC, *Growth of the United Kingdom Economy to 1966*, Tables 16 and 17.

disposable incomes. Traditional economic analysis, however, points to prices as being an important determinant both of relative quantities of final outputs demanded by consumers and as influencing the proportions in which different components, or inputs, are used in producing any output. Moreover, the prices are themselves influenced by the whole set of inter-relationships under discussion.

The most important aspect of prices as they affect input quantities is in the use of the basic factors of production, capital, labour, and land; and by capital is usually meant buildings and equipment, rather than shorter-term items, such as components and raw materials. There is undoubtedly scope for substitution among competing varieties of the latter items (e.g. artificial fibres or the natural product) which will be influenced by price, but in the case of raw materials, at least, inputs are more rigidly determined by technical considerations. The issue is also important as between capital and labour (though there is still controversy on the precise way in which price influences matters here) if we are discussing long-term growth, and it was precisely the inputs of capital equipment required for growth which was the starting point of this discussion. The fuller consideration of manpower requirements has been left for the next section, but the combination of issues has to be noted here.

The main point to be made is that in this kind of planning for growth the issues are fairly short-term, being concerned with the amount of capacity required in the next few years. General price relationships, especially those between interest rates and wages of labour, will have established habitually accepted rates of fixed capital to labour and of fixed capital to output; past changes of many sorts (including prices) may have built up a trend of change in these relationships, which any planning body might wish to encourage or discourage. At any one moment from which we are planning for a few years ahead, however, the relationships are not going to alter greatly or in a way which is sudden and unpredictable. For instance, particular prices will be relevant for particular industries, such as the price of fuel oil as compared with coal or nuclear plants in determining the nature of power installations, but these will be known to the industries concerned and can be taken into account by the planning body.

One of the important trend changes which would appear in the capacity and output plans of firms, as well as in the relationship between capacity and labour, would be due to progress in knowledge and technique which might be associated with relative factor prices or changes in them. It would be difficult to say whether favourable changes in the productivity of both capital and labour are likely to be more evident, and more helpful in the planning of growth, in a developed or an undeveloped economy. They might be more considerable in the latter, once increasing capital and education were available to the undeveloped country. This would be due more to the greater application of known improved techniques than to current activity in discovering improvements. Nevertheless, one of the characteristics of the British economy, though classed as a developed one, has been held to be tardiness in the application of knowledge. It is now reassuring to find the NEDC reporting that both the activities of application and discovery are taking place, and particularly that at the beginning of planned growth the investment boom of 1959–60 and the large sums spent in setting up research establishments in the years immediately previous to 1961 may be expected to begin bearing fruit. It is interesting to find it reporting a probable positive correlation between the research and development work in an industry and its rate of growth of productivity.

TABLE 2.5

Growth and Research in the United Kingdom, 1935–1958

Industry	Growth index 1935–1958 (1935 = 100)	Research expenditure as percentage of net output
Aircraft	974	35·1
Electronics	503	12·8
Instruments	472	6·0
Chemicals	382	4·5
Machinery	309	2·3
Non-ferrous metals	265	2·3
Other electrical	263	5·6
Rubber	239	2·1
Metal products	233	0·8
Vehicles	213	1·4
Ferrous metals	199	0·5
Food	170	0·3
Paper	148	0·8
Stone, clay and glass	134	0·6
Other manufacturing	123	0·4
Textiles and clothing	116	0·3
Timber and furniture	113	0·1
All above industries	200	3·1

Source: C. Freeman 'Research & Development: A comparison between British & American Industry', *National Institute Economic Review*, No. 20, May 1962.

Table 2.5 illustrates the relationship between research activity and the rate of growth of output of a number of industries in the United Kingdom. The growth index used is calculated from changes in net output between 1935 and 1958 indicated in the Census of Production. The correlation coefficient of research expenditure as a percentage of net output in the industries with their growth of output is 0·95.

6. *Matching with Basic Resources*

Capacity will set physical or temporal limits to the rate of growth attainable in the few years ahead. It is no use considering other things until those limits have been ascertained. Once that has been done, however, at least two questions become of major concern. Firstly, will the labour supplies available, and likely to become available, within the next few years, be sufficient to utilize the capacity selected? If not the capacity selected would have to be revised, or special attention given to increasing the size of the working population on to lenghtening the working week. Secondly, will there be enough saving to allow sufficient current capacity to be devoted to the planned new investment? Although this is a similar problem there is this difference. The plans for creating new capacity once adopted will go ahead as scheduled, whether or not sufficient resources are released from the production of current output. In fact they are likely to go ahead even faster if resources are not so released since, in that case, the current demand for goods and services will be exceeding the current supply at the then ruling price level and an inflationary rise in money incomes and prices will result.

Once the growth limits set by capacity plans have been ascertained, matching the growth rate chosen with resources of manpower and savings must be the job of a central planning body. This is apparent in the way the questions put to the seventeen industries by the NEDC were framed.

Although at the start of a growth programme capacity limits for the main types of goods must first be set and then manpower and savings fitted to them, as the programme proceeds capacities in future years are no longer fixed by past decision, and themselves become a variable. This clearly gives far greater scope, but the starting point for decision is no longer given. In fact it is likely, and it is desirable, for it to shift so that the circuit of determination is reversed, starting from manpower and savings possibilities, and from these determining investment plans. Manpower will then be the fixed item, savings will not be an absolute quantity but a function of income, and output will therefore to some degree, perhaps small, be controllable by government action.

Leaving aside this longer term sequence for which the aid of a fully developed social accounting matrix is probably needed, let us return to the manpower possibilities within the period prior to 1966.

7. *Manpower*

It is simple to talk of manpower as a whole in numbers which have some precision, but to utilize capacity specific types of labour are required, and this requires consideration of a further set of 'capacities', those for training the size or growth of which may be relatively inflexible for the next few years ahead. There are similar wide-spreading and circular relationships as those discussed before. The output of some training establishments will form the teachers in many other types and a growing part will also be needed as input to themselves, if their own capacity is to grow. While Britain has the advantage that the whole network already exists, its expansion, required not only by industrial growth but by the pattern of population and growth in final demand, is causing major concern. Since the process is predominantly labour-intensive rather than capital-intensive there are elements of flexibility, which may not exist for some types of industrial capacity although the period of process may be as long or longer. For instance, larger classes are possible but a teacher takes a full three years to train and this is longer than much industrial expansion requires.

While it may be counted one of Britain's successes that the period of process of some actual physical capacity such as school building, has been much reduced, there still exists a problem of physical capacity for the universities, which tend to be more capital intensive than other types of education, particularly for the training of scientists. The limits of existing expansion plans and those set by periods of process are important and are causing concern in this key sector. The emphasis placed on education by such countries as Russia which aims at a continuously high rate of growth, or the United States, which has experienced a high rate of growth, is significant here.

Some other developed countries achieving high rates of growth in recent years have been able to draw on labour supplies from the agricultural sector, the traditional source of workers for the towns and for industry. France, Italy and West Germany could draw large numbers of workers from the land, and Britain itself has drawn some, but the contribution in the case of the first three have been larger since the process had not gone so far as it had in earlier periods in Britain. Each has also had special features which are relevant. West Germany had a legacy of refugees, and, until recently, a sizeable annual inflow. Italy is virtually two economies, with move-ment from the south to the north to a great degree in place of emigration; this is, of course, its problem as well as its strength— the barriers which isolate the two parts still remain, with movement largely dependent on expansion in the north. In France, while total population has been almost static, the agricultural sector is particularly large and there have not been the same barriers to either the movement of capital or of labour as in Italy. In each case, whatever the new source of supply, there have been difficulties of training in a movement taking place over little more than a decade although France is often credited with having been particularly successful in overcoming them.

TABLE 2.6

Employment and Production in Agriculture, 1961–1962

Country	Percentage employed in agriculture (1962)	Percentage of G.D.P. at factor cost accounted for by agriculture, forestry and fishing (1961)
United Kingdom	5	4·1
Belgium	7	7·6
Netherlands	10*	9·8
West Germany	13	6·6
France	21	10·1
Italy	28	17·4

* 1961.

Source: *Basic Statistics of the Community*, Statistical Office of the European Communities.

The question may be asked, what of the agricultural output lost? The answer lies partly in technology; as in many less developed countries the physical marginal productivity of some agricultural labour was low, and was being reduced by improvements in technique. Over the years, as agriculture adapts itself, there need be no loss in physical output; in fact in France and Germany the problem is still one of agricultural surplus. More basically, perhaps, the answer lies in a comparison with the value of the industrial and other output which could be produced with the transferred labour, and bought with the rising incomes generated. It has been advantageous to meet the final demands, both home and export, for industrial goods since alternative supplies of cheap imported food have been available.

Whatever may have been the quantitative contribution of these sources to the growth of the countries concerned, it is clear that no such recourse exists, or exists only to a minor extent, for Great Britain, although there may still remain something to be accomplished in particular regions by movements of capital and labour between the agricultural and industrial sectors, or by analagous movements within the industrial and allied sectors themselves.

The estimated changes in the pattern of employment in the United Kingdom necessitated by faster growth are shown in Table 2.7.

TABLE 2.7
Changes in Employment, 1956–1966

Industry	1956–61 Percentage change per annum	1961–66 Percentage change per annum	Aggregate change (thousands)
Agriculture	−1·8	−2·0	−96
Coal mining	−3·4	−2·7	−85
Oil refining	+1·3	+0·1	—
Gas	−2·5	−1·2	−8
Chocolate and sugar confectionery	−0·7	—	—
Electricity	+1·6	+2·1	+24
Chemicals	+1·0	+1·4	+34
Iron and steel	+0·8	−0·9	−22
Machine tools	+0·2	+4·4	+22
Heavy electrical machinery	n.a.	+6·0	n.a.
Electronics	+4·6	+3·8	+49
Motor vehicles	+1·6	+3·0	+67
Wool textiles	−1·1	−1·7	−16
Paper and board	+3·2	−0·2	−1
Construction	+0·8	+1·1	+91
Postal services and telecommunications	+0·6	+1·6	+28
Distribution	+1·5	+1·3	+220
Total of the seventeen industries	+0·5	+0·8	+383
Rest of economy	+0·3	+0·8	+629
Employed in United Kingdom	+0·4	+0·8	+1,012

Source: NEDC, *Growth of the United Kingdom Economy to 1966*, p. 23, Table 6.

It has been estimated officially, on the basis of the projected size of different social groups and the likely proportions of employed persons in each, that the United Kingdom labour force will rise between 1961 and 1966 by 3·6 per cent, an average of 0·7 per cent a year. Purely by coincidence this is in fact the same rate of increase per annum as the total population. The aggregate increase appears to be a compound of two contrary tendencies; firstly, a trend towards a

F

rise in the number of married women in employment and, secondly, a rise in the numbers of both men and women above normal retiring age. The first tendency may be influenced by government policy if thought desirable; the second certainly is. The possible size of favourable changes is, however, problematic, and in fact the NEDC points to fuller use of labour in regions where activity rates are below the national level as a more likely source of greater supply, though one which may take careful and expensive planning to achieve. Projections of net immigration, taken as 50,000 per year for the years following 1962, the NEDC regards as uncertain. One trend may be regarded as certain if growth takes place at all, and that is a fall in unemployment as demand rises. All in all the NEDC is prepared to raise the officially estimated increase to 0·8 per cent per annum on the assumption that the 4 per cent per annum growth programme is under way.

To keep the matter in perspective it may be mentioned that the United Kingdom is already a highly populated country, having one of the higher densities per acre in the world—to many of its inhabitants it already seems crowded—and it has had in general in recent years, one of the lowest unemployment rates in the world, while the proportion of the time of women engaged otherwise than in the household is greater than that in many other industrial nations even though it may be low as compared with some peasant economies.[1]

The NEDC seem to have good grounds for their reassuring conclusion on the basis of their enquiry into the plans of the seventeen industries and their required capacity for the 4 per cent growth, and on the presumption that capacity and output will grow somewhat less in the remainder of the economy, that this increase in total manpower per year should be sufficient to match the increased capacity and produce the growth in output planned. This takes into account both the increase in output per man which will be associated with the new capacity, and also the increase to be expected in the next few years from new techniques and improvements in organization. If total manpower is to go up by 0·8 per cent per annum, and if total output is to increase by 4 per cent per annum, the clear implica-

[1] For some discussion of the wider aspects of the issue reference may be made to:

(a) *The Report of the Royal Commission on Population*, HMSO, Cmd. 7695, 1949.

(b) *Royal Commission on Population*, Papers, Vol. 3. Report of the Economics Committee HMSO 1950 (Reprinted 1956).

(c) International Economic Association. *Economic Consequences of the Size of Nations*. Ed. E. A. G. Robinson, London, Macmillan, 1960.

tion is a rise in product per man by 3·2 per cent per annum. It is one of the more striking of NEDC's conclusions that it should believe this relatively high rate of increase to be possible. It will be apparent from the foregoing argument, however, that it has a firm base in its study of the projected installations in the seventeen industries, which covers nearly a half of all industrial production, and nearly two-fifths of the total national product and employment. Support is also lent by the trend of productivity in the nation as a whole; this has shown an average growth of $1\frac{1}{2}$ per cent per annum in the inter-war years and for fifty or so years before 1914, an average of 2 per cent from 1951 to 1961, and an acceleration to $2\frac{1}{2}$ per cent from 1955 to 1961. These are calculations of the under-lying rate of change in productivity after account has been taken of the varying pressure of demand in some years which causes wide change in the rate due to variations in the degree to which plant and labour forces are utilized. As has been mentioned previously, a great number of firms in Britain do appear to have become convinced of the value of research and the application of knowledge, perhaps as a result of past strictures and of having seen the rapid advance of pioneers in the field among their fellows, and the economy is now beginning to reap the fruits of investment of this sort in the recent past.

This overall reassurance does not extend to the relative supplies and demands for expansion of specific types of labour, particularly for the scientifically or technically trained. Progress has already been made in increasing the output of highly qualified scientists and technologists, but there is still a great demand to be met, and, in view of expansion, more to come. Moreover, a problem which has been less discussed, but is now coming to light, is the need for technicians at a lower level, and more surprising still, perhaps, for considerably more workers skilled in the traditional crafts. The border-lines are blurred here, of course; in what category, for instance, does the 'electrician' come? In some respects it would also seem that demand requires other lines of demarcation to be less rigid. 'Design' is said to be lacking in the products of the machine-tool industry; in terms of recent (though not of distant) tradition it would be difficult to imagine the marrying of two more diverse arts. Perhaps it is not so strange however; colleges of art and technology have long remained together, and a new role is now set for them, in this and in other ways as, for instance, by technologists increasingly demanding education in the things which bear on business administration.

The need for a higher proportion of skilled workers, whether in new or old techniques, is again inherent in the adoption of new processes. The machines can easily displace the unskilled but they still need the skilled to design, build, operate and look after them. As they release the unskilled, and perhaps some workers trained for previous tasks, an opportunity is presented as well as a need. There is reason to believe that possibilities of training have not been fully exploited in the past, although it must be realized that the problem posed does involve time limits. It is not enough to enlarge the facilities for young students to learn skilled trades, and to reduce the periods of process involved. As in the other European countries mentioned, training or retraining of the old is necessary if the opportunities are to be taken. The experience of government training centres in Britain leads the NEDC to believe that the need can be met if sufficient attention is devoted to it, and the experiences of these other countries confirms their conclusion.

While on the subject of the use of manpower it is convenient to turn attention once again from the more physical needs and limits involved to the market and to prices. The processes of change described will involve some redundance (six of the seventeen industries questioned expected contraction of manpower needs). The problem here is to make technical changes acceptable to labour, minimizing opposition and speeding re-employment. Severance pay, higher unemployment benefits and speedy transfer to other occupations have long been discussed, and will remain important issues in any growth programme, particularly in the regional context. Perhaps more specifically linked with growth is the other side of the picture; rising expenditure leading to competing demands for particular types of labour in a general context of full employment. The general issue of wage stability has already been discussed; what needs to be brought forward here is one particularly intractable problem. In its attempts to establish a national incomes policy to which both bargaining parties, trade unions and employers, would agree and which would be in the national interest, the government started by asserting that one sort of wage increase to which both parties concerned might agree, namely one to make a particular industry or section of an industry more attractive to a certain class of worker, could not be regarded as in the national interest. This was because the government believed that either because of the working of the system of craft unionism in Britain or because employees in other industries would wish to re-establish their previous position, the rise for that particular type of worker would become general and stability be lost.

The National Incomes Commission sought to apply the above principle in the recommendations of their first report on the Scottish plumbers and builders agreements of 1962,[1] which were striking examples of a breach of the principle. It is possible to understand the government's intention as far as stability is concerned; it is even possible to see that such a sequence might eventually defeat its own end so far as the re-deployment of labour is concerned. The question still remains: how is the market for labour to operate without some means by which labour can be attracted to where it is most needed as the pattern of demand changes? In its second report on a number of agreements in the engineering trades,[2] the National Incomes Commission seems to have recognized the difficulty, and the government's third reference to the Commission (on salaries in university education), was specifically formed to take account of a particular need for expansion. Nevertheless, nobody would pretend to know yet the full answer to this problem of full employment. The hope is that, in order to avoid inflation, desirable rises for the operation of the market for labour may be kept within the limits prescribed by the growing average annual increase in output per man.

8. Savings and Investment

Let us turn to the other quantity which capacity plans have to match in the aggregate if a particular growth programme is to be viable, namely total savings.

So far only the key investments in industrial, educational and agricultural capacity have been discussed. Estimates for other investment for the years 1961 to 1966 have also been made (see Table 2.4). The case of transport may be singled out as one interesting and important case, since it affects most other industries. It is the sector, par excellence, from which external economies come in the earlier stages of growth. At a later stage, in crowded industrial areas, one begins to wonder whether it is not more a case of a costly and endless battle against external diseconomies. In many areas we have long reached the limit that past investment in roads will carry and additions involve costly and what sometimes seem disproportionately ingenious engineering projects. Between industrial areas the capacity of existing trunk routes has similarly long been reached; but here the motorways which have served the rapidly growing economies on the continent so well, may show that there are

[1] National Incomes Commission, Report on the Scottish Plumbers & Scottish Builders' Agreements of 1962, HMSO, April 1963, Cmnd. 1994.

[2] National Incomes Commission, Report on the Agreements of February–March 1963 in Electrical Contracting, in Heating, Ventilating & Domestic Engineering & in Exhibition Contracting, HMSO, July 1963, Cmnd. 2098.

still advantages to be reaped by the application of new constructional techniques.

The truth is, of course, that it is not merely the expansion in size of the economy as such which is throwing extra strain on the road system, but also a change in transport habits, both by firms and by final consumers, to the roads from the railways, and, to go further back still, from waterways as well. A great deal of some past investment is being rendered valueless at the same time as the strain on the other type grows. To what extent, by better organization and even by further investment expenditure, the capital tied up in the older system can still be used remains to be seen. The capital-using invention, the petrol-engine, has been available for a long time and more recently the rise in incomes has brought it within the reach of more firms and final consumers; its consequences are yet to be fully worked out. It would be interesting to know to what extent periods of process in distribution and the size of stocks have been reduced by it, to what extent it has conserved other forms of capital, besides adding to convenience and pleasure. At any rate the NEDC finds itself able to estimate an overall increase in investment in transport capacity of about 10 per cent in 1966 as compared with 1961, greater investment in roads, airlines, docks and harbours being restrained by a fall in shipping and little change in railway usage.

Investment in transport, and the change-over from rail to road, is of particular importance for the issues of regional development raised elsewhere.

One of the ways in which increased incomes due to growth could bring great benefits in convenience and pleasure is in housing. Unfortunately, there is a choice to be made here; though one of the earliest, housing remains a most costly form of investment. How much of the resources available for investment should be devoted to it seems a matter for political decision in many countries. The NEDC suggests a rate of construction of 350,000 dwellings a year—a little above that attained in the last few years, but below what could on reasoned grounds be thought desirable.

In addition to these items of investment in fixed capital, with which the foregoing argument has been mainly concerned, an increase in stocks of goods and work in progress is a necessary part of any growth in total output. The total value of stocks has stood consistently in the last ten years at 38 or 39 per cent of the gross domestic product and this gives some idea of their importance. Increases in stocks were just over 6 per cent of all investment in 1961. Comparison with other countries suggest that this total is too large, and that one of the major gains of better administrative techniques could be its reduction. The annual reports of some of the larger companies in fact show that increasing attention is being devoted to stock holdings and the related accounting issue of 'cash flow' (the conservation of working capital).

Since an adverse balance of international payments can be considered as dis-investment, that is, an addition to final output not coming from current production, and a favourable balance of payments as investment, that is, a subtraction from the output available for final consumption, a change from the former to the latter must be added to the total of investment before it is compared with probable saving. Since it is hoped to make such a change from an adverse balance in 1961 to a substantial favourable balance in 1966, provision of this sort is in fact made by the NEDC in the comparison with savings likely to be forthcoming.

The total gross saving required to finance investment as estimated by the NEDC for 4 per cent annual growth is £6,355 million in 1966 (19·5 per cent of the gross domestic product), as compared with £4,721 million in 1961 (17·8 per cent of the gross domestic product), assuming no change in the general level of money costs between 1961 and 1966, but allowing for some predictable and relevant changes in relative prices. The estimated move in the balance of payments is from −£77 million in 1961 to +£300 million in 1966:[1] a relatively small part of the total saving. The increase in the proportion saved of the gross national product reflects the NEDC's view that technical and managerial improvement alone is insufficient to achieve and maintain a 4 per cent annual growth in output. A rather greater proportion of current output will therefore have to be devoted to building up and maintaining capacity. That the increase suggested is so small (an addition of 1·7 per cent of total current output by 1966) while the rate of steady growth to be achieved is considerably larger than that experienced in recent years (4 per cent per annum as compared with 2·7 per cent from 1956–61), is a reflection of the NEDC's belief in the contribution that can be made by the technical and managerial improvements referred to previously on more than one occasion.

Fortunately there are trends at work which make feasible the saving required to meet this increased proportion of current output devoted to investment; and there is even the possibility that the tendency to save might run ahead of this. In 1961, savings after deducting stock appreciation, were subdivided into 43 per cent personal savings, 41 per cent company savings, 8 per cent by public

[1] In later UK balance of payments estimates this £77 million current account deficit for 1961 has been revised downwards to a negligible figure.

corporations, 10 per cent by local and national government, leaving an error of —2 per cent unaccounted for in the comparison between realized savings and realized investment in the national accounts. These figures are gross of depreciation allowances put aside during the year so that in the case of companies and public corporations they include more than undistributed profits for the former and trading surpluses (net of interest payments) for the latter.

It is personal savings which have been showing the most marked upward trend, so that they are now approaching the pre-war proportion to the total (48 per cent in 1938). Company and public corporation savings are somewhat lower than they were before the war (49 per cent in 1961 as compared with 52 per cent in 1938). The most striking change as compared with pre-war is the contribution now made by government budget surpluses; the surplus in 1961 was about as large as the deficit in 1938).

As a percentage of gross domestic product, saving by all the three groups (counting companies and public corporations as one) is higher than pre-war; personal 7·7 per cent in 1961 as compared with 5 per cent in 1938, companies and public corporations 8·8 per cent as compared with 5·5 per cent, government +1·7 per cent as compared with —1·5 per cent. The main change in the post-war years is the very marked rise in personal savings from 0·4 per cent of the gross domestic product in 1949–51, compared with a fall from 4·7 per cent for government and a minor change for companies and public corporations. In aggregate, savings grew from 14·7 per cent of the gross domestic product in 1949–51 to 17·8 per cent in 1961—a growth wholly due to personal savings more than off-setting a decline in government saving.

This surge of personal saving is interesting in itself. There were clear reasons why personal savings should be low in the immediate post-war years, as re-stocking took place in a period of relatively lower real incomes. There would necessarily be some recovery from this exceptional position. The swing in politics also favoured the change-over from government saving to personal saving. Pressure to keep dividend payments down was gradually removed. The early trend of government taxation policy towards heavy redistribution in favour of lower-income groups with higher propensities to consume was halted, and later reversed; the change in financial policy from cheap money and heavy budget surpluses as a means of controlling inflation (32 per cent of total saving was attributed to government in 1949–51, 4·7 per cent of the gross domestic product), to a greater emphasis on monetary policy favoured personal saving both by release from further rises in taxation and by the offer of higher interest rates. It is interesting that the holding back of government saving implicit in these later policies allowed personal incomes to rise, and in fact greater personal saving out of them balanced the reductions. The element of income transfer was aided by making the purchase of equities on the stock exchange more attractive at the same time as institutions and private investors were beginning to realize their value as a hedge against inflation, and later, by making many fixed interest securities such as National Savings Certificates more attractive.

It is remarkable that a period of inflation, traditionally held to be inimical to saving, should have been accompanied by policies and events leading to the opposite result. The major change which can be singled out was in the investment policies of the great financial institutions, such as insurance companies, as they sought to escape its effects. A lesser one was that of the more general public finding its way to the stock exchange in Britain, via the increasingly popular unit trusts. This nexus of events, however, covers one underlying feature which should not surprise the economist. Real incomes were rising and inflation brought a rise in money incomes as well as in prices accompanied by an increase in the average propensity to save. This rise in money and real incomes was over and above the redistributive transfers already referred to, though saving out of the latter also occurred.

It has seemed worthwhile to give this account of the genesis of new personal savings to emphasize its importance and its firm base, and perhaps to point to conclusions about their future course as growth proceeds.

Although it may be expected that the level of personal savings will continue to be high and continue to rise, their rate of increase is likely to be reduced, since some of the special forces which gave rise to it will have spent their effect.

Company savings will depend very much on political influences, firstly because the total amount of profits may come under greater political control as part of an incomes stabilization policy. The question here is what means of control can be devised that would not at the same time conflict with a policy of expansion. It would have to be selective; and so a good guess might be that the effects would not be strong in a period of growth. Secondly, the amount to be distributed on ordinary shares out of profits is much more effectively capable of government control, and will naturally affect the amounts put to reserves. Since 1958 the proportion distributed in this way has tended to increase; for the next few years an assumption that there will be no change in the proportion distributed seems the safest on which to base plans, and this is in fact the one chosen by the NEDC.

If present government thinking on the financing of investment in the nationalized industries is maintained, then it may be expected that public corporations will move more into line with the private sector, and finance more of their capital needs out of their own accumulated resources, rather than making demands on the treasury, and its borrowing powers, for loans. This was the suggestion of the important White Paper of 1961 on 'Financial Obligations of the Nationalized Industries' (Cmnd. 1337). It does have implications for their pricing policies which give rise to political issues, but the financial realities of the situation suggest that in future the nationalized industries will have to rely more on themselves, and therefore points to a rise in saving by public corporations.

The final picture for savings likely to be available during the next few years and in 1966 looks like this:

TABLE 2.8
Total Savings, 1961 and 1966

	£ million		Per cent	
	1961	1966	1961	1966
Persons	2,031	2,730	43	43
Companies	1,954	2,480	41	39
Public Corporations	381	720	8	11
Government	461	580	10	9
Statistical error	−107	−130	−2	−2
Total:	4,721	6,380	100	100

Source: NEDC, *The Growth of the British Economy to 1966*, p. 49.

Since the savings estimated to be required in 1966 to balance domestic capital formation and the balance of payments surplus is £6,355 million compared with £6,380 million likely to be available, the two totals match sufficiently well, at about 19½ per cent of gross domestic product, for there to be reasonable assurance that a growth rate involving this amount of new capital formation is feasible.

9. Land Resources

So far capital and manpower requirements have been discussed. There has been a tendency to neglect land, or national endowment in general, in discussions of the growth of developed economies although it is a relevant factor determining the capabilities of particular regions within an advanced economy and less developed countries as a whole. The reasons for passing over these important resources for developed economies as a whole are two. Firstly, being 'advanced' is associated with manufacturing industry which is predominantly capital-using, not directly land-using. Secondly while the product of land, either in the form of raw materials or of food and clothing for workers is essential for all industries there is always the possibility of importing them for the economies which are advanced at present, if the necessary capacities are not available within their own borders. The 'at present' needs emphasizing; availability, cheapness and plentiful supply, depend on a particular structure of world trade which has grown up over many decades, but which may not survive indefinitely.

Advanced economies differ widely in the extent to which they have recourse to trade for the direct products of land. All countries require to import some items and all find advantages in trade. Some, however, such as Britain, seem to live off trade, in that a large part of their food and much of their material for the supply of power is bought from abroad, and a good deal of their manufacturing activity consists in adding value to materials bought from abroad. The problem of land requirements for any given rate of growth then reappears in the guise of physical export capacity coupled with the ability to earn foreign currencies with the goods, or services, exported; that capacity and earning power will have to be sufficient to purchase the extra imports which will be demanded as the economy grows. In Britain, in present circumstances, they must also be sufficient to relieve current balance of payments difficulties and achieve a surplus which will allow for aid and investment abroad.

The long-term problem should not, however, be exaggerated. (The harsher realities of the current problem will be discussed shortly.) It is not only the case that a country may require to import if some standard of living or growth rate is to be achieved; it may merely be that with the existing relation of world and home prices it is advantageous for her to import, and to export to do so, as the theory of comparative advantage in international trade would suggest. Moreover, the reasons for international trade may lie in particular patterns of consumer tastes or in fashions which may be ephemeral and far removed from trade to overcome deficiencies in basic land resources.

It would be misleading to think of an economy even such as that of Great Britain having recourse to food imports solely because the manpower needed for sustaining and improving her standard of living could not be supported off the product of her own land. Much food is imported from abroad merely because it is cheaper to do so with the existing pattern of world economic development; yet, even though it would be cheaper, some importation is avoided because of the drive to protect a highly developed home agriculture. At present for the fortunate advanced countries the situation still tends to be one of food surplus. It perhaps may remain so for them and become so for countries where the present situation is far from one of surplus. Advanced industrial countries do possess land, and whatever purely economic advantage might suggest, seem to want to use it. Since they are advanced they have the ability to use it productively, both in terms of yield per acre and per man, and are impelled so to use it for it to progress at least some way to being competitive in price with imported products. The process may be carried even further when major industrial countries are also major food producers and exporters as is the United States, or wish to become so, as does France.

The import of mineral raw materials stands on rather a different footing. They may be 'required' for growth in a stronger sense than in the case of food, since advanced industrial processes often need, for instance, relatively scarce metals which may not exist within the country's borders. Growth, with its capital construction, may also require basic metals such as steel which do not exist in sufficient quantity or have already been exhausted within the country's own borders. The advanced country may be relatively lucky in these respects, as for example, North America, or not so fortunate, as Britain, and some of the other Western European nations.

Though their home supplies of raw materials may be less satisfactory than their supplies of food the present advanced industrial nations have the advantage that, at the moment, they are the only large-scale consumers of these products of land. It is here perhaps that one might expect the greatest change in the world market situation as the present underdeveloped countries grow, and themselves begin to use mineral products in larger quantities, since, unlike agriculture, the scope for improvements in 'yield per acre' is small.

This section may be concluded by repeating the old lesson that it is by foreign trade as well as by technical improvement that an advancing country beats the tendency for returns to its own material endowments to diminish, which Ricardo otherwise foresaw as setting a limit to growth. The variety and scope of trade itself may defer this for some considerable time, before its limits are in turn reached. Much depends on the world situation as well as on the needs and capacities of the countries concerned. For an advanced economy such as the United Kingdom it is probably still fair to say that the balance is in its favour, as far as the supply of the products of land from the rest of the world is concerned. What may happen in the future, and whether there are limits set to expansion in the world as a whole, as each nation attempts the same relief is perhaps a question which can be left.

10. *The Balance of Payments*

The previous section discussed what might be called the hard core of foreign trade allowing the import of the more direct products of land required for growth. But the sort of distinction it implied has significance only in thinking about the influence of 'natural endowment' on the output and growth rates that an economy can achieve. It may have some special significance in certain circumstances, such as a country at war, when foreign trade has to be minimized, or when a country is developing under socialist direction. Even in this second case, however, and it may be in the first as well, there is no particular virtue in as complete self-sufficiency as possible, and land products to which considerable value has been added abroad, such as manufactured goods, may be imported with advantage. One of the important products that the USSR has to obtain from abroad is natural rubber, and this item therefore occupies a special position in her trade balance, but it is quite customary also for her to import advanced technical goods which are not sufficiently provided for in her own immediate production plans. By this means a developing economy can avoid for the time some of the waiting which the development of her own capacity in that particular line would require, and therefore make greater output possible sooner.

There is a further reason why an economy such as that of the United Kingdom might find it advantageous to import some manufactured products, at any stage of the process of production from capital equipment to finished products, and that is to act as a standby if a part of its input-output plans miscarries for some reason. In view of the vast complication of the relationships themselves and the extent to which they depend on unpredictable factors it is not surprising that shortages occur which may hold up the rest of the plan. Foreign trade offers an element of flexibility and insurace in carrying out a complicated operation.

On top of the 'hard core' foreign trade then, there may be another layer of imports which depends, not on the scarcity of land, but on the wish to conserve capital, and the need for an element of insurance. Although this second set of needs has been brought out by considering an economy developing under socialist direction it forms a second category of imports for any growing economy. Import needs of this sort emerge quite naturally as an addendum to any input-output analysis for growth of the sort described above. First having worked out input-output requirements for each good and capacity for a particular rate of growth, taking into account at this stage only 'hard core' import requirements, the planning body might reach the conclusion that a desired growth rate could not be reached unless more planned capacity were devoted to exports, and some otherwise missing items were imported.

For a predominantly free enterprise advanced economy such as Britain there is a whole lot of other trade added to the core and the layer just distinguished. There is the sort of trade which finds its justification primarily in the theory of comparative cost advantage, rather than absolute advantage. On top of this there is the sort of trade which depends largely on the free exercise of consumer choice as a political feature of the economy; for instance, some people may rather like to own a car made in France, and many people like Danish bacon.

To achieve a full integration of thinking about foreign trade and thinking about growth is a difficult task. What planning for growth has done so far in the United Kingdom is to take the whole existing structure of international trade for granted, to make predictions on its basis, and to work out its implications for the desired 4 per cent growth rate. Final demands for various classes of commodities have been predicted for each year and over a period of a few years. The situation of goods for export is indeed somewhat different from that of goods consumed domestically, since it is necessary to predict both foreign demand curves and foreign supply curves; and then to consider how much attention home manufacturers will devote to export markets, and now their level of costs and prices will enable them to compete abroad. In the case of the home market physical calculations of demands and requirements can proceed without paying too great attention to the monetary units in which they are expressed. But this is obviously not sensible in the case of the goods which will be demanded for export. The success of internal policies for price stability, the course of external prices, and the value of foreign currencies, are clearly relevant, as well as the assessment of trends in the demand schedules for different classes of commodities in the world markets. The probable course of tariff negotiations with all their political overtones are also of major importance.

In order to bring out the problem let us make some relatively simple assumptions about the size of final export demands. The simplest one to take is that there will be the same increase at constant prices over the whole category as for domestic final demands and within that total account could be taken of any obvious shifts between different commodities or destinations. This would then be in conformity with the desired rate of growth, at constant prices, of the whole of domestic output.

From this rate of growth may be calculated sets of import requirements for any input; the only difference in this case being that imports are the output of no domestic industry but are input for the economy as a whole. The predicted requirements will be on the basis of past relationships, and any observed trend in them. In this case there is one set to be added; that is the proportions of any good which will be imported and the proportion which will be produced at home, for those goods which are not wholly imported. This proportion again depends on complications such as tariff reductions or the relation between internal and external price levels. For a few years ahead, however, it may be possible to make some physical estimate, and perhaps to take account of probable changes in the external factors mentioned.

The import requirements will come from three sources. These are (1) requirements as direct items of final consumption; (2) requirements as raw material, fixed capital, or components in industries producing other items of final consumption; and (3) requirements as raw material, fixed capital, or components by industries exporting their products. This last source merges into the second since a very large number of industries will export some part of their product, even if they would not normally be thought of as export industries. It is convenient to distinguish here two classes of goods for home consumption and for export, even though they do not correspond to any industrial division, in order to clarify the issues involved. It is, of course, the input of imports into exports which corresponds to the consumption by an industry of its own products in the earlier discussion, since the exports may be thought of as the means by which the imports are provided. The demand for imports which are directly, or almost directly, consumed will be influenced, in its relation to the rest of the items of final demand, by all the issues previously mentioned such as external prices and tariff reductions. Again it may be possible to estimate some relationship between growth in final demand (that is, the overall growth in output and incomes) and the rate of growth in final demand for the various classes of this sort of import, on the assumption, used for the rest of the analysis, that reasonable price stability is maintained at home, and taking account of any trends in that relationship which seem clear from the past, or probable in the future.

Having formed some estimate of the import demand and requirements for the desired rate of growth, the set of figures, if in physical terms, may then be translated into a total value for imports, now taking account of any available forecast of world prices and exchange rates. If the rates of demand and requirements for groups of commodities have already been assessed in value terms, then these external factors will already have been dealt with, and it only remains to aggregate the items.

At this stage it would be appropriate to use similar forecasts of exchange rates and world market conditions to obtain the total of exports valued not at constant prices, but at the prices (in domestic currency) expected to be current at the dates to which the growth plan refers. It is the then current value of exports in domestic currency (the export earnings of the country) which have to be compared with the value of imports (in domestic currency) required and demanded, to see how the particular growth programme chosen works out in terms of the current balance of international payments of the country. (It may be presumed that 'invisible' imports and exports have been included in the calculations.)

For a growth plan which runs in terms of gross domestic product this is as far as we need go. A further objective of a balance of payments surplus, to allow for aid or investment abroad, or to build up reserves, which refers to the use made of the growth in output when it has been attained, may be included in the programme of the government made known to the planning body, and the investigations of the NEDC for the United Kingdom do, in fact, include it as an additional aim. But there is the danger, of course, of an excess of the value of imports over that of exports. If this was the result of the calculations it would be a clear indication that growth of the form envisaged, that is a given rate of growth at constant prices over the whole of final output including exports, was not feasible.

The first thing to be done if this were the outcome of this first type of calculation, would be to re-examine the figures for export production. In a free enterprise economy there is no particular reason why production for export (at constant prices expressed in domestic currency) should advance in exactly the same proportion as output as a whole. It might advance less, in which case matters would be worse, but the possibility of its advancing more, and so forming a larger proportion of total output at the expense of that going to the home market, would have to be considered. The survival of the particular total growth rate envisaged, would then imply a smaller growth of output produced and sold at home, which might possibly be made up by the increased imports, depending on whether the increased aggregate value of imports was due wholly to increases in quantity, or partly to increases in external prices. If such a relative expansion of production for export was not to be expected of its own accord then the possibility of government measures either to encourage exports or to diminish imports would have to be considered. Such measures, which could include anything from devaluation to internal deflation, tariffs, import controls, export assistance of various sorts, and propaganda campaigns, might or might not be internally and externally acceptable, according to their degree. This is one of the most difficult problems of economic policy with which a free enterprise economy has to contend.

The alternative, in this matter of import and export values not matching, would be to declare that the particular rate of expansion, involving that particular level of import requirement, was not feasible. At some point, with some values of the relationships involved, this might have to be the conclusion, to be weighed in the balance with the use of the measures of government influence and control mentioned. A lack of balance in external payments due to growth may come either from a failure of foreign demand to expand sufficiently to accommodate the increased export production, if it advanced in line with the rest of output, or from a more than proportionate rise in imports demanded as internal output and incomes rose. On top of this there might be predictable movements in the terms of trade, and the general situation in world markets which could lead to the same trouble, but would have nothing to do with the growth programme of the country concerned. A reduction in the size of the growth programme would be a remedy for the former, and that is all that need be said as far as the problem of planning for growth considered purely by itself is concerned.

Nevertheless, planning for growth takes place within a certain context of events and so it is natural that a body commissioned to assess the feasibility of a growth programme would in fact do so taking into account all factors which might cause difficulty for the economy whether there was growth or not. It would, in the course of its work, attempt to assess all influences on the balance of payments and any difficulty that was likely to arise, even though it was not the growth itself that was responsible for the changes. In fact, in the particular situation from which the programme started expansion might help in solving some of these other difficulties which already existed. For instance, if any existing deficiency in exports lay more in home output and in costs than in potential marketability abroad, the domestic expansion might give a fillip to export production along with the rest; it might reduce costs by the higher replacement rate

G

of old equipment, increase investment in improved techniques which it would make possible, increase the extent to which existing capacity was worked, and in the long run increase capital formation out of the larger incomes.

On the other hand growth might make for instability in the short run, which would be detrimental to costs in export industries, and in the long run (perhaps very long indeed) generate limits to itself via the balance of payments. Just as growth as a remedy for unemployment is one that is delicately balanced, so is growth as a remedy for balance of payments difficulties.

So far this has been a general discussion of the connection between growth and the balance of payments for an advanced industrial economy, designed to bring out the issues involved. In many ways the considerations brought forward by the NEDC for the United Kingdom are reassuring, as were those in the case of the balance between investment and savings, though, to an outsider, it does seem that the balance of payments issue is the one which gives the greatest concern to the NEDC among the many requiring its attention.

One obvious basic difficulty is the fact that quantitative assessment of even the most rudimentary sort has to do with prices and market situations, and cannot be confined, even in the short run, to an analysis of physical limits on capacity. Since the markets concerned cover the whole world the degree of uncertainty in prediction must be high. However, the NEDC starts out by assuming that Britain's terms of trade remain roughly the same over the years to 1966 as they were in 1961 (by the end of 1964 this assumption had not been falsified), and by assuming also that there will be a continuing reduction in tariffs in the European Free Trade Area but that there are no other tariff reductions, nor entry into the European Economic Community. This is a conservative basis for prediction, though, of course, tariff reductions cut both ways. An improvement is anticipated in the invisible balance to be expected, giving a surplus on invisible items of £230 million in 1966, largely due to a continuation of the recent increase in investment income from abroad and a continual reduction in home interest rates although by the end of 1964 this seemed a misplaced hope.

It was initially estimated that the net deficit on current account in 1961 was £77 million but later estimates have revised this to almost zero. For many years it has been the declared aim of successive governments to achieve a net surplus on current account of £300 million a year, £250 million of which would allow for private and government investment and aid abroad, and, say, £50 million to build up gold and foreign currency reserves which, of course, not only serve this country but the rest of the sterling area as well. There are obvious and sound financial reasons for this. Although it is not part of a growth programme relating to gross domestic product, the NEDC has taken over this general aim to convert a relatively small deficit into a substantial surplus. As an objective it is related closely to the purely domestic programme, not only by imposing some demand on home output, but in a more vital way as well. The world knows the smallness of British reserves in relation to short-term external commitments, and the recurring domestic difficulties created in recent years by their inadequacy. If a drain on reserves becomes serious either because of lack of confidence or of deeper difficulties the government must take action, and the action which has been most immediately effective both on overseas opinion and on underlying factors is to increase bank rate. This incidentally may serve, together with other deflationary measures adopted, to reduce the rate of expansion domestically, whether that expansion was inflationary or not. Achievement of a more assured balance of payments, and the world's view of it, is a pre-condition of a programme for internal growth. Internal growth may help in both assuring confidence and solving underlying problems, and this is one of the more reassuring factors in the situation. At any rate recent United Kingdom governments have, from past experience, become convinced that the balance of payments problem must be approached in a context of growth and that the growth programme must be such as not itself to aggravate it over any length of time. The consequences of any imbalances which do develop in the short run (for example, a rapid rise in imports due to re-stocking as the programme gets under way) should apparently be borne in the interest of longer-run development and an assured solution of the problem. To this end there has been preliminary activity in co-operation with other central banks and the International Monetary Fund, to provide immediate reinforcement of the reserves and generally to inform world financial opinion of the policy and its aims.

Furthermore, it is interesting to note the increasing importance of private capital flows, both in and out, during recent years. This is not only short-term capital attracted by interest-rate differences but also long-term capital. In 1961 there was a net inflow, but in preceeding years the balance had been quite substantially in the other direction, so that the NEDC has thought it prudent to enter a debit figure in the capital account of £150 million a year by 1966, and, as has been said, to double it to allow for a net outflow of government capital of £200 million—£20 million to repay old debts, £180 million to lend to underdeveloped countries—and to provide for an increase in the reserves of £50 million.

The reasoning by which the NEDC reached its conclusions about the implications of growth and the achievement of this favourable balance of payments in the years to 1966 is not clear from the document itself. As will have been apparent from the preceding discussion one needs to know the level of exports before the volume of imports can be fully assessed, and to know the level of imports before one can assess the level of exports needed to secure the balance of payments objective. The NEDC's report begins by discussing the level of exports needed to secure the desired balance of payments, but as prior knowledge of the level of imports in 1966 is a major requirement for calculating this, it seems convenient to start by discussing the import prediction first. In doing this we, as does the NEDC report, will leave on one side the awkward but quantitatively minor point that exports also have an import content.

On the assumption made earlier of roughly constant terms of trade and only certain planned tariff reductions taken into account, the NEDC's First Report estimated that the growth in the volume of imports from 1961 to 1966 could be in the same proportion as that of gross domestic output and incomes as a whole, that is 4 per cent per annum. Constant terms of trade seem here to imply constant import prices, over the whole range of goods, since the total is in money terms. The figures for 1966 of £5,345 million c.i.f. and £4,870 million f.o.b. represent an increase of 4 per cent per annum both c.i.f. and f.o.b. over the 1961 figures. This growth rate was later revised to 4·7 per cent.

It is assumed that the relative fall in the price of food will not continue, and that this will so moderate the tendency for growth in incomes to increase food consumption that it will only increase by 1·7 per cent per annum. It might also be expected that the marginal propensity to consume food would be falling as incomes rose to any considerable extent, though there might be some substitution of the more expensive varieties of foreign food. On the other hand a substitution away from the cheaper varieties of foreign food in favour of home products is equally to be expected; and, in fact, an upward trend in the rate of increase in food production at home is expected to continue.

It is interesting and reassuring to see that the relationship between increases in output and rising imports of raw materials has tended to be a declining one in recent years, and is expected to continue. This trend could take some considerable part of the sting out of the analysis of what might happen, as set out in the previous sections on land resources and on the implications for the balance of payments. It does not mean, however, that imports of materials will not have to increase, and for them the NEDC takes a rate of increase of 3·3 per cent per annum. This figure is supported by the enquiry into the needs of the seventeen industries. Imported fuel, mainly oil, is an item of some importance, though considerably less than the two categories already mentioned (in 1961: food, £1,435 million and materials £1,131 million compared with fuels £484 million). Oil imports are expected to grow at a somewhat faster rate than imports in general (4·4 per cent per annum), but the rate of increase as compared with that in recent years is expected to fall off, mainly due to a slower increase in its use in electricity generation.

The major expansion is expected to be in imports of manufactures. At a rate of 7·0 per cent per annum this is a continuation of the upward trend of the preceding ten years. These years were remarkable for a general expansion in world trade in manufactures, though the underlying significance of this cannot yet be assessed since they were also a period of rapid removal of import controls and other restrictions on trade. Some restrictions still remain, and are much discussed; whether the expansion will continue at so high a rate when there is less scope for major de-restriction is a matter for conjecture; whether, for instance, world trade in manufactures will advance at a slower, the same, or faster rate than the continuing fairly high rate of increase in world production of them ($4\frac{1}{2}$–5 per cent per annum) which is to be expected. For the long term what happens is important since it affects the continuing ability to grow of the expanding number of already advanced economies.

The NEDC's estimates are worked out on the basis of 1961 prices, and it is assumed that there will be some slight improvement in our competitive position, through a slight fall in the domestic price of manufactures relative to world prices—an assumption to be discussed more fully in connection with exports, but which is relevant here. If it were not fulfilled then the rate of growth of our imports of manufactures might be even higher.

In order to purchase this increased volume of imports (£4,870 million f.o.b. in 1966 at 1961 prices), an annual rate of increase of 4 per cent, and in order to achieve the aim of turning a current account deficit into a surplus of £300 million in 1966, the NEDC initially estimated that exports and re-exports would have to grow to £4,940 million f.o.b. at 1961 prices, requiring by 1966 an annual rate of increase of 5 per cent. This is on the assumptions that there would be no change in the terms of trade, and that only already planned tariff reductions would come into effect, but it may be that these assumptions are somewhat conservative.

The main interest centres on the rate of expansion and the state of foreign markets, and on our competitive position in them, and it is the markets for manufactured goods that are particularly relevant. Since it is almost impossible to predict the course of recession and expansion from time to time, even for a few years ahead, discussion has necessarily to settle round the trend, even though this may be to discount difficulties which are very real in Britain's existing balance of payments situation. The world trend itself is encouraging, even if allowance is made for a falling off in the rate of expansion which might naturally follow the particularly rapid progress in the 1950's when controls on trade of all sorts were considerably reduced. If we follow the NEDC in thinking that a trend rate in international trade in manufactures roughly equal to that in world production of manufactures is neither over-cautious nor over-optimistic, then we would have a predicted average annual growth rate of $4\frac{1}{2}$ to 5 per cent, this being based on a continuation in the next few years of the same rate of increase of production as in the second half of the 1950's.

In the past Britain's share of trade in manufactures has been falling, and this at a time when trade in them was expanding faster than production. If we were to continue predicting on the basis of trends, then the prospects of achieving a 5 per cent per annum growth in exports would be gloomy. It is at this point that the NEDC calls most decisively for action; action to halt this particular trend towards a falling share of world trade in manufactures. If some help is given by tariff reductions we may reasonably aim at the 5 per cent per annum figure. What most needs remedying to attain it? The range of goods we export is wider than that of many countries whose trade has grown faster. It is true that a great deal of Britain's trade has been directed to markets which have not been the fastest to grow and, for technical reasons, the benefit of discrimination through Commonwealth Preference has been declining. The NEDC's assessment, however, is that this would only account for a small part of our relative decline and is in any case not expected to work so strongly in the future. It is worthwhile quoting the NEDC's conclusion: 'Our exports have been hampered by a comparatively low level of investment and slow rate of increase in productivity at home, and it is assumed that there will be improvements in both respects in the future. Measures to improve selling methods, design and the speed of innovation would also help'.[1] Furthermore in its study,

[1] NEDC, *Growth of the United Kingdom Economy to 1966*, p. 52.

Export Trends, the NEDC showed a clear correlation between Britain's falling share of world trade and a rise in her export prices relative to those of other countries.

While this is a call to action, a more technical point, which has already been referred to, is included. The NEDC is entitled to assume an improvement in costs of production of exports merely by virtue of its own growth programme. This is one of the more reassuring aspects of the situation, backed up by another feature of recent trade in manufactures, namely that some of the best performances in exports were by economies whose over-all rate of expansion was the greatest. It is essential, however, that the possibility of any such favourable outcome of growth is not hindered by instability of incomes tending to push up internal costs. The NEDC suggested, rather cryptically, that, in order to widen profit margins on exports, which have recently been becoming dangerously small, prices of home manufactured goods should be allowed to fall relatively to external ones. In other words, growth with stability should mean such a degree of stability that any increase in home prices would be less than that of external prices. This is quite a restrictive condition unless, alternatively, it is read as an oblique way of advocating devaluation. Actual price reductions of manufactures in the home market consequent on increases in the productivity of labour, capital or management have not been the rule in recent years, though they are far from being ruled out logically, and have sometimes occurred as in the case of electric lamp-bulbs.

Whether so high a rate of increase in exports can be achieved within the NEDC's time-table remains to be seen; as long as a growth programme is in motion the longer-term prospects of achieving it are, of course, better than the shorter, world economic conditions permitting. With the data of the NEDC's 1963 Report the United Kingdom balance of payments would look something like this in 1966:

TABLE 2.9

The Balance of Payments, 1961 and 1966

	£ million		Rate of increase per cent per annum
	1961	1966	
Imports f.o.b.	−4,006	−4,870	4·0
Exports and re-exports f.o.b.	3,863	4,940	5·0
Net invisible items	66	230	
Current balance	−77*	300	

* Subsequently corrected to virtually zero.

Given the British government's declared policies of maintaining the international position of the pound as regards the fixity of its exchange rate and its role as a world currency, and of pursuing greater freedom in world trade, the British balance of payments position will prove crucial for the success of NEDC's plan. If exports fail to rise sufficiently, and imports rise too quickly, either 4 per cent growth must be abandoned or a drastic reappraisal of priorities in policy objectives must be undertaken.

11. *Conclusion*

With the United Kingdom two-thirds of the way through the period over which the target rate of growth set by the NEDC was 4 per cent per annum, has the performance of the economy matched up with the NEDC plan? From 1961 to 1963 the rate of growth of gross domestic product was well below the NEDC target. During 1963 and continuing into 1964 the growth of the gross domestic product was greater than 4 per cent per annum. Despite this increase in the growth rate during and since 1963, the United Kingdom did not achieve in 1964 the level of production that is required if an average annual growth rate of 4 per cent is to be achieved for the whole planning period. It is necessary, therefore, that the growth rate for the remainder of the period (1964–66) should be in excess of 4 per cent per year if the target for the whole period, 1961 to 1966 is to be achieved.

As already in early 1964 there were signs that inflation and balance of payments crises were lurking not far around the corner, the situation did not look encouraging for achieving the NEDC growth target. These portents of balance of payments crises were borne out in the Autumn of 1964 when the pound was under severe pressure and it was feared that the 7 per cent bank rate and other measures would mean the postponement of 4 per cent growth. The previously expressed fear about the balance of payments limitation in a year when export values rose by 4 per cent and import values by 15 per cent was all too speedily justified. Even if the annual average rate of growth between 1961 and 1966 did turn out to be 4 per cent, the achievement of this result would not appear to be a result of long-term planning of a steady rate of growth, but the result of the statistical accident that the short-period boom of the latter part of the period cancelled out the stagnation of the economy in 1961 and 1962. In short, the pattern of economic activity between 1961 and 1966 is unlikely to look much different from the fluctuations that were to be found in the 1950's, except that these fluctuations were about a more rapidly rising trend.

If this be the case, it seems that the NEDC is in danger of becoming an irrelevancy in that the pattern of activity would have been similar if the NEDC had not been created. Critics of the NEDC have made conflicting criticisms that on the one hand the target for growth has been too high to be achieved by a steady growth rate, while on the other the target has been too low in that it looks as if it is possible to achieve the average growth rate over the whole period without doing anything to remove the phenomenon of the rolling readjustment in Britain's economy. Perhaps the creation in October 1964 by the Labour Government of the Department of Economic Affairs was partly to give more purposeful direction to the British economy and its growth.

It is important to remember the nature of the NEDC and to realize what it is possible and impossible for this organization to do. First, the NEDC is an independent body in that it is not a part of any government Ministry, and of course in no way akin to a Ministry of Planning. The functions of the Council are largely fact finding and consultation between different industries and between labour and management. Secondly, the NEDC has no powers to enforce any of its targets upon different sectors of the economy. In this respect there is a significant difference from the French planning machinery where the planning organization has subtle and indirect powers to secure acceptance of its targets by virtue of control over capital issues. The achievement of any NEDC target, if not by accident, must rely on industrialists accepting the NEDC targets, which they have helped to formulate, and co-operating in making of the plans a reality.

The success of this type of planning depends, therefore, on co-operation between the various interests represented on the NEDC in formulating a feasible rate of growth for the economy as a whole and for individual industries, and in persuading industry to follow the plans. The innovation that has come about by the creation of the NEDC is that industrialists and trade unionists have become involved in planning on a wider basis than previously, when their horizons were restricted to those of an individual firm or an individual industry.

Because the success of the Council's plans depends on their acceptance by various interests on the Council, and because the plans are created by the various interests on the Council, one might argue that the outcome would be the same with or without the deliberations of the NEDC. This indeed could be true if the NEDC ceased to function as a committee so that the ideas and plans of each individual on the Council were in no way influenced by the discussions of the Council. As long as the organization functions efficiently as a committee, however, what any one party regards as a feasible rate of growth for his own industry is likely to be modified in the course of conference. As it is not unreasonable to believe that these modifications to the notion of a feasible growth rate will be upward, and as long as the members of the Council then go away and use their influence in an attempt to achieve the modified growth rate for a particular industry, the NEDC has justified its existence. If an average 4 per cent per annum growth rate is achieved for the period 1961 to 1966, much still remains to be desired in achieving a steady annual rate of growth within the period; but at least a 4 per cent average growth rate is an improvement on the 2·6 per cent of the period from 1950 to 1960.

CHAPTER III

Regional Development in the United Kingdom

by M. J. PULLEN

1. *The Concept of Regional Development*

As we have seen, the economic development of a nation state may be measured in a crude fashion by calculating the income per head of population. This measure, apart from all the inherent difficulties in calculating national income and the even greater difficulties of making any meaningful statements about the level of economic welfare, masks variations in the level of income per head within the nation state. It is with the extent of these regional variations in income per head, the reasons for the variations and possible policies to bring about a more egalitarian regional distribution of income, that this chapter is concerned.

The differences between countries with high and low incomes per head are frequently explained in terms of how far the resources of the nation are being fully employed. A modification of this argument is that the income differences are a result of the factors of production not being combined together in the optimum proportions in the low income countries (e.g. over-population of the land so that the marginal product of labour is extremely low). Such reasoning, however, is misleading.

First, there is no one optimum combination[1] of factors of production. The optimum combination of factors of production to produce a given output will vary according to the local relative scarcity of the various productive factors. This applies to methods of production in regions within a country as well as between countries. Secondly, the idea that differences in the level of economic development are due merely to different factor employment levels ignores the given nature of the natural resources of a particular country or region. However fully employed labour and capital may be, if there are no water resources available in a region, the region is unlikely to prosper

[1] In the sense of the least cost combination of factors to produce a given output.

as an agricultural region! We must expect, therefore, differences in income per head between countries and between regions within a country for no other reason than that they are unequally endowed with natural resources. This argument will apply with greatest force to countries or regions which are engaged in primary production (agriculture, forestry, mining and quarrying). In the United Kingdom, however, where 94 per cent of the working population is employed in manufacturing and service industry, and where in these industries transport costs are a relatively insignificant proportion of the total costs of production, the natural endowment argument is not so relevant—a fact which considerably increases the scope for government intervention in planning the location of private investment in new industrial capacity.

In applying the concept of economic development to a region (a section of a nation state), the limits on development imposed by the natural resources of the region must be remembered. Where, however, industry in one region is at no cost disadvantage compared with industry in other regions, the existence of factor unemployment is a sign that national income per head could be raised by using these unused resources. Regional studies which highlight variations in the level of unemployment are relevant, therefore, to formulating a *national* policy for economic growth. There is obviously scope for increasing the national output by employing factors, especially labour, in regions where unemployment is relatively high. In the United Kingdom, where the government since the Second World War has been relatively successful in maintaining a 'high and stable level of employment', the possibility of raising national output by using any regional pools of unemployed has been limited. The NEDC Report *Conditions Favourable to Faster Growth* suggests that, using data for 1961, an increase in national employment of 200,000 would be possible by drawing upon the unemployed in the less prosperous regions. This would represent an increase in the total labour force of 0·9 per cent. The major contribution to the NEDC growth target of 4 per cent between 1961 and 1966 would seem to be in raising labour productivity, although the removal of the considerable under-employment in the older industrial areas would be an important means of achieving this increase in productivity.

A static concept of economic development, in terms of either an optimum combination of factors of production or full employment of the factors in a particular region, is misleading. Economic development implies change. The process of change in technology and the demands of final consumers means that static equilibrium optima are of limited value, and that there is no particular pattern of regional income differentials which can be said to be an equilibrium.

As technology and consumer tastes change, the fortunes of different regions will also change depending upon the location of different forms of economic activity. Regions where declining industries are concentrated will have falling income per head—if not an absolute fall, at least a relative fall compared with regions with a large share of expanding industries. The rise and fall of different industries will mean that different demands are made upon the resources of the nation; new factors of production and new combinations of factors may be required. Because of the uneven spatial distribution of a country's resources, the growth and decline of industry is not spread evenly, so that there will be a kaleidoscopic pattern of differentials in income per head between regions over time. Any concept of regional development must, therefore, take account of the changing environment in which the economic system is expected to function.

Economic development tends to be a cumulative process because the causal relationships are not of the Humeian billiard ball type, where event A causes event B and that is the end of the matter, but as Myrdal emphasizes in *Economic Theory and Underdeveloped Regions*, are circular in nature. Event A is not an independent variable but determines and is determined by event B. Increasing (or decreasing) economies of scale play an important part in the cumulative process by which the rich regions tend to become richer and the poor regions poorer. To quote Myrdal:

'Within broad limits the power of attraction today of a centre has its origin mainly in the historical accident that something was once started there, and not in a number of other places where it could equally well or better have been started, and that the start met with success. Thereafter the ever increasing internal and external economies—interpreted in the widest sense of the word to include, for instance, a working population trained in various crafts, easy communications, the feeling of growth and elbow room and the spirit of new enterprise—fortified and sustained their continuous growth at the expense of other localities and regions where instead relative stagnation or regression became the pattern.'

The growth or decline of income per head in a region within a country is more likely to be a cumulative process than the relative growth and decline of income per head between rich and poor countries. Assuming that there is no government interference in regional development, the more perfectly the individual regions of a country are integrated in the nation state the more likely is the cumulative growth or decline in income to take place. Among the conditions that are necessary for the cumulative mechanism to operate between rich and poor regions is that there must be no state interference in influencing factor mobility—labour and capital funds (not stocks of real capital) must be free to move from region to region to maximize their earnings—nor in the movement of goods within the country. Secondly, the factor markets must be national and not reflect purely local supply and demand conditions within each region. In terms of the United Kingdom situation this condition is not unrealistic in that the collective bargaining procedure by which national standard wage rates are fixed has removed many of the regional differentials in the payments to labour that existed at the beginning of the century,[1] and in that the market for capital funds is national in extent and does not reflect the regional demand and supply conditions for capital funds. Labour will maximize its earnings by moving to the regions where it will be employed instead of remaining unemployed; while capital funds being raised on a national market will be used for investment projects which show the greatest return on capital.

The rich region will tend to attract labour and capital funds away from the poorer regions. New capital funds will be invested in the rich region where the rate of return is highest. Much of the investment of capital funds in the rich region will be at the expense of the level of investment in the poor region. These changes in the levels of investment will, of course, cause the rich region's income to rise in the subsequent time period and the poor region's income to fall. Labour will be attracted to the rich region by the better prospects of finding and keeping a job than in the poor region.

An accelerator and subsequent multiplier effect will result from the rise in the income of the rich region and the fall in the income of the poor region. The interaction of multiplier and accelerator will tend to make the change in the level of regional income a cumulative process. The development of economies of scale in the rich region as a result of the growth in economic activity may also aggravate the cumulative process by putting the rich region at an increasing cost advantage compared with the poor region.

It is likely that, although we have ruled out the downward adjustment of factor prices in the poor region as a means of stopping the cumulative process, an effective ceiling on the growth of the rich region at the expense of the poor region will result from what can be

[1] Not all regional differences in earnings have been removed, of course, by the development of a national pattern of wage rates.

called a one way factor price effect by which factor prices will rise in the rich boom region. There will come a point in time when, as labour becomes scarce, the earnings of labour will rise in the boom area, until the higher labour costs make businessmen seriously consider locating their businesses in other regions. How soon this point would be reached would depend on how far there was scope for migration into the rich region, and how easy it was to pass the higher costs per unit of output on to the consumer by raising prices.

The boom in the rich region would after a time also result in inflation of other prices as the demand within the region outgrew the available resources. If the boom in the rich region is then brought under control by the national government applying a restrictionist economic policy to the whole country, further growth in the rich region will be prevented; but also the poor region will be further depressed. All too often the less prosperous regions of the United Kingdom have suffered for the sin of inflation that has appeared in the South-East and the Midlands.

A poor region within a nation state is in many ways worse off than a poor nation state in the sense that it is more restricted in the policies that it can follow to correct a falling level of regional income. A region within a country cannot prevent capital funds flowing out across the regional frontier, nor can it impose restrictions on interregional trade, nor can it follow an independent monetary and fiscal policy.

It will be useful here to mention a few factors that are relevant to the problem of how far the cumulative process of growth and decay of regions within a country should be allowed to proceed unchecked. First, the value judgements underlying the economic system and the extent of state action will determine how far the cumulative processes are permitted to go. The United Kingdom government is committed to the concept of the welfare state which aims at bringing about greater equality of opportunity. Since one's place of birth is just as fortuitous as one's social class of birth, on grounds of equality of opportunity an individual should not be penalized because he was born in a development district, any more than he should be penalized because he comes from what is labelled a 'working class family'. Large inequalities in income per head between regions are as undesirable as large inequalities between the incomes of individuals. The inequality of opportunity between the older industrial areas and the growing industrial areas is also often heightened by the contrasts in the quantity and quality of the social capital to be found in different parts of the country. To some extent how far a country can afford equality of opportunity on a regional basis will depend upon the level of economic development already achieved. Only the rich countries can afford to forfeit the national output that is not produced as a result of bolstering up the poor regions by preventing migration to the most productive locations.

Secondly, it is not possible to follow a policy of equalizing regional income or a policy of national economic development as if they were completely independent of each other. With large pockets of regional unemployment, where labour is immobile, development on a regional basis may be the main means of achieving an increase in the National Income, although this is not true for the United Kingdom. To a large extent the success of a regional development policy will be tied up with the performance of the national economy in achieving growth. Myrdal uses the term 'spread effects' to describe the process by which the cumulative growth of a rich region is likely to increase the demand for products of the poor regions, as well as of the rich region, so that the growth of income will be shared by the poor regions; and the term 'backwash effects' to describe the process by which the rich region becomes richer at the expense of the poor regions by the concentration of labour and capital in the rich region. Theoretically, whether the cumulative growth process should be allowed to continue will depend upon whether the backwash effects outweigh the spread effects or vice versa. If in the United Kingdom the spread effects of allowing an increasing amount of economic activity to be concentrated in the South-East outweigh the backwash effects, a case can be made on economic grounds for allowing the drift to the South to continue unhindered.

Thirdly, in resolving the possible conflict involved in policies to equalize regional incomes and policies of national economic development, the inadequacy of income per head as a measure of economic development should be remembered. Estimates of national income or regional income include only those items that have a market price and those items for which, although not involved in market transactions, it is possible to estimate their market value if they had been sold. Factors which promote welfare, such as clean air, the sense of belonging to a community, or access to the countryside, do not find expression in the national income accounts. Because these factors do, however, contribute to welfare just as much as the production of washing machines or cars, it is irrational to exclude consideration of social benefits and costs when considering government policy on the pattern of regional growth.

It is possible, therefore, that in following a policy of national economic growth with no regard to the relative fortunes of different regions, the social disadvantages from increasing congestion in the growing regions and the decay of the old industrial areas could out-weigh the gain in national output resulting from the increased production of goods and services with market values. When social benefits and costs are considered together with private benefits and costs (reflected in the pattern of relative prices), conflict may arise as to whether the government should in following a policy of national economic growth also take action to ensure that the growth does not take place at the expense of the less prosperous regions. The economic justification for government interference in protecting the poor regions from the cumulative growth of the richer regions must take into account both the private and social costs and benefits involved in allowing the free market mechanism to determine the pattern of regional economic development.

These introductory remarks on the concept of economic development as applied to a region have so far skirted around the problem—in the United Kingdom a very real one—of what meaning can be attached to the term region. The limits of a nation state are clearly defined by the change in currency, by the restrictions on the movement of goods and factors of production, and by changes in the laws of the land as one crosses the international frontier. There is no such clarity when it comes to delimiting regions within a country. Ideally, the regional division of a country should be based upon the distinctive nature of different parts of the country—that is, the divisions should be into regions of significance, not merely into regions of convenience.

Regional studies were pioneered by the French school of geographers, who wrote the geography of France on a regional basis—the country being divided into a number of distinct regions or *pays*. The limits of each *pays* were drawn after examining the various elements in the geographical environment and deciding the area within which there existed a distinct geographical unity (in terms of physical and human geography).

In terms of economic activity, however, it is often more meaningful to consider regions of diversity, where the regional boundary contains diverse but complementary elements. A micro-illustration of a region of diversity would be a downland parish in the South-East of England. In the past, when each parish was virtually a self-sufficient community, it would be necessary to include within the parish as diverse a selection of resources as possible; hence the elongated downland parishes which lie astride the chalk scarps and include the sands and clays of the lower land for arable farming as well as the grazing lands of the chalk. Such a region is a region of diversity from the point of view of the physical environment; but

H

from an economic viewpoint it is really a region of unity in an age of self-sufficiency when few demands were made on surrounding areas.

In studying regional economic development, the most useful definition of a region will not be based directly upon the physical background, but upon whether a particular area is more or less self-sufficient. It will immediately be appreciated that the division of a country into regions of significance will be more satisfactory in a country of subsistence agriculture, where trade is relatively small and where there is a close relationship between human activity and the physical environment, than in a highly specialized, urban, industrial country.

In many ways any division of the United Kingdom into regions must be arbitrary because of the high degree of specialization in economic activity, and the large volume of internal trade. How can one draw any meaningful line around London as a distinct economic region when it is remembered, for example, that London's milk supply is drawn from as far away as Cornwall and Carlisle? A regional division of the United Kingdom would seem to be a division of convenience, not of significance. One such division of convenience is that based upon the major conurbations (now officially described as 'city regions') and their immediate hinterlands. There would be a considerable overlap between such regions depending upon the economic activity selected as the criterion for delimiting the hinterland. The use of regions of convenience means that, as a great deal of inter-regional trade is necessary for all consumer wants to be satisfied, the inter-regional balance of trade assumes importance in regional economic development studies.

The regional division of the United Kingdom used in this chapter is truly a division of convenience in that the regions are the standard regions for which the government publishes statistics. The standard regions do, however, to some extent correspond to the major conurbations and their hinterlands; the Northern region, the North-West region, Yorkshire and Lincolnshire, the Midland region and the London and the South-East region all contain a major conurbation recognized in the Census of Population statistics.

2. *The Pattern of Regional Development in the United Kingdom*

The best available measure of the level of economic development in the regions of the United Kingdom will be estimates of regional income per head. In comparing the economic fortunes of the standard regions, the usual distinction made is that between the North and the South. In many ways, however, it is a more relevant distinction if a line is drawn from the mouth of the River Tees to Exmouth to divide the Highland zone from the Lowland zone of Great Britain, including the South-West and Wales in the Highland zone. The distinctions made by Sir Cyril Fox in *The Personality of Britain* between the cultural continuity to the north and west of the Exe–Tees line and the process of cultural change to the south and east is valid in terms of the industrial structures of the two zones— the Highland zone having an undue proportion of the old, declining industries and the Lowland zone having more than its share of new growing industries. This feature is illustrated in Table 3.1 where the

TABLE 3.1

EMPLOYMENT IN EXPANDING INDUSTRIES IN EACH REGION, JUNE 1962

Region	per cent
London and South-East	52
Eastern and Southern	49
Scotland	46
South-West	45
United Kingdom	45
North-West	44
Northern Ireland	41
Midlands	40
Northern	40
Yorkshire and Lincolnshire	39
Wales	39

Source: Table 2 in 'The Regional Problem', *The National Institute Economic Review*, No. 25, August 1963.

percentage of employment in seven expanding industries is shown for each region. The expanding industries (professional and scientific services; distributive trades; insurance, banking and finance; engineering and electrical goods; other manufacturing industry; paper, printing and publishing; and construction) are those in which employment rose at a faster rate than total employment between 1952 and 1962.

The figures show the Lowland zone (London and the South-East, and the Eastern and Southern regions) as having an above-average proportion of their labour forces in the seven expanding industries. The proportion of the working population in the expanding industries in Scotland is very similar to that for the United Kingdom. Nevertheless other indicators put Scotland in the less prosperous area category. The South-West region has the average United Kingdom proportion of employment in the expanding industries because, compared with the national industrial structure, it is relatively specialized in the distributive trades and professional and scientific

TABLE 3.2

UNEMPLOYMENT RATES BY REGION 1962–1964

Region	June 1962	Jan. 1963	June 1963	Jan. 1964
	Percentage unemployed			
London and South-East	1·1	2·2	1·2	1·3
Eastern and Southern	1·1	3·3	1·2	1·4
Yorkshire and Lincolnshire	1·4	3·0	1·7	1·7
Midland	1·4	3·2	1·6	1·3
South-West	1·4	3·7	1·6	2·1
North-West	2·3	3·9	2·8	2·6
Wales	2·6	5·7	3·0	4·1
Northern	3·2	6·5	4·3	4·3
Scotland	3·3	5·9	4·3	4·7
Northern Ireland	7·2	9·5	7·5	8·0
Great Britain	1·8	3·6	2·1	2·2

Source: Ministry of Labour Gazette.

TABLE 3.3

POPULATION CHANGES BY REGION, 1951–1961

Region	Increase per year per cent	Natural increase per year per cent	Migration* per year per cent
Eastern	1·88	0·54	+1·34
Southern	1·44	0·54	+0·90
North Midland	0·73	0·55	+0·19
Midland	0·72	0·59	+0·13
South-West	0·54	0·30	+0·24
England and Wales	0·51	0·44	+0·08
Northern	0·35	0·62	−0·27
North-West	0·17	0·33	−0·17
East and West Ridings	0·17	0·40	−0·24
Wales	0·16	0·35	−0·19

Source: *Census of Population 1961*, Preliminary Report, Table C.

Note: The standard regions in this table are those used prior to April 1962 when the regions Midlands and Yorkshire and Lincolnshire were formed from the regions Midlands, North Midlands and East and West Ridings.

* + indicates net gain: − indicates net loss.

services. Because of a lack of employment in the rapid growth service industries, the Midland region in Table 3.1 has joined company with the less prosperous regions, Northern, Wales and Northern Ireland.

The official unemployment figures (Table 3.2) illustrate the differing degrees of vulnerability of the regions to a recession despite post-war government interference in the location of industry. The lack of employment opportunities is a more severe problem in the Highland zone than in the Lowland zone. The unemployment problem in the South-West shows a markedly seasonal pattern as a result of the dependence on agriculture and the tourist industry. The Highland zone's lack of employment opportunities is also reflected in the pattern of internal migration in England and Wales (Table 3.3).

Social accounts on a regional basis are still in Britain at an embryonic stage. The figures that are used here as an estimate of the income per head in different regions of the United Kingdom are those from the survey of personal income (before tax) in the 105th Report of the Inland Revenue Commissioners. These estimates, although suffering from a number of major defects, do make some attempt to assess both income from employment and investment income. The information in the survey is a summary of total income and the number of taxpayers for various types of income on a regional basis. The first defect is that all incomes of below £180 per year are excluded, as also from the regional figures are the incomes of civil servants, the armed forces and merchant seamen. The exclusion of incomes below £180 per year is unlikely to make any difference to the relative position of the regions in Table 3.4, although it could well over-estimate the poverty of Northern Ireland where a much greater proportion of the population is engaged in semi-subsistence agriculture[1] resulting in incomes which are low and in kind.

Secondly, the Inland Revenue returns are based upon the place of business and not the place of residence. This means that the place where the income is created and where it is recorded for taxation purposes need not necessarily be in the region where the income is finally received and spent. The distortion due to this factor is particularly important in the Greater London area where a considerable amount of the income recorded in the London and South-East region will in fact be spent at the place of residence in the Southern and Eastern regions. There is also considerable difficulty

[1] See Isles and Cuthbert, *An Economic Survey of Northern Ireland*, HMSO 1957, chapters 2 and 5 and Appendix A.

in dealing with investment income. For taxation purposes, company profits are included in the income of the region where the company headquarters is located. The regional figures do not, therefore, indicate where the economic activity creating the investment income

TABLE 3.4

REGIONAL AVERAGE INCOME PER TAXPAYER 1963

Region	Average total net income £	Average earned income £	Average investment income £
London and South-East	812	745	390
Midland	751	717	275
Southern	733	664	394
United Kingdom	732	684	334
North Midland	718	683	234
Eastern	715	673	293
East and West Ridings	711	675	263
North-West	708	672	247
South-Western	690	629	336
Northern	686	655	240
Wales	678	649	195
Scotland	675	629	369
Northern Ireland	600	569	236

Source: *Report of the Commissioners of Inland Revenue*. 105th Report, 1963, Appendix II

Notes: The regions are those used in Table 3.3.

Average total net income = Total income divided by number of tax cases.

Average earned income = Earned income divided by number of cases.

Average investment income = Investment income divided by number of cases.

Married couples are counted as one person.

takes place, nor where the investment income is received when profits are distributed. For this reason the investment income in the London area, where company head offices are concentrated, will be overestimated. Table 3.4, which shows the average income per taxpayer in the regions, gives some indication—bearing in mind the limitation of the data—of the variation in income per head between the regions.

The figures of average total net income, used as a guide to the level of regional income per head, clearly fit into the pattern of Highland and Lowland zones. The Lowland zone regions—London and South-East, Midlands and Southern—have average total net incomes above the United Kingdom average; while the Highland zone regions—Northern, South-Western, Wales, Scotland and Northern Ireland—are congregated together at the foot of the table. The level of economic development, as indicated by these estimates, is not simply a contrast between old, nineteenth century, industrial areas and new twentieth century industrial areas. A per capita level of income below average is also connected with a proportion of employment in agriculture above the United Kingdom average.

The estimates of average earned income show a change in ranking amongst the more prosperous regions. The relatively low positions of the Southern region and the Eastern region are, however, a result of the over-estimation of the London and South-East region income by not allowing for the commuting between the place of work in London and the place of residence in one of the other standard regions. The familiar group of low income regions remains: Northern, Wales, South-Western, Scotland and Northern Ireland. Little significance can be attached to the figures of average investment income. The location of the registered offices of companies does not give any indication of where the investment income is received and spent.

Because a factor of production often performs its services in the productive process in a different location from where the income recipient is located and where the income is spent, it is worth considering how the mobility of labour and capital, and the flows of income to the owners of these factors, can affect the level of income in different regions.

With a specific region it is more likely that the supply of labour is provided by persons living within the region than is the supply of new capital funds. It is more likely, therefore, that income from employment will be spent within the region where the income is created than income from investment in real capital assets. A region which is unduly dependent on a flow of external capital funds (i.e. from other regions) will, therefore, have a greater degree of uncertainty as to the future level of economic activity in the region, depending upon where the income from the ownership of capital is spent or reinvested. To maintain stability of income within the region it would seem desirable either for the region to be self-sufficient in providing capital funds and for those who own the funds to be parochial in their outlook as to where they should be invested, or for a greater share of the income in the region to be paid to the factor of production, labour. Both of these possibilities are undesirable, however, for achieving the optimum allocation of resources in the country as a whole.

The greater mobility of capital funds, compared with labour, in moving to where they can obtain the highest return, brings the problem of regional development before the public, as labour becomes 'stranded' without work in regions where the business outlook is poor. Unless the government intervenes, the flight of capital and the growth of unemployment becomes a cumulative problem.

3. *Analysis of the Regional Pattern*

Some of the reasons for the pattern of regional development, as indicated by the estimates of income per head, and for the persistence of this pattern, will now be examined in more detail. Northern Ireland is in a peculiar position compared with the other regions of the United Kingdom in that it has its own separate government, which is not free to follow its own fiscal and monetary policy; in that it is separated from the rest of the United Kingdom by the Irish Sea; in that it is dependent on the other regions of the United Kingdom for supplies of raw materials and for markets for its manufactured goods; and in that it has a high rate of natural increase of population. These factors make the position of Northern Ireland as a 'less prosperous region' a more difficult one to solve than the position of the other less prosperous regions in Great Britain.[1]

Because the negotiation of wage rates in the United Kingdom is increasingly carried out between trade unions and employers on a national basis, during this century there has been a narrowing of geographical wage rate differentials; but there still remains considerable variation between the regions in the actual earnings which amongst other factors tend to reflect the relative scarcity of labour in the regions. Because of the shortage of labour in London and the South-East and in the Midlands, where for most of the post-war period the ratio of unemployment to unfilled vacancies has been less than one, earnings are higher than elsewhere. The relative scarcity of labour, therefore, is one reason for differences in the money income per head between the regions. Because the markets for many manufactured goods in the United Kingdom are national in which uniform prices are charged, the differences in money income per

[1] For further details of the position of Northern Ireland see Isles and Cuthbert, *Economic Survey of Northern Ireland* and *Report of the Joint Working Party on the Economy of Northern Ireland* (Hall Report), HMSO, Cmnd. 1835, 1962.

head are also differences in real income per head. Table 3.5 compares the average weekly earnings for all male workers in manufacturing industry for each region with the average weekly earnings in manufacturing industry for the United Kingdom. Apart from the surprising position of Wales[1] on a par with London and the South-East, the

TABLE 3.5

INDEX OF AVERAGE WEEKLY EARNINGS BY REGION, OCTOBER 1962*
(Men manual workers in manufacturing industry only)

Region	Regional average weekly earnings as percentage of UK average weekly earnings	Unemployment/Unfilled vacancy ratio (December 1962)
London and South-East	106	1·8
Wales	106	6·9
Eastern and Southern	104	1·8
Midland	104	2·2
North-West	96	4·7
South-West	95	2·5
Yorkshire and Lincolnshire	95	2·7
Northern	95	12·1
Scotland	92	11·6
Northern Ireland	82	n.a.†

Source: *Statistics on Income, Prices, Employment and Production*, No. 4, March 1963.

* See also the first results of a new Ministry of Labour survey into earnings in engineering and other metal-using industries (published in Ministry of Labour Gazette, May 1963).

† The Northern Ireland ratio was 50·0 in June 1961.

index of regional earnings mirrors the relative scarcity of labour in the various regions. Of fourteen manufacturing industry groups, while London and the South-East had above the United Kingdom average earnings in all fourteen groups, and the Eastern and Southern regions had above the average in twelve groups; the South-West and Northern regions had earnings below the United Kingdom average in twelve industry groups, and Scotland and Northern

[1] This very high figure is largely the result of high earnings in the South Wales iron and steel industry which together with other metal manufacture employs 9 per cent of the total insured population.

Ireland had below average earnings in all fourteen industry groups. Although the differences in earnings between the regions are largely due to the demand and supply conditions of the labour market, it should be remembered that where piece-rate and bonus schemes are in operation, part of the regional difference in earnings could represent differences in labour productivity.

As a result of different industrial histories, and different endowment with the factors needed for various forms of industrial activity, there are considerable differences in the industrial structures of the standard regions of the United Kingdom. The pattern of industrial employment in each region can explain much of the difference to be found in income per head in the regions. There is considerable variation between industries to be found in the value added in the manufacturing process (net output). Remembering that it is net output which forms the fund from which the factors of production are paid, it will obviously depress the level of regional income if that region has a concentration of low net output industries. Regardless of whether the net output varies in one industry from region to region, the uneven distribution of employment in different industries will in itself result in differences in regional income per head.

Some guide to how far the concentration of employment in low net output industries is a cause of low regional income per head can be derived by comparing for each region the percentages of total employment in those manufacturing industries where the net output per head is above the United Kingdom average net output per head for all manufacturing industry. (The data is confined to manufacturing industry because the source of information is the Census of Production.) In 1958 the industries with net output per head above the average were: chemicals; food, drink and tobacco; metal manufacture; paper and printing; vehicles; and engineering and electrical goods. For the United Kingdom 24·5 per cent of total employment was in these six manufacturing industries. Three of the regions had a greater percentage of their total employment in these six groups: Midland 30·9 per cent; North-West 26·4 per cent; and Eastern and Southern 25·9 per cent. Although the pattern of employment in the Midland and the Eastern and Southern regions would seem to be a factor in explaining the relatively high regional income per head to be found in these regions, it obviously does not explain the relatively poor position of the North-West in the regional income per head league table. The regions with a lower than average percentage of total employment in the six industry groups are:

Region	Per cent
Yorkshire and Lincolnshire	23·9
Northern	22·1
Wales	21·9
Scotland	20·9
Northern Ireland	14·4

The figures for London and the South-East and the South-West regions are omitted since these regions specialize in the service industries and so the present figures, using manufacturing industry only, are misleading. The pattern of employment in different industry groups is important in explaining the low regional income per head of the Northern region, Wales, Scotland and Northern Ireland— especially when it is remembered that the Northern region, Wales and Scotland specialize in mining and quarrying, an industry with a low net output per person employed, which is not included in the figures above, and that Northern Ireland and Scotland specialize in agriculture, another industry with a low net output per person employed.

In the modern industrial state the process of technical innovation is continuous. Technical advance will mean that new goods and new methods of production are making their appearance on the market and that the nation's resources will be re-allocated to produce the new products rather than the old products for which demand gradually falls off. The speed with which an industrial country can re-allocate its productive resources from declining industry to growing industry is an obvious factor in determining the national rate of economic growth. The same argument can be applied to regions within the nation state. If in the United Kingdom some regions have continued to rely heavily on declining industries while other regions have been able to retain dynamic industrial structure by having their share of new growing industries, differences in the rate of economic development and in income per head are going to arise between the regions. The lower income per head in regions heavily dependent on declining industries with rapidly shrinking markets can be due to the higher net output per head in the new, growing industries compared with the old industries (e.g. cotton textiles compared with electrical engineering), and to the rising unemployment as the declining industry shrinks.

How far does the empirical evidence support this picture of certain regions with low income per head failing to adapt their industrial structures to changing conditions? If the growth of employment is used as a measure of the growth of different industry groups,[1] for the period 1952–62 the most rapidly growing industry groups were: professional and scientific services; distributive trades; insurance, banking and finance; engineering and electrical goods; other manufacturing; paper, printing and publishing; and construction. All these groups had a percentage increase in employment greater than the percentage increase of employment in all industries between 1952 and 1962.[2] In the United Kingdom these seven rapidly growing industries accounted for 45·1 per cent of total employment. London and the South-East, however, had 51·8 per cent of its total employment in these rapidly growing industres, and the Eastern and Southern regions 49·1 per cent. This fits in with the pattern of high income per head in these regions. The above-average proportion of employment in the seven rapidly expanding groups in Scotland (45·9 per cent) and the South-West (45·4 per cent) does not fit into the pattern, however. The Northern region, Yorkshire and Lincolnshire, and Wales have marked divergencies in the proportion of employment in the growing industries.[3]

The differences in income per head between regions as being due to the imbalance of expanding and contracting industries in the regions is perhaps more clearly illustrated by examining how dependent the various regions are on industry groups where there was an absolute fall in the numbers employed between 1952 and 1962. The most important absolute falls in employment were in textiles, shipbuilding and marine engineering, mining and quarrying, and agriculture, forestry and fishing—the staple industries of the past. For the United Kingdom 27·7 per cent of total employment was in the nine industry groups where an absolute fall in employment was recorded. It is significant to rank the regions according to increasing proportion of employment in the nine contracting industry groups. The regions with less than the United Kingdom percentage of total employment in these industries are, apart from the South-West region, the prosperous regions in terms of income per head; while those with more than the United Kingdom percentage are the less prosperous regions. (Because of a change in the definition of the standard regions it is not possible to make a close comparison of the rankings of the regions in Table 3.4.) The low income per head in the

[1] This measure of course has its drawbacks in that it underestimates the importance of capital intensive industries such as oil refining, nor does it take into account changes in labour productivity. The employment measure is used because it can be applied to all industry groups including service industries.

[2] Figures taken from Table 1 in 'The Regional Problem' by Mrs M. F. W. Hemmings in the *National Institute Economic Review*, No. 25, August 1963.

[3] See Table 3.1.

Highland zone of Britain can partly be ascribed to the lack of new growing industries which, as they tend to be scientifically based,[1] have high net output per person employed, and to the relatively high rates of unemployment. The regions ranked in order of their ratio of unemployment to unfilled vacancies[2] are in the same two groups as in Table 3.6, with the lack of employment opportunities being more severe in regions where specialization is in the declining industry

TABLE 3.6

EMPLOYMENT IN INDUSTRIES WITH AN ABSOLUTE FALL IN NUMBERS EMPLOYED
1952–1962

Region	Per cent of total employment in Region
London and South-East	22·3
Eastern and Southern	24·1
Midland	24·6
South Western	27·6
United Kingdom	27·7
North-Western	29·5
Scotland	31·9
Wales	32·7
Yorkshire and Lincolnshire	33·9
Northern	35·5
Northern Ireland	39·3

groups. To stop the cumulative decline of certain regions it is necessary for the government by one means or another to persuade new industry to locate in the less prosperous regions so that the resources of the region can be re-allocated within the region instead of involving the social hardship and waste of a mass migration such as that which took place from South Wales in the inter-war years.

Another possible reason for differences in regional income per head connected with the industrial structure is that certain regions specialize in capital intensive industries where a greater proportion of the net output is paid to capital than in more labour intensive industries. Because, as has already been argued, capital funds before being invested in real capital are more mobile than labour and seek out the location where their earnings are highest, there is a greater likelihood that the earnings of capital will flow out of the region where they

[1] See list of rapid growth industries in the NEDC Report, *Growth of the UK Economy 1961–66*, p. 3.
[2] See Table 3.5.

are created. A large slice of income going to owners of capital could, therefore, conceivably cause a big leakage in the income of the region if that region was a heavy net importer of capital funds.

A crude measure, using the 1958 Census of Production data of the percentage of net output that goes in wages and salaries for the major manufacturing industry groups, hints that the proportion of net output going to labour may help explain differences in income per head. There are four industry groups where the proportion of net output going in wages and salaries is particularly low: food, drink and tobacco; chemicals; metal manufacture; paper and printing—all industry groups where large amounts of capital are necessary. It is interesting to note that Yorkshire and Lincolnshire, the North-West region, the Northern region and Wales have a greater proportion of total employment in these four industry groups than has the United Kingdom; while London and the South-East, the Eastern and Southern regions, the South-West and the Midlands have a lower proportion than the United Kingdom. A great deal more analysis is required to measure how far the flow of income out of the less prosperous regions as a result of their specializing in capital intensive industries is an important factor in explaining regional income differentials. The problem of an income outflow to owners of capital funds will, of course, only be of consequence for the level of regional income if there is no corresponding inflow of new capital funds for investment purposes into the region.

Differences in the income per head between regions could also come about if the types of labour predominantly employed differed between the regions. For example, because wage rates are related to the skill required in a particular job, a region which specialized in industries employing unskilled labour would have a lower income per head than a region where the industries employed all skilled labour. A similar difference in income per head might arise as a result of the traditional difference between male and female rates of pay, where one region specialized in industries employing females while another specialized in industries employing males, or where in one industry in a particular region female labour was substituted for male labour. For the pattern of male/female employment to be responsible for lowering the income per head in a particular region, for reasons of differences in wage rates between the sexes, it would be necessary that the traditional roles of man and wife as wage earner and housekeeper be reversed; if there were two wage earners per family the income per family and per head of population would be higher than in a region where there was less female employment and only one wage earner per family. Other things being equal, a region where the male population was fully employed, and where employment opportunities for women also made possible high female activity rates in the working population, would have a higher income per head than a region where female employment opportunities were missing. It is significant that the low income per head regions—the South-West, the Northern region, Wales, Scotland and Northern Ireland—all have low female activity rates.[1]

All the reasons put forward so far for regional income per head differences have depended on the pattern of employment between different industries in the regions; it has been assumed that plants in any particular industry have been equally efficient in whichever region they have been located. In formulating a policy for regional economic development therefore, there is a great deal of scope for 'equalization' of regional income by changing the industrial structure of the regions—although the choice of a particular industry to be encouraged in a particular region so that the maximum benefit is given, is not as easy as it may appear at first sight. Because, however, the natural and man-made resources of regions differ, to follow an equalization of regional income per head policy to the length of trying to make the pattern of employment in each region a microcosm of the United Kingdom pattern of employment would be nonsensical. As the scope for altering the regional pattern of employment may be severely limited, the following section will examine some of the other possible explanations of income differences between regions that are not concerned with the industrial structure in itself.

Differences in productivity between the regions may be a cause of the range of income per head to be found in the United Kingdom. In other words, the assumption that any particular industry will be equally efficient in whatever region it is located must now be dropped. The pattern of industrial location indicates in itself that all locations are not equally suited to a particular form of economic activity. Better quality raw materials, a supply of skilled labour, the presence of linked industries in an industrial complex, the quality of transport facilities and the proximity of the market are all factors which would make some locations more attractive to a particular industry than other locations. The cost advantage of particular locations will, of course, change over time as there are changes in sources of supply, in technology and in the nature of the market. At any point in time, however, some location may be especially favourable to an industry and so mean that either labour productivity, or capital productivity,

1 See Table I in NEDC Report, *Conditions Favourable to Faster Growth*, HMSO, 1963.

or both, is higher than in other locations. In terms of the empirical evidence available for a regional comparison, differences in productivity between the regions will be reflected in differences in the net output per person employed. A crude comparison of the value of net output per person employed in, say, the paper, printing and publishing industry group would not tell one anything about differences in productivity between the regions, because the figures also reflect the industrial structure of the regions, showing whether they specialize on high net output activities within the broad industry groups. For example, in 1954, the region with the largest net output per person employed for the paper, printing and publishing industry group was London and the South-East; but this was a result of the specialization of the region in the high net output trades within the industry group such as paper and board manufacture, and printing and publishing (especially newspapers). It is possible by constructing an index to remove the influence of differences in the industrial structure from figures giving the net output per person employed, so that the remaining differences would indicate differences in productivity between the regions. But even if the more detailed industrial classification of the Census trades is used as the basis of the adjusted index there is still a great deal of scope for specialization in different products within the trade. For example, there is little meaning in comparing the value of net output per person employed in the paper and board manufacture trade when the product can vary from cardboard and coarse packing papers to fine quality drawing papers. Regional comparisons of productivity are therefore thwarted by the familiar problem of ensuring that like is being compared with like.

Assuming that not all the variation in net output per person employed can be explained in terms of differing specializations in the regional industrial structures, what factors might account for differences in productivity in similar industries between the regions?

First, greater productivity, as has already been mentioned, could be the result of nature being particularly bountiful in endowing certain regions with natural resources. The favoured region is therefore able to produce a given output with a smaller input of other factors than in the less favoured regions. One region may have a higher productivity in an industry because of certain acquired advantages—one of the most important being the existence of a reservoir of skilled labour of the required type. A new firm entering the industry will tend to locate its plant in the traditional area where the acquired advantages are already available rather than in a new area where the firm will have to provide many services itself instead of their already being available externally within the industrial complex.[1] The government could help to make certain regions of the country more attractive to new industrial firms if it undertook the job of industrial training in these regions (or paid a subsidy to firms to train labour in the skills required) instead of leaving the task of training to individual firms, many of whom either show no inclination to train their own labour when 'poaching' is an alternative method of acquiring skilled labour, or are not in a position to train labour even in the boom areas. This form of subsidy to the less prosperous areas would have the advantage that if it did not entice sufficient firms into the region, at least it would enable the labour to find more worthwhile employment elsewhere.

The more specific the demands an industry makes upon the factors of production, the more likely it is to find certain locations where productivity is greater, so that it has a narrow range of locational choice. In these industries (industries such as coal mining, cement manufacture, iron and steel production, mainly involved in processing raw material) there is less scope for public policy to use them as means of equalizing regional income without seriously impairing their industrial efficiency.[2] Recent empirical studies[3] suggest that many manufacturing industries are sufficiently footloose to enable them to be located in any of the regions of the United Kingdom (though not at any site within a region) without suffering any significant cost disadvantages. Where the cost disadvantages in locating a new factory in the North of England exist only in the mind of the businessman, it is pertinent to question how far public money should be used to bribe a firm to settle in the less prosperous region.

The factor of production capital, which has not been specifically mentioned in the above section, may also be responsible for differences in productivity. Two regions similar in other respects may have

[1] The location decision could be reversed if, as a result of scarcity, the extra cost of factors in the traditional area outweighed the extra costs of providing services internally to the firm in the new area. A firm might also choose the new area if restrictive practices by labour in the traditional area prevented the firm from feeling the advantage of the labour's potentially greater productivity.

[2] By distributing this type of industry equally in each region, not only will the costs at a given scale of output be much higher in some regions than in others, but also the fragmentation of the national production between regions will involve a serious loss of economies of scale. T. Scitovsky in *Economic Theory and Western European Integration* (p. 121) states: '... the advantages of economies of scale may often be unobtainable without sacrificing balanced growth; just as balanced growth may have to be paid for by sacrificing economies of scale'.

[3] For example see W. F. Luttrell, *Factory Location and Industrial Movement*, Vol. I (National Institute of Economic and Social Research, 1962).

I

different levels of labour productivity because the amount of capital per worker is much higher in the one than in the other. Differences in labour productivity would also appear if there were variations in the quality of capital equipment between the regions. The process by which private capital funds are invested in the more prosperous rather than the less prosperous areas could result in the less prosperous areas being starved of capital for new investment, and also, because the business outlook is more pessimistic, continuing to use obsolete equipment which would have been replaced by new more efficient equipment in the more prosperous areas. The failure of the Lancashire cotton industry to re-equip itself until the government introduced its Cotton Industry Reorganization Scheme is an example of obsolescent equipment continuing in use in the face of un-certainty about the future of the industry. Where there is a long run decline in the major industries of a region, therefore, a pattern of circular causality is likely to be established by the failure of the industries to make themselves competitive in conditions of changing demand. Failure to maintain the quality of the social capital of the region may not have a direct effect upon regional productivity; but indirectly, by making the social infrastructure of a region inadequate to meet modern requirements, it can again help to accelerate the cumulative process of decline in the less prosperous region.

The poor performance of industries in a region in training labour and in replacing obsolete equipment may be closely related to the predominant form of industrial organization in the region and the quality of entrepreneurial ability to be found within the region. Differences in productivity between the regions might, therefore, be connected with the form of organization and managerial ability in a particular region. As small family-controlled firms are more likely to be conservative in the use of the firm's resources than a public joint stock company which is management-controlled, an industrial community where the family firm is dominant is likely to have a greater degree of capital immobility because of a reluctance to change the firm's 'line of business'.[1] The small family firm is also more likely to hit the 'financial barrier' in the process of change within the firm than a large joint stock company.[2] The small family firm is less likely to be able to afford specialized top quality managers —the specialization of management function may be in an embryonic

[1] See E. T. Penrose, *The Theory of the Growth of the Firm* for a discussion of the process by which the main line of business can change radically in the process of development.

[2] See the case studies in A. S. Mackintosh, *The Development of Firms* (CUP, 1963).

stage—and the firm often tends to be parochial and inward looking, especially in considering the use of new management techniques and in the adoption of technical innovations.[1]

If, in a particular industry, one region has a predominant firm-size smaller than in other regions, the region may be put at a disadvantage compared with the other regions because it has forfeited various internal economies of scale. The inability of the firm to grow may be due to a variety of factors ranging from the limited objectives of many family-controlled firms to inadequate finance arising from relying on purely local resources. The effect of the form and quality of the industrial organization upon the rate of economic development within a region should be investigated in assessing the scope for raising the level of income per head in the less prosperous areas of the United Kingdom.

One further factor may be mentioned in accounting for productivity differentials between regions, and that is the degree to which firms gain external economies of scale from congregating together in an industrial complex. The extent to which external economies of scale are available to firms located in an industrial conurbation will depend upon the extent of inter-industry relationships, and the extent to which the process of disintegration has taken place,[2] as shown by the appearance of highly specialist firms performing services that in the absence of an industrial conglomeration would not have been undertaken or would have had to be performed internally by the firm on a non-optimum scale. The external economies to be gained or lost in different locations underline the importance of carrying out a detailed analysis of inter-industry relationships within the individual industrial conurbation, within a region and between different regions, if government interference in regional development is to be as effective as it might be in raising regional income per head. The loss of internal economies of scale mentioned in the previous section might well be more than balanced by external economies of scale if all the small firms were located closely together in one conurbation where the different industries are closely interlinked. In the metal-working conurbation of the West Midlands and in the two textile conurbations on either side of the Pennines, the predominant size of the firm is relatively small, the industry is highly localized, and there is a great deal of specialization of function between individual firms.

[1] See Carter and Williams, *Industry and Technical Progress* (OUP, 1957).

[2] The process of industrial disintegration is illustrated by the pottery industry of North Staffordshire where there are specialist firms who mix the 'slip', manufacture transfers and glazes, or manufacture barrels for packing.

To conclude this section, two other factors will be mentioned. First, the uneven distribution of persons receiving incomes from capital may help explain the persistence of the regional income per head differentials. Although the figures published by the Inland Revenue of regional investment income are of little use here, one would suspect that the South-East of England has a higher proportion of the population receiving investment income, and that the South-East receives, compared with its share of the population, an undue proportion of the total investment income of the United Kingdom. If this be true—it has yet to be proved—then the flows of investment income between the regions will be an important influence on the level of regional income. If the outflow of investment income from one region in a particular period is not counterbalanced by an inflow of spending power from the other regions, the level of income will decrease in the next period. An unequal geographical distribution of the ownership of capital funds coupled with a reluctance to invest in regions where business conditions do not appear so favourable would help explain the persistence over time of regional differences in income per head.

Secondly, it is possible that the failure of much of the Highland zone to adapt its industrial structure to current economic conditions may be a result of resistance to cultural change and a great inflexibility in the pattern of consumer demand. The slower pace of change in the Highland zone (the nineteenth century was a brief interval in history when the process of change was much more rapid in the Highland zone than elsewhere[1]) conceivably could be a social factor underlying the differing rates of economic development.[2]

4. *Regional Economic Planning*

The concept of regional economic planning is still in process of evolution. It has arisen from the desire to remove large pockets of unemployment that persist in certain parts of the United Kingdom. The forerunner of a policy for regional economic development in the United Kingdom has been the government location of industry policy, which since the inter-war years has been dominated by the need to solve an unemployment problem. For regional economic

---

[1] The previous period when the process of change was dominant in the Highland zone was when the metal-working cultures were evolving around the Irish Sea in the Early British Bronze Age.

[2] The inflexibility of the Western European pattern of demand compared with that of the USA, Scitovsky suggests, is one reason for the higher level of income per head in the USA than in Europe. (T. Scitovsky, op. cit., p. 131.)

planning to develop further it is necessary to look at problems of regional development on a broader basis than local unemployment rates. Government recognition of this principle has slowly emerged in the publication of the plans for the North-East of England and for central Scotland in 1963, and in the plan for the South-East published in 1964; and more recently in the Labour government's proposals for Regional Economic Planning Councils.

For regional development policies to be fully effective, planning is needed on at least three levels. National economic planning is necessary to set the stage for specific plans for individual regions. Policy decisions at national level, for example on the rate of growth of the national product, are basic inputs in any regional analysis. To persuade businessmen to expand their productive capacity in the less prosperous areas, it is essential that the national business prospects should be sufficiently encouraging to induce a strong desire for expansion in the businessman. There is then, in a mixed economy where private enterprise is still important, a need to create a favourable national economic environment if location of industry policy in its present form is to be effective.

The second level of planning is regional economic planning proper. This will involve an understanding of the operation of individual regional economies. Differences in industrial structure in different regions will mean that a particular national policy will have different effects according to the regional environment. The need for policies to fit the needs of a particular region is clearly understood by the less prosperous areas of the United Kingdom, where there is a large amount of excess capacity and which have suffered from national anti-inflation policies that ideally should have been restricted to the South-East and the Midlands.

The third level of planning is land-use planning or—to use a more comprehensive title—town and country planning. This third level of planning is concerned largely with the design of the social infrastructure. Apart from aesthetic considerations, this level of planning, in determining the layout of urban areas, the design of a transport network, and the design of other public utility services on a local basis, is going to play an important part in making the less prosperous areas more attractive. Town and country planning, for example, by enabling a built-up area to perform its urban functions more efficiently, is a source of external economies for firms deciding to set up business in these areas. From the regional planning point of view all three levels of planning are important, and even more important, there should be co-ordination between these planning levels.

In Section 1 of this chapter the case for state interference in regional development was considered. The choice between the alternative policies of interference and non-interference can more rationally be made if some estimate of the gains and losses to the national community of the alternative policies are made. For example, if a model of the economy represents what would happen with no state interference in the decision to locate a particular project in a prosperous region, the decision-making process would be aided if the extent of spread and backwash effects were estimated. Using an incremental approach, that is, considering the location of one investment project, one might be dubious about the desirability of state interference with the choice indicated by the existing market conditions if the increase in income in the rich region plus the spread effects in the poor regions were greater than the backwash effects in the poor regions. If the backwash effects outweighed the spread effects and the increase in income in the rich region, state interference to even out the rates of growth in the regions would seem to be justified. This is assuming that the initial income distribution between the regions was acceptable to the community.

To estimate the spread and backwash effects would necessitate input-output analysis on a regional basis. The input-output tables for each region would show the inter-industry relationships and the imports and exports of each region. From this data (ignoring the practical problem that much of the necessary information is not available to enable the construction of true regional input-output tables) it would be possible to estimate the effect, say, of a 4 per cent growth in output in a rich region upon the economic activity in the other regions of the country. The whole procedure could be made more sophisticated if, besides involving the production of goods and services with market prices, estimates were made of the magnitude of various social costs and benefits involved in a particular growth pattern between the regions. Assessment of some of the social costs involved, such as costs of congestion in the rich regions or waste of social capital in the poor regions, could well tip the balance between the desirability and the non-desirability of state interference in regional development.

A combination of input-output analysis and cost-benefit analysis can aid decision-taking by the Board of Trade as to whether a particular investment project should be allowed in the congested South-East or should be moved to one of the less prosperous areas. The policy indicated by such analysis will, of course, be open to reversal on the basis of any social or national security factors, such as the desirability of preserving rural communities or the deterioration of human capital as a result of prolonged unemployment, that cannot be quantified and cannot therefore be incorporated into the cost-benefit analysis. The assessment of net gains could be done in terms of the effects of individual investment projects or in terms of a general growth of activity in the rich region at the expense of the poor region.

Depending on the level of the decision to be made, whether a blanket approval or disapproval of state interference in boosting the level of economic activity in the poor regions or whether approval or disapproval of a particular investment project, there will be a number of policies available to the government to bring about the desired location of new economic activity. If state interference is aimed at increasing generally the level of income per head in the less prosperous regions, the policies should be chosen with due attention to the reasons for the low level of income in the region; some of these reasons were discussed in Section 3.

If the low income per head in a region is the result of its industrial structure, there are a number of measures that the government can take and has taken in the United Kingdom to alter directly the industrial structure so that it compares more favourably with the pattern of industry in the rich regions. In the United Kingdom the policy of modifying the regional industrial structures has been embodied in the Location of Industry Acts and now the Local Employment Act, and in the Town and Country Planning Acts— the government using a combination of coercion through the industrial development certificate mechanism and persuasion by offering various inducements in cash and kind to firms willing to locate new capacity in the less prosperous regions.[1] The granting of subsidies to firms locating in the less prosperous regions can be justified on the famous infant industry argument usually used to justify restrictions to international trade. There is a strong case for granting a subsidy to a new undertaking in a less prosperous area

[1] Under the 1960 Local Employment Act the Board of Trade was empowered to:
(i) make loans and grants to firms extending or building new capacity in the 'development districts'.
(ii) build factories for sale or leasing.
(iii) give grants to cover any unusual initial expenses that have to be met as a result of going to a development district.
Powers are also given to various government departments to improve the infrastructure of the region by, for instance, clearing derelict land and improving basic services. Further inducements have been made available to firms going to development districts by the 1963 budget by, for example, increasing the depreciation to 100 per cent in the first year after investment in plant and machinery. Also standard grants to all firms setting up or expanding in development districts of 25 per cent of the cost of buildings and 10 per cent of plant and machinery costs are now paid by the Board of Trade.

where, because of the absence of economies of scale in the early days of operation, it is at a cost disadvantage compared with established firms in the rich regions. The infant industry argument would not justify the continuance of the subsidy once the firm was established whether or not costs were now as low as those of the established firms. The tax relief for the first ten years of operation given by the Eire Government to firms establishing themselves at Shannon Airport is an example of a policy helping industrial undertakings to become established.

A subsidy to a firm setting up in a development district is also justified if the net private loss involved in the location is outweighed by a net social gain. Assuming the private and social losses and gains remain constant, this subsidy would be a permanent feature of the firm so that it was at no private cost disadvantage compared with its competitors. It would seem, however, wasteful of public money to pay a subsidy, in whatever form, to a firm if it is at no private cost disadvantage by settling in a development district. In such a case there is a stronger case for using coercion rather than a bribe to influence the location.

Where coercion is used, by, for instance, the refusal to grant an industrial development certificate in certain regions, the co-ordination of national economic planning and regional economic planning becomes of paramount importance. If the government attempts to coerce private firms to a location that they would not otherwise have chosen, in conditions where the national economy is stagnant, the government interference in the private location decision is more likely to bring about the 'no investment response' than to result in a new factory in a depressed area.

In an economy where more manufacturing industry is becoming footloose in the sense of having a wider range of locations which are equally attractive in terms of private costs, the choice of a particular location may easily be decided on the general attractiveness of an area to the businessman and his family; this will, of course, be true only if the person taking the location decision is going to find himself in the region where the new factory is located. An important part of a regional development policy should be to improve the social infra-structure of the less prosperous areas. These are inferior not only in terms of urban environment but also in health and education services such as the availability of maternity beds, the incidence of chronic bronchitis and the incidence of slum schools and large classes. Improvement should not only increase the external economies of scale by redeveloping city centres, for example, so that traffic movement is more efficient, but also make the urban areas more attractive places of residence. A welcome new emphasis has been placed recently on the improvement of the social infrastructure of the less prosperous regions in the government plans for the North-East of England and for central Scotland. It is in the improvement of the social infrastructure that town and country planning becomes of vital importance in formulating a regional development programme.

Rather than attempt to change the industrial structure of a less prosperous region, the government may attempt to revive industrial activity by pumping extra demand into the regional economy. This could be done by the strategic placing of government orders to benefit firms in the less prosperous regions (it is desirable for the government and the public to realize whether any hidden subsidy is involved in such a policy), or for the government to step up its public investment programme in a region with a low income per head. Another alternative is for the government to aid an industry which is heavily concentrated in the less prosperous regions (the government credit scheme to the shipbuilding industry would fall within this category).

The effectiveness of the extra demand pumped into the regional economy in raising the level of income per head would depend upon the regional balance of payments and the size of the regional multiplier.[1] For example, the increase in regional income resulting from a particular public investment project will be greater if the inputs of raw materials or semi-manufactured goods required for the project are available from within the region, rather than if all the inputs are imported from outside. A high regional marginal propensity to import will mean that the regional multiplier is low so that the secondary increases in income, resulting from an investment project or from increased exports, are felt in other regions which are supplying the inputs. This effect is well illustrated by the Northern Ireland economy, where natural resources are limited, and where most of the industrial raw materials must be imported. Much of the multiplier effect of investment in Northern Ireland does not benefit Northern Ireland but creates extra income in Great Britain.[2] A consideration of the marginal propensity to import is especially important when the investment in a region is in an assembly industry such as motor vehicle manufacture, when the component parts are supplied from outside the region; the new Ford plant at Halewood is an example,

[1] The regional multiplier is equivalent to the foreign trade multiplier which includes domestic saving. The regional multiplier (K_r) is equal to $\dfrac{1}{MPM_r + MPS_r}$ where MPM_r is the regional marginal propensity to import and MPS_r is the regional marginal propensity to save. This ignores governmental activity.

[2] See Isles and Cuthbert, op. cit., Ch. XVII.

with many component imported from the Dagenham works. It is not sufficient, however, to say that any industry importing its inputs from outside the region is unsuitable for implementing a policy of raising the level of income within a region. It may well be to the region's advantage to stimulate an importing industry with a comparative cost advantage, if by so doing the demand for the region's exports are stimulated so that the increased imports are more than offset by increased regional exports.

The third set of policy measures may be described as indirect attempts to change the industrial structure of a region and attempts to increase the productivity of factors in their use within the region. Such policy measures would be aimed at increasing the occupational mobility of the factors of production and at creating an awareness of more efficient production methods. The predominant form of industrial organization in a particular region could play a decisive role in determining the economic adaptability of a region's economy. For example, specialization in industries where small, family-controlled firms predominate could help explain the absence of re-allocation of factors into their most productive uses. Because of the tendency for the small, family firm to be conservative in its attitude to changing or extending the range of its product, to the introduction of innovations, and to the employment of outside managers and new management techniques, such an industrial structure could well tend to freeze the allocation of resources within a region in a pattern that is not in sympathy with a changing economic environment.

Government industrial training schemes and payment of removal expenses are ways in which labour may be persuaded to change occupation and place of residence within a region. In a case where it was to the community's advantage to encourage the growth of activity in the rich regions, this policy would also help to accelerate the redistribution of labour between the regions.

For the government to encourage a more productive use of capital funds in regions or industries where the outlook of the firm tends to be parochial, it seems necessary to develop government information services to industry in the field not only of technical matters but also in the field of management techniques that are able to improve small-firm efficiency. Where research activity in a small-firm industry appears inadequate, the government could remove one excuse for the lack of innovation if research organizations, financed by a compulsory levy on firms in the industry to provide an incentive to use the results of the research, were established not only to under-take research, but also to distribute new ideas to the firms in the industry.

The success of any policies in this group will depend upon how strong is the resistance to change by labour and owners and managers of firms. A more direct solution by subsidy to encourage re-equipment with efficient machinery could be used in the form, for example, of the 1959 Cotton Industry Reorganization Scheme, or the specially favourable depreciation and investment allowances that are available to firms in the development districts under the 1963 Finance Act.[1]

For regional economic development policies to be fully effective it has been argued that there is need for the development of three levels of planning and of co-ordination between these levels. There have been a number of attempts to make the machinery of planning more effective since October 1964. The national economic planning machinery has been remodelled with a new Department of Economic Affairs taking over some of the functions of the National Economic Development Council. The Minister of Economic Affairs has also taken the first important step in constructing machinery for planning on a regional level by announcing that Regional Economic Planning Councils are to be established.[2] The Regional Councils will not be elected representative bodies, but their members will be selected by the Department of Economic Affairs. The Councils will not have any executive powers and at present the town and country planning function is to remain in the hands of numerous County Councils and County Boroughs.

A regional planning structure that is relevant to modern industry and traffic movement could evolve by an amalgamation of large numbers of the present local authorities and by the granting of much greater powers to the new authorities, or by a process of decentralization of government departments from Whitehall (i.e. more power to the regional offices of the various Ministries). The signs at present are that regional planning is more likely to come about by the latter process. The crucial function of co-ordinating the activities of the various regional offices of the government departments involved in regional development is to be in the hands of an Under-Secretary of State mainly responsible for regional planning at the Department of Economic Affairs, the Regional Councils acting in an essentially advisory capacity.

[1] Measures aimed at speeding the process of re-equipment will of course not be as effective as they might be if firms select investment projects on a pre-tax rather than a post-tax basis, or if firms persist in using the payback period method of investment project selection. See R. R. Neild, *Replacement Policy*, NIER, November 1964.

[2] So far six regions have been officially announced: Northern, North-West, Yorkshire and Humberside, East Midlands, West Midlands, and the South-West.

TABLE 3.7

THE PATTERN OF EMPLOYMENT IN THE REGIONS OF THE UK, JUNE 1962
(Percentage of total employees)

Industry Group	London E. & S. & SE.	SW.	Mid-lands	Yorks. & Lincs.	NW.	N.	Scot-land	Wales	N. Ire-land	UK
Agriculture, Forestry and Fishing	1·1	5·0	1·9	3·1	0·8	2·4	4·4	2·3	3·3	2·5
Mining and Quarrying	0·2	1·4	4·7	6·1	1·6	11·0	3·8	10·7	0·8	3·1
Total Primary Ind.	1·3	6·4	6·6	9·2	2·4	13·4	8·2	13·0	4·1	5·6
Food, Drink and Tobacco	3·2	4·8	3·2	4·1	4·3	2·7	4·5	2·2	6·2	3·7
Chemicals	2·1	0·9	1·3	2·1	4·2	4·5	1·6	2·5	0·4	2·3
Metal Manufacture	0·6	0·4	5·2	5·3	1·3	4·4	2·5	9·1	0·1	2·6
Engineering and Electrical Goods	10·4	6·6	11·8	8·2	10·0	8·2	7·8	5·2	4·8	9·4
Shipbuilding and Marine Engineering	0·3	1·7	—	0·4	1·2	4·2	2·8	0·5	3·6	1·1
Vehicles	2·4	6·0	7·9	2·3	3·7	1·1	1·8	1·8	1·6	3·8
Metal Goods N.E.S.	1·8	0·6	6·4	3·3	1·9	0·9	1·2	2·1	0·5	2·4
Textiles	0·5	1·2	4·4	9·0	8·5	1·5	4·8	1·8	11·5	3·7
Leather, Leather Goods and Fur	0·3	0·3	0·3	0·3	0·3	0·2	0·2	0·2	0·1	0·3
Clothing and Footwear	2·4	2·0	3·0	2·9	3·4	2·5	1·4	1·5	5·6	2·6
Bricks, Pottery, Glass, Cement, etc.	1·0	0·9	3·2	1·6	1·6	1·4	1·1	1·1	0·9	1·5
Timber, Furniture	1·6	1·3	1·0	1·2	1·0	0·9	1·1	0·7	0·9	1·3

Paper, Printing and Publishing	4·2	3·1	2·7	1·5	1·9	2·9	1·2	2·7	1·1	1·3	2·7
Other Manufacturing Industry	1·6	1·4	1·2	1·5	0·6	2·0	0·8	0·9	1·3	0·5	1·3
Total Manufacturing Industry	32·4	35·5	30·6	50·7	43·2	46·3	34·5	34·4	31·1	38·0	38·7
Construction	6·6	7·6	8·3	5·9	6·2	6·0	7·4	8·4	8·3	9·8	6·9
Gas, Water, Electricity	1·8	1·8	2·0	1·6	1·8	1·6	1·6	1·4	2·1	1·5	1·7
Transport and Communication	9·1	6·1	7·2	4·8	6·4	8·1	7·0	8·1	8·3	6·2	7·3
Distributive Trades	14·5	12·7	13·3	10·3	11·8	12·9	12·3	13·8	11·0	13·0	12·8
Insurance, Banking and Finance	5·0	1·9	1·9	1·4	1·6	2·1	1·4	1·9	1·5	1·8	2·5
Professional and Scientific Services	9·5	12·1	11·4	7·9	8·4	8·5	8·6	10·4	10·1	9·8	9·5
Miscellaneous Services	12·8	9·9	11·4	6·2	6·9	7·5	8·0	8·0	8·0	8·5	9·1
Public Administration	6·8	6·6	7·5	4·5	4·5	4·6	5·8	5·3	6·7	7·3	5·8
Total Service Industry	66·1	58·7	63·0	42·6	47·6	51·3	52·1	57·3	56·0	57·9	55·6
Grand Total	100·0	100·0	100·0	100·0	100·0	100·0	100·0	100·0	100·0	100·0	100·0

Source: Ministry of Labour

CHAPTER IV

Indian Economic Development

by S. K. NATH

1. *Introduction*

India is a large and poor country. Her population of 438 million (in 1961) is the second largest in the world. But her land area is only the eighth largest, so that the average density is comparatively high in India. India has 136 persons per square kilometre. The comparable density figures for some other countries are: Brazil 8; Ghana 31; China 68; Britain 215; Japan 252; and the Netherlands 342. The overall world density is 22 persons per square kilometre of land.

India's national income per capita in 1960, expressed in US dollars, was 68. This places India among the poorest countries. Similar figures for some other countries are: Ceylon 120; Federation of Malaya (as it was in 1960) 206; Ghana 225; Japan 341; Yugoslavia 480; Britain 1,085; USA 2,286. There are also other indicators of the low standard of living in India. For example, the number of physicians per 10,000 of population in India is 1·9. Similar figures for some other countries are: Brazil 4·1; Britain 8·7; Japan 10·6; USA 12·4; and the Soviet Union 18. Again, consumption per head in India of energy per year (in coal equivalent) is 140 kilograms, and of crude steel, 11 kilograms. Comparable figures for some other countries are: Yugoslavia 858 and 92; Japan 1,164 and 208; the Soviet Union 2,847 and 246; Britain 4,920 and 425; and USA 8,013 and 501. Lastly, only 23·7 per cent of India's population was literate in 1961.

India is largely an agricultural country. 82·2 per cent of her population is rural, living in about 56,000 villages. About 48 per cent of India's national income is contributed by agriculture, on which 70 per cent of her population depends for livelihood.

It is also worth remembering that India is a federation consisting of a number of semi-autonomous states. All matters relating to defence, foreign affairs, communications, currency and coinage, banking and insurance, and customs duties are the exclusive responsibility of the centre while all matters concerning law and order, public health and sanitation, education, agriculture, forests and fisheries are under the exclusive authority of the states. There is also a concurrent list of subjects, on which both the centre and the states have authority. That list includes economic planning, social security, trade and industry, and electricity.

We shall start by examining in detail the performance of the Indian economy during the past few years. Sections 3 and 4 will be devoted to a discussion of the more important problems of the Indian economy which hinder rapid economic development. Then in Section 5 we shall discuss the underlying strategy of Indian economic planning and in Section 6 the impact of population increase and unemployment.

2. *The Recent Record*

India became independent of British rule in the second half of 1947. As soon as the massive refugee problem created by the partitioning of the country had been brought under control, the indigenous government resorted to economic planning to promote economic growth and to reduce poverty. But the First Five Year Plan (lasting from 1950–51 to 1955–56) was not an exercise in any systematic planning; it was much more a collection of schemes or projects already started or envisaged by the various government departments. With the Second Five Year Plan (lasting from 1955–56 to 1961–62), an attempt was made to do more systematic planning. India is currently implementing her Third Five Year Plan (to last from 1961–62 to 1965–66). We shall later examine the nature of Indian planning. Let us now examine the record of the Indian economy over the last thirteen years.

Though there have been some encouraging features in the recent economic history of India, and though the overall rate of growth over the past thirteen years has turned out to be more or less according to the plans, yet one cannot describe the performance as anything but disappointing. The reasons for this generalization should be clear by the end of this section.

First, the encouraging features: these relate to the tremendous increases in the production of some important industrial products. In 1950 India manufactured only 7 steam locomotives; by 1960 the number has reached 295. In 1950 only 4,600 diesel engines were produced; by 1961 the figure had become 44,400. The output of power transformers in 1950 was 172,000 k.v.a.; by 1961 the figure had risen to 1,775,000. The output of electric motors in 1950 was 82,000 h.p.; the figure had grown to 824,000 in 1961. In 1950 machine tools to the value of 2·7 million rupees were produced; in 1961 the figure had soared to 76·1 million. The output of finished steel in 1950 was 1 million metric tons; by 1961 it was 2·9 million. Cement production increased from 2·7 million metric tons in 1950 to 8·2 million in 1961. The production of crude petroleum rose from 264,000 metric tons in 1951 to 442,000 in 1961; and the production of petroleum products, such as kerosene and diesel fuel, over the same period increased from 249,000 to 6,100,000 metric tons. Over the same years the output of ammonium sulphate increased from 48,000 metric tons to 395,000 and of caustic soda from 11,000 to 120,000.

Not only some industries producing capital and intermediate goods but also some consumer-goods industries expanded rapidly. The output of sugar increased from 990,000 metric tons in 1950 to 3·03 million in 1961. The number of bicycles produced in 1950 was 103,000; by 1961 the figure had risen to 1,047,000. The figure for sewing machines rose over the same period from 31,000 to 317,000; for electric fans from 193,000 to 1,074,000; and for radio receivers from 44,000 to 326,000. The overall increase in industrial output between 1950 and 1960 was 94 per cent.

According to the projections embodied in the First Plan, national income in 1962 was to be about one-third higher than in 1950. But in the Second Plan targets were revised upwards, so that national income in 1962 was expected to be about 61 per cent over the 1950 level. This target implied a planned compound rate of growth of about 4 per cent per year. The actual compound rate of growth over the twelve years from 1950 to 1962, worked out at 1948 prices, has been about 3·5 per cent; national income in 1962 was 51 per cent higher than in 1950, both being estimated at 1948 prices. Some observers think that these calculations, for various reasons, under-estimate the actual rate of growth, and it may be that the difference between the planned and attained rates of growth is even smaller than that between 4 per cent and 3·5 per cent.

We see then that there have been tremendous increases in the output of some industrial products, and that the overall rate of growth till 1962 has been more or less according to plan. Why has the performance none the less been disappointing? There are many reasons for this. The rate of growth of per capita income has been only about 1·5 per cent over the years when the overall rate of growth has been about 3·5 per cent. This actual rate of growth of per capita income has been less than was planned in 1956 because at the time it was thought that the population was growing annually at only about 1·25 per cent per year. This was over-optimistic because there already were indications that the population was growing much faster. The 1961 census showed that population during the 1950's was growing at over 2 per cent per year. While the Indian per capita income has been growing at about 1·5 per cent, the Chinese per capita income between 1950 and 1958 grew at an annual rate of 11·5 per cent; the annual per capita rate of growth for Yugoslavia between 1952 and 1959 was 9·2; that for the Soviet Union between 1950 and 1959, 8·7, and that for Japan between 1955 and 1959, 8·1. A few observers draw some comfort by comparing the recent Indian overall rate of annual growth of about 3·5 per cent with the Japanese rate of 4·6 between 1878 and 1907, or the Japanese rate of about 3 per cent between 1893 and 1912. But the more relevant comparisons of the recent Indian rate of growth are with the recent rates of growth of similarly placed economies such as those of China and Yugoslavia.

Another reason for disappointment is that while the last decade or so has seen the genuine beginnings of something like an industrial revolution in India, Indian agriculture continues to be stagnant. Between 1951 and 1963, income from agriculture increased by only one-third; whereas income from all other sectors grew by 70 per cent. The progress in the agricultural yield per acre has been even more disappointing; in 1960 the yield per acre was only 18·3 per cent higher than in 1950. Agricultural output has been growing annually at a rate not much above 2 per cent; this low rate of growth of a sector whose relative share in the national product has continued to be about 48 per cent has naturally depressed the overall rate of growth of the economy. We shall be examining in detail the reasons for the failure in agriculture in the next section.

Even the modest annual increase of about 1·5 per cent in per capita income does not represent an equivalent rise in the level of consumption by the people. The relative shares in national income of both net capital formation and government consumption expenditure have been rising. In 1950, their combined share was 12·5 per cent of the national income; by 1955 it had gone up to about 17·5 per cent; in 1960 it stood at 20 per cent; and after the Chinese attack and the consequent growth in defence expenditure, the combined share of net capital formation and government defence expenditure had reached almost 25 per cent of the national income. The growth of such expenditure has naturally squeezed the relative share of private consumption. Still, up to 1961, there seems to have been some annual rise in per capita consumption. But there is reason to suspect that only the better off sections of the community benefitted from this; the rural and urban working classes do not seem to have benefitted—except perhaps the workers employed in factories.

K

Let us turn now to education and health. These may be described as parts of the social welfare programmes; though, since education and good health increase the personal efficiency of workers, they can also reasonably be described as possible fields of productive social investment. In both education and health the record has been disappointing. In 1951, the percentage of children between the ages of six and eleven that attended school was 42·6; in 1961 this percentage has only risen to 61 per cent; and the similar percentage for the age group from eleven to fourteen rose even more slowly from 12·7 to 22·8. Further, according to most observers the standards of education at all levels have been dropping. This drop in standards has been particularly marked at the university level. Indian university education has always had a heavy bias in favour of arts subjects as opposed to scientific subjects or vocational training. This bias has continued, so that today though there is an acute shortage of trained people, there is also a growing number of graduates who cannot find jobs. In health, too, progress has been slight. In 1949 there were 2,700 hospitals; by 1958 the number had risen to only 3,400: and the number of hospital beds rose over the same period from 109,000 to only 160,000. The poor progress in education and health are only faintly indicative of the total lack of any progress in giving aid to the destitute. The streets in Indian towns have as many handicapped people lying about uncared for as they have ever had. The seventeen years of the country's independence have brought no improvement in their condition.

Where the unemployables are uncared for, it is no wonder that there is no relief provided for the unemployed. Moreover, the size of unemployment has been growing right through the thirteen years of planning and conscious efforts for economic development. The present unemployment of about 12 million works out as about 7 per cent of the total number of workers (agricultural and industrial) in the country. Apart from this unemployment, there is also under-employment in agriculture, and in traditional trades and occupations. For obvious reasons it is more difficult to estimate this under-employment but there can be no doubt that it continues to be substantial.

The record has been disappointing in two other important respects: exports and birth rates. With both of these it is easy to slip into complacency or an attitude which insists that government action can do very little about them. Though it is true that both in export promotion and in the promotion of the idea of family planning there is a large, unpredictable and uncontrollable element, it is also true that with respect to both of these much more can be done by education, propaganda and inducements than has actually been done. Over ports have risen only slightly while birth- ... d of falling.

... f the very recent past, i.e. the last three ... ese first three years of the Third Plan has ... much worse than the previous record, is ... uring the current Plan, national income is ... e by about 6 per cent per year. Since population ... at least 2·2 per cent per year, the planned annual ... pita income is of about 3 per cent. But according to the ... appraisal of the Third Plan, published towards the end of ... ational income during the first half of the Plan was rising at an annual rate of only a little over 2 per cent. With population annually rising by at least 2·2 per cent, the latest record of the Indian economy is of virtual stagnation. The greatest failure has been in agriculture. Since weather has not been helpful and since there has been no real change in agricultural methods, the production of most agricultural products has suffered. Over the last three years, overall agricultural output has at best remained constant. And over the last two years the total output of food-grains has in fact declined; in 1962 it was 2·8 per cent less than in 1961; and in 1961, it was 1·4 per cent less than in the year before.

But agriculture is not the only sphere in which ambitions have remained unfulfilled. In industry too, especially in the publicly-owned industries, performance has been far below expectations. In a number of projects, construction is woefully behind schedule, so that actual output in the last year of the current plan is going to be much below that proposed. Of finished steel, the actual output in 1965 is likely to be 5·8 million tons instead of the target of 6·8; of alloy, tool and stainless steels the actual output is likely to be nil instead of the target of 200,000 tons; of steel forgings the actual output is likely to be just over half the target; of nitrogenous ferti-lizers, the actual output is now likely to be 500,000 instead of 800,000 tons; and of phosphatic fertilizers, only half the target. The delays in the execution of projects in the public sector are more or less matched by the similar delays in the privately owned industries—especially the heavy industries.

The real cause of these delays is simply inefficient implementation. Delays in obtaining the necessary foreign exchange can be a possible cause only in some cases. This factor was not relevant in at least twenty highly important large-scale publicly owned projects lagging seriously behind schedule; in each of these projects the necessary foreign exchange was already arranged by the end of the Second Plan, and some of them had already begun to be constructed by the beginning of the current Plan. These projects concern such things as heavy electrical equipment, precision instruments, machine tools, fertilizers and so on. Needless to say, lagging behind schedule in such basic industries has cumulative effects. For example, early during the Second Plan the Soviet Union had offered substantial aid for a heavy-machinery complex. If this work had been quickly taken up and completed, a great deal of the equipment for further expansion of steel manufacture could have been obtained at home.

We noted earlier that the relative shares in the national income of capital formation and government consumption have been rising; we noted a little later that per capita income over the last three years has stood still or declined a little. It follows that during the last three years, per capita consumption has been declining. There is no reason to believe that this decline has been equally shared by all classes. In fact, nearly all observers agree that the decline in the standard of consumption of the poorest, especially in urban areas, has been much greater than the overall average.

The last three years have been a period of rapidly rising prices. The index number of the wholesale prices of food articles (with 1952–53 = 100) stood at 124·3 in August 1961; by August 1962, it had risen to 131·5; in August 1963 it had reached 138·6; but the rise was greatest during 1963–64, and in August 1964 the index had reached 165·1. Prices of manufactures and raw materials also rose, but by much smaller percentages. This steep rise in food prices has caused widespread distress, especially in urban areas. Various suggestions about reforming the system of distribution of food-grains are being currently discussed in India. We shall be examining them in the next section.

3. *Backward Agriculture*

As we have noted, agriculture is the single most important economic activity in India; it contributes about 48 per cent of India's national income, and about 70 per cent of the working population depends on agriculture for a livelihood. Yet for a number of years now, Indian agriculture has not been able to produce enough to meet the internal demand. In the very recent years, India's dependence on imported food has been increasing. Though the imported food forms only a very small percentage of the total food consumed, it is a large absolute amount. Therefore, even though a great deal of it comes as a gift under the United States Public Law 480, there is still a significant wastage of foreign exchange.

Moreover, with India's large population and its high rate of increase, agricultural production has to increase rapidly if there is to be any improvement in the majority's nutritive standards without increasing further India's dependence on imported food. With population increasing by at least 2·2 per cent per year, that rate is the minimum at which agricultural production must increase if the country's dependence on imported food is not to increase, and if the already low nutritive standards are not to decline. In order to raise the nutritive standards, and to eliminate the dependence on imported food, agricultural output should increase by at least 4 per cent per year. This is, roughly speaking, the target of the Third Plan. Moreover, the only way of raising the standard of living of the 70 per cent Indians who depend on agriculture is to raise the agricultural yield per acre, since the possibilities of bringing more land under cultivation are very limited now.

Over the ten years from 1951 to 1961, the overall agricultural yield per acre has risen by about 18 per cent; that is, by less than even 2 per cent per year. The record of the increase in the yields per acre of specific crops like rice and wheat was little better; between 1951 and 1961 the increase for rice was about 24 per cent and for wheat about 22 per cent. Between 1961 and 1964, yields per acre for most crops have at best stood still. In other words, for the first three years of the Third Plan, the target of a yearly rise of 4 per cent in the agricultural yield per acre has not been reached; there has been no increase in yields per acre over these years. Further, there is no sign that the planned annual output is going to be achieved for the next two years either.

That is the actual record; but the potential for growth in agricultural yields would seem to be very great. A number of agricultural experts who have studied Indian conditions consider that the yields for most crops could increase by 8 per cent per year. A Ford Foundation Agricultural Production Team which visited India during the Second Plan, concluded that cereal output in India during the Third Plan could increase at a cumulative annual rate of about 8 per cent. Such rates of growth have been achieved recently in other countries, notably Yugoslavia.

The reason for this great potential rate of growth of agricultural yields is that while the productive methods in stagnant agricultures have remained traditional, there have been great advances in the scientific knowledge about agriculture. Perhaps the most important single contribution of science to agriculture in this century has been the development of the systematic application of chemical fertilizers. The great potential increase in the Indian yields per acre is indicated by what has been achieved in other countries, of which some at least have no natural advantage over India. For example, India produces only 1,400 kilogrammes of rice per hectare, whereas Japan produces 4,620 and Australia, 5,950. Again, India produces only 790 kilogrammes of wheat per hectare, whereas France produces 2,600 and Denmark, 4,130.

These figures show the potential increases in Indian agricultural yields that are *technically* feasible. It is with some such comparisons in mind that it has been argued recently that we should consider agriculture in backward economies to have a great deal of excess capacity. But whether any reasonably quick method of exploiting this excess capacity can be devised is a different question. The necessary changes in methods have been adopted by some farmers, so that in a number of states in India some farms now have yields per acre about five to seven times the local average. And the innovations which these farmers have adopted are well-known and simple enough. They are: using improved seeds; increased weeding and hoeing; much greater use of green manure and fertilizers; rotation of crops; better guarding of crops against wild life and other pests; better storage; and the construction of new as well as the repair of old water tanks, wells and canals.

All these measures are relatively simple in themselves; given a moderately worldly-wise farmer, expectation of rising or at least stable agricultural prices, some access to capital to finance minor investments and a fairly steady availability of chemical fertilizers, improved seeds and the other inputs which come from outside the village—given all these things the necessary measures to raise agricultural yields 100 per cent or more could be adopted within a few years. Unfortunately, none of the preconditions we have mentioned has in fact existed in anything more than a very partial way.

First, and most important, the worldly wisdom of the farmers: there are necessarily differences of opinion on this issue, but a number of observers think that many of the Indian farmers are fatalistic and therefore in a vague way quite content with their present way of life and standard of living. The results of an intensive study of two villages (in the Economic Review, August 7, 1962, published from Delhi) showed that in one village about one-third, and in another about one-half of the farmers showed lack of any interest in a higher income. Further, in one village only 40 per cent, and in the other as little as 25 per cent, of the farmers realized that higher output was a means to higher income. Perhaps these results are not exactly representative of the whole country. But it cannot easily be denied that there definitely is some apathy for adopting changed methods in the Indian villages. Apart from the bonds of religion, the other factors responsible for this attitude are the class structure of the rural society and the system of land tenure. The inhibitions placed on individual enterprise by the class (and caste) structure have been only slightly weakened in rural India; so that even now if a poor farmer tries to improve his lot in an impressive way, he runs the risk of incurring the displeasure of his social superiors. Also, in spite of all the talk about land reform, the real reform in the landlord-tenant relations has been negligible. This is largely because landlords are politically strong—having close ties with the governments of a number of states in the Indian federation.

Further, whatever the motivations of the Indian farmers, till recently the price incentive for increasing yields per acre has definitely been weak. Up to about 1959, agricultural prices followed a downward trend; during the First Plan they fell by 13 per cent. Though they have been rising since 1960, there is reason to believe that this has not increased the incomes of farmers as much as could be desired. This is because a great number of farmers have not the staying power to withhold their stocks until that part of the agricultural season when prices begin to rise. It has been estimated that about one-third of the rice crop is sold by farmers in the harvest and the immediate post-harvest season at prices a great deal below the average. A number of experts, especially visiting American experts, are of the opinion that the lack of price support to agriculture has been one of the major causes of agricultural stagnation.

Acting on that advice, and also in order to try to control the rise in the prices of food-grains to the consumer, the Indian government has recently announced a system of declaring in each agricultural season minimum and maximum price limits for the producer and maximum price limits for the consumer. It is proposed to administer these price limits through the Food Corporation of India. It will not be a monopoly. It will have statutory powers to requisition stocks from the private wholesale traders and sell them through government-owned fair price shops, if the retail price in the free market threatens to rise above the declared ceiling. Otherwise, it will compete with private wholesale traders in buying stocks from the traders. Provided it has sufficient storage capacity, it should be able to maintain realistically fixed price floors. Again, provided it can build up sufficient stocks, it should also be able to maintain the announced price ceilings unless there is a gross failure of crops any year.

The amount of food-grains sold by the farmers annually is estimated at between 30 and 35 million tons; and it has been estimated that if the corporation is to perform its functions effectively, it will need a storage capacity of about 5 million tons. But the storage capacity so far available is only 2 million; hence a great deal will depend on how soon a programme is started to increase quickly that capacity. This then is the government plan for the related purposes of providing price incentives to agricultural producers (of food-grains at least) and of ensuring some price ceiling for the consumers. Whether the latter can really be ensured without effective rationing remains to be seen; on the other hand, it is doubtful if the Indian administrative machinery in its present state can bear the burden of large-scale rationing.

As for the fear that the price support policy for agricultural producers may provoke a complete lack of response or a negative response, there is ample evidence to suggest that in the aggregate food farmers as well as non-food farmers are positively responsive to price changes. But before any substantial incentive effects can be expected, there will have to be a definite commitment that the minimum prices announced will not be revised downwards for at least five years. So far no such commitment has been forthcoming.

The other important precondition for a dramatic rise in yields which is lacking is the steady supply of inputs which the farmer cannot supply himself; namely such things as finance, better seeds, fertilizers and irrigation. It is possible to write a long chapter about each of these problems, but we must be content with a few words. The traditional source of finance is the village moneylender; he is unsuitable for the task of financing agricultural improvements because of the very high rates he demands. Credit co-operatives have been tried in India, but the idea has not worked; the degree of sophistication and literacy required from the members for the successful working of such institutions is just not available. The few co-operatives there are have largely been worked by the most influential local families in their own interests. (The co-operative farms—with joint cultivation, or just joint buying or selling—have proved even less successful for similar reasons.) The problem of rural credit still remains to be solved.

There are similar failures of organization in the supply of better seeds, fertilizers and irrigation. There is undoubtedly need in the country for more fertilizer production and more irrigation projects (especially small-scale projects), but the astounding fact is that there are at present under-utilized irrigation facilities as well as unsold stocks of fertilizers. In each case the cause is organizational. Irrigation is not fully utilized because the distribution channels have not been constructed in the right time in the right places; similarly not all the amount of fertilizers gets sold because often it is not available in the right place at the right time.

Is too little being spent on agricultural development as compared with the other industries? The public expenditure on agriculture amounted to 31 per cent of the First, 20 per cent of the Second, and 23 per cent of the Third Plan expenditure. But in absolute terms, the expenditure on agriculture grew from Rs. 6,010 millions in the First, and Rs. 9,500 million in the Second, to Rs. 17,181 million in the Third Plan. Hence it cannot be maintained that agriculture has been deprived of public funds.

What agriculture has missed is the close government and public attention which has been devoted to the programme of industrialization. In some respects, agriculture is one of the minor ministries in Delhi; there is less glamour attached to being an officer in that ministry than in some others. Again, the various officials appointed under the Community Development Projects (which have been going on for years with the basic aim of increasing yields per acre) have been poorly paid and have had a markedly low status compared with other members of the Indian administration. Consequently, they have lacked self-confidence, courage and drive. The worker at village level, the main link between the planners and the farmers, is usually a poorly trained person with so many villages and tasks to look after that often no village or task gets proper attention.

According to the Third Plan, the output of food grains at the end of the plan should be about 100 million tons; but in fact during the first three years of the Plan output has remained at around 80 million tons. There is every reason to believe that this is due as much to failure of administration as to the lack of enthusiasm on the part of the farmers. For, other agricultural objectives—in the fulfilment of which farmers play no role—are also now unlikely to be attained by the end of the current Plan. For example, by the end of the Plan, there were to be 16·3 million acres of irrigation potential and 12·8 million acres of utilization; but now it is expected that by the end of the Plan the respective achievements will only be 11·1 million and 10 million acres. Again, while the objective over five years for the soil conservation programme is 11 million acres, the achievement during the first two years was only 2·5 million acres. In the vital matter of area under improved seeds, while the Plan proposes an addition of 148 million acres, in the three years so far the achievement has been only 46 million acres. In almost every item of the agricultural programme, the achievements in the first three years have been well below what they should have been.

4. *Low Savings and Shortage of Foreign Exchange*

Underdeveloped countries usually save only a small percentage of their annual incomes. Since most of the necessary measures to promote economic development require increased annual investment, it is customary to put a great deal of emphasis on the obstacle of low savings. But it is now gradually being recognized that more can be done by the countries themselves to overcome this particular obstacle. It is clear that, in a number of underdeveloped countries, incomes are so unevenly distributed that though the majority of people are too poor to save much or pay much in taxes, there is a small minority to which a large proportion of the annual national income accrues. Therefore, given enough determination, the governments of most such countries can raise the proportion of at least public savings within a short time. More serious obstacles to growth are backward agriculture and shortages of certain kinds of inputs—largely equipment, components, some raw materials, and skills; linked with these shortages is the important shortage of foreign exchange.

Let us examine the behaviour of total national savings in India. When the First Plan started, domestic investment and savings were both about 5 per cent of the national income; by the end of the Plan, investment was 7·3 per cent, and savings, 7 per cent. By the end of the Second Plan, investment had risen to 11 per cent and savings to 8·5 per cent—the gap being filled by foreign assistance. By the end of the current Plan, domestic savings are scheduled to rise to 11·5 per cent and investment to 14·5 per cent. Domestic savings are planned to catch up with domestic investment by 1975, when both will be 18–20 per cent of the national income.

The rise of domestic savings from 5 per cent of the national income in 1951 to 8·5 per cent after ten years in 1961 is a disappointing record—not that the planning authorities could have done a great deal to raise the private propensity to save. But they could have increased the level of taxation of certain classes much more than they did; in other words, the percentage of national income saved through government taxation could have increased considerably more. Taxation in India could be made much more progressive than it is at present. Professor H. F. Lydall calculated in 1960 that whereas in the United Kingdom the top 1 per cent, 5 per cent and 10 per cent of population (arranged in order of income) are respectively left after taxation with 5 per cent, 15 per cent and 25 per cent of the national income, in India the top 1 per cent, 5 per cent and 10 per cent of the population are respectively left after taxation with

10 per cent, 22 per cent and 33 per cent of the national income. Only if a further 8 per cent of national income is taxed away from the top 10 per cent of the population in India, will the taxation of that part of the population be as progressive as it is in the United Kingdom.

An Indian's annual income has to be more than twelve times the per capita income of the country for him to pay income tax. The corresponding ratio for Australia is 0·9, and for Japan about 2. But for India to lower appreciably the level of taxable income is uneconomical, because the tax will have to be collected in small amounts from an exceedingly large number of people—a great proportion of whom are self-employed and keep no regular accounts. There is no similar administrative argument for the low rates of taxation at the middle and high ranges of incomes. For example, when a British tax-payer has an income fifty times as high as the national per capita income, he pays 67 per cent of his income in tax; an Australian in the same relative position pays 57 per cent of his income; but an Indian in that relative position, pays only 7·3 per cent of his income in tax.

While the rates of taxation are lower than in many other countries, tax evasion is widespread. Most income tax is collected from urban incomes; though these increased at an average rate of 3·5 per cent per year between 1948 and 1957, the revenue from the income tax as a percentage of national income *fell* from 1·83 to 1·37 per cent. Even if this outcome was not entirely due to tax evasion, this and other evidence strongly suggests the prevalence of income tax evasion on a large scale. (Revenues from indirect taxes and non-tax revenues over the same period were much more income-elastic.)

A great deal more revenue can be obtained by more effective administration of the taxes. This has been proved by the Rs. 700 million excess over the budgeted amount collected from corporation and income taxes in 1963; this excess has been mainly due, in the words of an official report, to 'better collections of advance tax, incentives for prompt payment and completion of a larger number of assessments'. But there are still many people who completely escape paying any direct taxes even though they have assessable incomes. This is suggested, among other things, by the fact that while there are 3·6 million radio licence holders in India, there are only 0·9 million tax payers; in the Indian conditions, anybody who can afford to buy a radio is most likely to have an assessable income. The government has recently started door to door surveys in some areas in order to discover new assessees. Such a survey in Calcutta recently uncovered about 70,000 persons who had been evading the payment of any direct taxes.

A recent unfortunate development has been encroaching upon the amount of resources available for investment for development purposes; this is the steep rise in the proportion of the national income devoted to defence expenditure. India is now spending annually on defence about 6 per cent of her national income. A number of other countries restrict their expenditure on defence to only 2 to 4 per cent of their national incomes. As India's relations with her neighbours improve, it should be possible to effect some cuts in defence expenditure.

Let us consider now the shortage of foreign exchange. Provided the marginal propensity to import is at all positive, an increase in the national income of a country necessarily leads to an increase in imports; but there is no necessary reason for exports to increase by an equal amount. A country going through the initial phases of economic development is particularly import-hungry, with its high need for equipment, materials and skills of the type that cannot be provided locally. This would not create a serious problem if the country could simultaneously increase the value of its exports. But the world market for the products of underdeveloped countries (which are largely primary producing) has been sluggish ever since the end of the last war. India's own exports of agricultural products and related manufactures decreased from about Rs. 4,970 million in 1950 to about Rs. 4,740 million in 1960.

There are two broad groups in India's exports: agricultural commodities and related manufactures, including cotton and jute manufactures—broadly the traditional exports; and other manufactures and minerals—including new engineering products. India's relative share in world exports declined for almost all her traditional exports between 1950 and 1960. Her share in world exports in jute manufactures fell from 97 per cent in 1948–50 to 76 per cent in 1958–60; and in tea from 50 per cent to 43 per cent. Before the last war, India supplied 45 to 50 per cent of world exports (excluding China) of groundnuts and groundnut oil, but in 1958–60, her share had fallen to 3 per cent. During 1948–50, India and Japan each accounted for about 11 per cent of world exports in cotton textiles; in 1958–60 Japan had increased her share to 18 per cent, while India's share had fallen to 10 per cent. Dr Manmohan Singh has estimated that if India's relative share of the world market for her principal traditional exports had remained constant, her export earnings would have been higher by about Rs. 1,000 million each year. India's relative share declined because in the earlier years there was a lack of appreciation among planners of the need to increase exports at all costs. At the same time the rising demands at home for most goods weakened exporters' incentives.

A few years ago a great deal of hope was placed on developing the exports of one particular item in the 'non-traditional' category, namely, the new engineering products. They can be divided into three types. First, light engineering products—such as utensils, steel trunks, electric fans, sewing machines, and bicycles. Second, industrial machinery—such as oil mill, shoe, jute, and textile machinery. Third, intermediate products—such as iron and steel, cast iron pipes, diesel engines, and sheets of non-ferrous metal. In 1960 the exports of all these new products amounted to only about Rs. 90 million. More than half of them were of light engineering products; about a tenth, of industrial machinery; and about a quarter, of intermediate products. Most of these exports (62 per cent) went to African and Asian countries.

Recently it has been realized that, though every effort should be made to develop these new exports, it will be unrealistic to expect to increase easily such exports to the other underdeveloped countries. There are two reasons for this. Firstly, since light engineering products are not essential imports, most of these countries are unlikely to allow them to grow fast and increase their own balance of payments difficulties. Secondly, since the manufacture of these products is relatively simple, these countries are likely to start their own manufacture of them. We can already see both these courses in operation. Burma banned the import of aluminium utensils in 1957, and more recently Iran and Iraq have been setting up their own plants to make electric fans.

In a more sanely organized world economy, India, and other newly industrializing countries, would be able to sell greatly increased amounts of the relatively simple manufactured products to the industrially advanced countries, where a large market for these products exists; in return, the industrialized countries would specialize much more than they do now in the more difficult kinds of manufacture. But, as things are at present, the advanced countries restrict their imports of simple manufactures by means of tariffs, quotas, high internal excises, and by negotiating agreements with underdeveloped countries so that they themselves restrict their exports of such products.

Since industrial machinery and intermediate products are both more essential imports and more difficult to produce in the early stages of industrialization, India's chances of increasing her exports of these to other underdeveloped countries are good—even though she has to compete with the exports of these things from the industrially advanced countries which are in a better position to offer credit. But the irony is that for some years to come India will have less than sufficient of a number of these products for her own needs; and if she is to increase her productive capacity of them in order to increase her exports, then in the short-run she will have to increase further her imports of equipment and materials, thus making her foreign exchange position even more difficult.

That India's foreign exchange position is difficult can be gathered from the following facts. According to the Third Plan, the need for foreign loans and grants during its course of five years will amount to about Rs. 26,000 million. According to present estimates, the Fourth Plan will have about an equal need for foreign aid; during the Fifth Plan, ending in 1976, it is hoped that this need will be smaller. These estimates are based on the assumptions that during the Third Plan exports will increase by 40 per cent, and that by 1970 exports will be more than twice as large as they were in 1960. During the previous ten years, from 1950 to 1960, exports increased by only 3 per cent.

A recent estimate is that by 1980, the traditional exports of the non-communist underdeveloped countries can at best double. On the most optimistic deductions about the prospects of India's traditional exports from this estimate, India would need to increase by 1970 her 'non-traditional' exports (i.e. exports of minerals and of all kinds of manufactures, other than cotton and jute) to at least four times their size in 1960, if she is to fulfil her total export objective for 1970. Over the ten years from 1950 to 1960, India's exports of these non-traditional exports nearly doubled, rising from Rs. 820 million to Rs. 1,580 million. By 1970 they will need to rise to about Rs. 6,800 million a year.

Such a dramatic increase in total annual exports will be achieved only by a combination of sustained efforts on many fronts: negotiations with developed countries to persuade them to import more manufactures, effective quality control not only for manufactures but also for agricultural products, inducements to exporters, and check on the domestic demand for exportables—this applies particularly to agricultural products. Quality control and the related tasks of studying the designs, patterns and types of products wanted in foreign markets have been largely neglected in the past by India, even though they have been repeatedly recommended. There is now, however, an Export (quality control and inspection) Act which is gradually coming into full operation.

Regarding the exports of new products to other underdeveloped countries, India's chances are best for those products which are considered essential by these countries, and which are not usually sold by advanced countries with aid and loans tied to them. Such products are essential consumer goods like drugs and medicine, intermediate goods like fertilizers and cement, and some kinds of public utility equipment.

Though the years 1963 and 1964 have been in most respects a period of economic gloom for India, the one encouraging development has been that at last the Indian exports have begun to increase at a helpful rate. India's total exports in the first six months of the financial year 1964–65 were Rs. 380 million higher than those in the corresponding period of the last financial year. This increase is more or less evenly spread over the items in India's exports—traditional and new. Exports in the last quarter of 1964 were at the rate of Rs. 9,000 million a year. The projected target for annual exports during the Fourth Plan is Rs. 10,000 million a year. Till recently this seemed optimistic, but now it is beginning to look well within the reach of the economy. This shows that India's recent quality control measures, institution of credit facilities for exporters (through the Export Credit and Guarantee Corporation), and export promotion councils have begun to produce some results.

Since, however, the bulk of India's exportables (tea, textiles, cotton, leather goods, oil seeds and light engineering products) are such that the domestic demand for them increases fast with a rise in domestic income, the country will have to devise measures to prevent buoyant domestic markets preventing a fast growth of their exports. Further, since a number of important exportables are of agricultural origin, the possibility of progressively increasing their exports at competitive prices is tied up with the performance of the agricultural programmes. There should be no complacency with regard to the exports yet: in 1963–64, only 78 per cent of India's imports were financed by exports.

5. *Strategy of Indian Economic Planning*

India is not one of those countries where all or most means of production are state owned. All agricultural land is privately owned; similarly most of manufacturing industry is privately owned. Again, though the government formulates five year plans of economic development which include targets for the privately owned sector too, there is no direct and continuous control by the government over private enterprise to ensure that it does fulfil the targets. The government has the power to exercise direct control in, or even completely take over, a firm if there is gross mismanagement or evidence of fraudulent activity; but this is quite different from the kind of control a government has over state-owned enterprises. In short, India is a mixed economy.

Though further industrial expansion in some industries, such as munitions, atomic energy, iron and steel, heavy engineering and heavy electrical plant, is more or less reserved for state enterprise, private enterprise is still left with the responsibility for looking after a large number of industrial products. The reasons for the state to have reserved certain fields of industrial activity for itself are such as these: strategic considerations, knowledge that in those spheres private enterprise for various reasons had been sluggish, and a desire to prevent an excessive concentration of power which may result from large and basic industries being owned privately.

Starting from the Second Plan, there has been a marked emphasis on projects for basic industries in India. The reason for this has been the realization on the part of the Indian planners that in a vast country like India, the absolute total size of consumption goods industries is going to be so large that their demands upon basic industries will also be large. But India cannot expect to import large amounts of basic industrial products continuously for the next three or four decades because nobody has been able to see any possibility of India being able to increase her exports to the required extent. This long-term viewpoint dictates the strategy of planning for a large foundation of basic industries at home. But since the import require-ments of a programme of new heavy industries in an underdeveloped country are much larger than most other conceivable programmes, the strategy of the Indian planners has made India's foreign exchange requirements in the relatively short-run bigger than they might otherwise have been. There is, however, no escape from this decision. Quite apart from the planners' objective of diminishing in the long run the economy's dependence on imports of heavy industrial products, some basic industrial capacity such as power and an extensive system of road and railway transport must be increased because these can never be imported.

It may be asked why there should be the need in India for govern-ment planning of economic development. The answer to this question has many parts. Firstly, some guidance of the working of the national economy now takes place in all countries and under all kinds of political parties. The importance of a 'healthy' economy to the welfare of each individual in a country, and the possibilities of an economy which is working entirely on its own getting into a mess, are so widely recognized now that most people in most coun-tries expect their governments to 'do something' about keeping the economy 'healthy'.

In underdeveloped countries the major economic problems are not confined to avoiding inflation and fluctuations in employment, and preventing a recurring deficit in the balance of payments (as is largely the case in developed countries), but also include the basic problem of changing a stagnant, tradition-bound economic system into an expanding economy. This last problem is much more difficult than is sometimes assumed. It is not simply a matter of offering monetary and fiscal inducements designed to raise the proportion of annual investment in national income. Monetary and fiscal inducements would have some hope of being sufficient if there were in the country a sufficiently large middle class, an entrepreneurial group of the required vitality in that middle class, and the necessary financial and economic institutions. But these conditions are not satisfied by India; otherwise, she would not have been an underdeveloped country.

An idea which went out of fashion some time ago, but the importance of which is now once again being increasingly realized, is that the underdeveloped countries need a cultural revolution before the character of their economies can fully change. And a cultural revolution which has to take place soon and fast is not really possible without active support by the government of new trends in art, literature, education, customs and ways of living.

Further, since there is not a sufficiently large entrepreneurial class, the government in a country like India has to start a number of enterprises on its own. This would inevitably give rise to some amount of planning of economic growth by the government. But what makes comprehensive and detailed planning of the economy necessary is simply the fact that in an underdeveloped economy so much needs to be changed and created. It is easily recognized that most economic activities are interdependent: production of steel, for example, depends on the steady availability of iron ore, coke, transport facilities for the raw materials and finished products, an expectation of a fairly steady demand and some confidence that the necessary components of machinery and equipment which are not available at home could be imported from abroad. A potential investor in such an industry in a developed country can usually take most of these things for granted. The trouble with underdeveloped countries is that, firstly, there are not so many potential investors and, secondly, the few potential investors there are cannot take the availability of supplementary facilities for granted. Left to themselves many important investments do not get made. The government has itself to plan such investments, work out their supplementary requirements and plan for these to be met in good time.

Because so much needs to be done to create new economic units

L

in a short space of time, the repercussions are widespread and important. There could easily be vast, unnecessary waste and suffering: new factories without raw materials, new products without customers, finished goods waiting for transport, completed industrial units without the necessary fuel or power, new industrial labour without anywhere to live, new towns without sufficient water, or large industrial complexes working below capacity for lack of foreign exchange with which to import the required raw materials or components. In an economy undergoing large-scale change there has to be a great deal of advance planning to ensure that the various important requirements and provisions are balanced sufficiently to prevent too much waste or suffering. During rapid economic development this need for balance, which cannot, particularly in an underdeveloped economy, be provided by the market except with significant time lags—this need is the basis of the case for government planning in a country like India. This case is strengthened when it is recalled that these are some investments for which private and social returns differ in most economies. Examples are: investment in irrigation, power, transport, education, health, the first few industrial units in a backward region and so on. And these investments form a substantial part of the new economic activity in an underdeveloped country undergoing change.

The foregoing arguments necessarily assume that the aim of social policy is to further the welfare of individuals at the fastest possible rate; otherwise it would not matter if there were waste or suffering. Further, it is assumed that the political nature of the country is such that the detailed planning for the whole economy which is entailed and the necessary powers of inducement and control, would only be entrusted to the government and not to any powerful private organization. Unless this last assumption is made, the arguments we have developed are those for planning rather than government planning.

How well has Indian planning been satisfying the need for balanced economic development? The First Five Year Plan, though no less bulky and verbose than those which were to follow later, largely consisted of bringing together some major projects which were already under construction, and of some aggregative projections of national income, investment and savings over the next two decades or so. Systematic planning began with the Second Five Year Plan. But the basic approach was far too aggregative, being based on the use of capital-output ratios for large sectors of the economy. Though there were output figures for various sectors for the end of the five-year period, no attempt was made to work out, from these final targets, yearly figures of output of at least the more important primary, intermediate and final goods, and of the necessary resources to be used. Many difficulties resulted from this failure to work out the implications for various sectors in each year. The most striking complications were in the balance of payments. Since no careful budget had been made of each year's requirements of imports, the government found itself making available the total allocation of foreign exchange for private investment right at the beginning of the plan. For their own reasons, private investors used up most of this allocation in the first two years of the Plan. The result was the severe foreign exchange crisis of 1957–58. That crisis necessitated cutting down a number of essential imports, with results— especially in power capacity and in coal washeries—which have hindered growth ever since. There were similar mistakes in other respects; cement capacity was installed well in advance of the need for it, while there has been a continued shortage of coke.

Coupled with the failure to ensure that the output requirements of at least the most important things were carefully balanced each year, was the failure to grasp the significance of time lags for economic planning—the fact that most investments produce the required output only some years after the decision to undertake them has been made, so that there is a constant need to try to forecast the demand for the more important requirements many years in advance, and in the light of the forecasts to prepare and actually undertake investment schemes well in advance. Failure to undertake such exercises during the First Plan led to having to start building steel factories during the Second Plan, when the need for steel had become much greater than the domestic output, instead of having started at least one such factory during the First Plan. There seems to have been a similar failure in the latter half of the Second Plan to start projects which will come into production in the early years of the Third Plan. It will not be surprising to discover that part of the explanation for the very slow annual rate of growth of the national output during the first half of the Third Plan, as revealed by the recent mid-term assessment, is to be found in just this factor.

But the basic cause of the poor performance during the current (the Third) Plan is that while perhaps the enthusiasm of the various groups concerned with the implementation of the Plans has been sagging, the planning technique itself has not evolved to make plan implementation vigorous and effective. India's plan documents are too much like advisory reports and not enough like documents detailing in a systematic way the necessary actions to be taken by identified agencies to realize the multifarious targets and subtargets.

Most of this is due to the lack of sufficient disaggregation already mentioned.

Perhaps some of it is also due to the very nature of the Indian Planning Commission. That body is largely advisory. The Prime Minister is its Chairman and it usually has one or two other Ministers as members. The Commission has largely to depend on the co-operation and enthusiasm of these Minister members to ensure that its recommendations are carried out. Moreover, the Commission does not continually review, evaluate and check the implementation of the programmes formulated by it. In an economy where so much needs to be changed, perhaps there is a need for some top Ministers to have the sole responsibility for formulating plans and continually checking their implementation.

Lastly, Indian planning has obviously not in practice been able to achieve balanced growth in one important area, namely agriculture. We have noted earlier the steep rise during 1963 and 1964 in the prices of food articles. Given the shortage of foreign exchange in India and the relative importance of agriculture in her national income and her occupational structure, a rapid rise in agricultural yields per acre is of fundamental importance to her development effort. Here again, as we noted in Section 3, the real failure has been that of implementation rather than of planning as such.

6. *Population and Unemployment*

India's population nearly doubled between 1901 (when it was 235 million) and 1961 (when it was 438 million). The increase was greatest between 1951 and 1961 when population increased by the best part of a hundred million. Its present rate of growth is at least 2·3 per cent per year. This high rate of growth is the result of the phenomena which are common in underdeveloped countries: modern public health measures as well as anti-famine measures (through modern transport links) have greatly reduced death rates while the birth rates continue to be high.

In the First Five Year Plan Rs. 4·5 million were spent on the family planning programme. It was an exceedingly modest beginning—more in the nature of a token programme than anything else. Indeed, the First Plan revealed rather surprising complacency about the need for popularizing birth control; it conveyed the impression that government hospitals should give advice about mechanical methods of birth control only to women whose health would be endangered by further births.

In the Second Plan, the outlay for this purpose was raised to

Rs. 50 million. The objective was to start 300 urban and 2,000 rural clinics. But this too was wholly inadequate. The underlying assumptions about population growth were far too optimistic, and this lack of a sense of urgency was reflected in the family planning programme envisaged. In the formulation of the Second Plan it was assumed that population during the 1950's would be increasing at the rate of 1·25 per cent annually. But the 1961 census showed that population had been growing at about 2·2 per cent annually during that period. In the Third Plan the allocation for family planning was still quite small, being Rs. 270 million. In the Fourth Plan it is to go up steeply to Rs. 950 million.

So far there has been no impact on birth rates from the family planning programme. Clearly much more vigorous action on a much larger scale is required. One country which has recently been able to achieve a remarkable decline in the rate of growth of its population is Japan. Its birth rate in 1959 (17·55 per thousand) was ouly half the figure it had been twelve years earlier. In 1948 Japan had taken the historic decision of legalizing induced abortion and sterilization. From 1949 to 1955, the number of registered induced abortions increased five times. It seems that now contraceptives have largely replaced abortion as a method of family planning in Japan.

There are naturally differences of opinion regarding the future rate of growth of India's population. It is safe to assume, however, that until 1966 there will be no decline in birth rates, and only a nominal decline in the five years after that; perhaps after 1970 there will be a greater decline. Working on some such assumptions, it has recently been estimated that India's population in 1966 will be about 494 million, in 1971 about 560 million, and about 695 million in 1981. According to these estimates, the density of population in India in 1981 will be about 53 per cent higher than in 1961.

One serious consequence of the rapid rate of growth of population is the large annual increase in the labour force: this increase is serious because for a long time there has been a large amount of unemployment in the economy. For example, at the beginning of the current Plan, 9 million persons were unemployed. This Plan expects to create about 14 million new employment opportunities. But since during the five years of this Plan fresh entrants to the labour market will be about 17 million, by 1966 the number of the unemployed will have increased to 12 million. And it is estimated that a further 23 million will enter the labour market during the five years of the Fourth Plan. If unemployment were to be abolished during the Fourth Plan, then that Plan would have to provide employment opportunities for 35 million persons. According to the Memorandum on the Fourth Plan which became available recently, about 16 million employment opportunities are expected to be created in the non-agricultural sector and about 4 million in agriculture. Thus at the end of the Fourth Plan, there will be a backlog of unemployment of about 15 million. It is further estimated that during the period of the Fifth Plan, the labour force will further increase by about 30 million.

Nobody argues that it is impossible at any cost for India to abolish unemployment within the next few years. If the country were to use all its savings and foreign exchange to equip each person with sufficiently simple implements, importing such increased amounts of goods demanded as she could not produce at home, she could certainly have full employment. But it is generally believed that given the limited supplies of such prerequisites as land, capital and foreign exchange, the techniques which would have to be used to provide everybody with employment would probably result in a total output smaller than could be produced with the same resources, using better techniques but giving employment to fewer people. In other words, though in the developed economies maximization of output often requires maximization of employment, in an underdeveloped country, with limited investible resources but overpopulation, maximization of employment and maximization of output are considered incompatible objectives.

The question arises as to whether that allocation of investible resources which maximizes output is necessarily the best. This depends on the social objectives of the economy; more specifically, it depends on what relative importance society places on output and on employment. If little importance is attached to employment and hence also to the distribution of incomes, or if it is assumed that whatever the level of employment resulting from improved techniques it is always possible to redistribute the accompanying output, through such instruments as unemployment relief payments, without affecting its size, then the allocation of investment which gives maximum output is necessarily the best.

On the other hand, if it is assumed that in an underdeveloped country with widespread unemployment it is difficult to organize systematic relief for the unemployed, and if it is assumed that an important social objective is to guarantee some minimum for everybody, then the allocation which maximizes output need not necessarily be the best. The best allocation may well be the one which attempts to strike a compromise between maximum output and maximum employment.

But there is another consideration relevant to this choice, and that has to do with the rate of growth of total output. It can seldom be assumed that an economy is interested only in the size of its present output; usually some importance will also be attached to the rate of growth of that output. Now, it is possible that the techniques of production which give relatively little employment but large output are also the ones which lead to a relatively high rate of growth of output. This may be so not only because such techniques produce greater amounts of savings, or investible surpluses, but also because they introduce the local workers, technicians and managements to new methods and thus make future innovations more likely. Therefore, in any investment allocation, there has to be a decision with respect to three considerations: total output, total employment and the rate of growth of output.

We have noted earlier that India's long-term export prospects necessitate a large heavy industry component in her current investment programme, if she is not to run the risk of having to slow down her rate of growth. Such investments have a relatively small employment potential in the short-run. Output-capital ratio is also much smaller in these investments than in some other possible investments. Yet the requirement that the rate of growth of the economy over the next decade or two should not be jeopardized, dictates some investment in heavy industry. At the same time, since the present population must have some reasonable amounts of consumer goods, there has to be adequate investment in the industries that produce such goods.

Since it seems likely that in a vast country like India, where the administration is in need of streamlining before it can undertake any additional burdens, any systematic relief for the unemployed will be difficult to organize for many years yet, there has to be a significant component in the investment programme which will be employment-oriented rather than output or growth-oriented. The investment in this category need not take the form of workers digging useless holes and then filling them up again. In India there is plenty of digging and building to be done of a kind which will also help greatly to increase output, though it does not necessarily follow that capital allocated to such uses could not have contributed more by way either of output or of growth potential in some other uses. Examples of useful products which employ many people but little capital are: simple but well designed houses built with indigenous materials, simple furniture, roads, wells, tanks, canals, school buildings and so on.

A high degree of unemployment also persists among the educated in India; it was recently estimated to be about 16 per cent among those with school leaving certificates and about 9 per cent among graduates. At the same time there are shortages of doctors, nurses, engineers, technicians, firemen and many similarly qualified workers. The high unemployment among the educated in India is the result of the irrational educational system which we have already noted. An excessive number of students, both at schools and colleges, do non-scientific subjects, and come out with a kind of education for which demand is very limited. Of course, this demand could be increased if the educational system itself were properly rationalized and greatly expanded. As at least primary education becomes universal, there is bound to be increased demand for teachers even in the non-scientific subjects. And with literacy there are always possibilities of re-training.

Apart from the shortage of fixed and circulating capital, there is in India also a shortage of wage goods. If more employment is created over the next few years than is planned at present, there will be increased purchasing power in the hands of the people and unless the amounts available of at least the necessities can be increased, there will be a wholly unwelcome rise in prices. As we noted earlier, prices have already been rising fast during 1963 and 1964. Moreover if the increased incomes raise the demand for and the prices of exportables (like tea, coffee, oil seeds, spices, tobacco, etc.) and this reduces their exports, that too would be an unwelcome outcome. If a programme of providing much more employment within a short period is to succeed, measures such as the following will have to accompany it.

A large buffer stock of food-grains and other essential commodities should be built up in advance, utilizing all foreign gifts of such commodities as can be obtained. (The USA has been, and it seems will continue for some time to be generous to India with gifts of its surplus food under Public Law 480.) Wasteful consumption by those who buy more of essential items than they really need should be eliminated; this is likely to require rationing and price control. These measures do not, of course, increase total supplies of necessities, but by limiting unnecessary demand they do alleviate the shortages. The spare capacity in industrial plants should be used by running more shifts. Improved storing and transport of crops to reduce wastage, better weeding, hoeing and guarding of crops, gathering of manure, composting of refuse, and any other such measures as can improve productivity per acre within a single season would need to be adopted widely, with labour applied generously but in a systematic and sustained way. With the remaining part of the hitherto unemployed, work should be started at the same time on such projects as require little capital but would increase total output in the long-term. Some of the endless list of possible jobs have already been mentioned such as the construction of wells, tanks, canals, roads, and small dams.

Employing India's unemployed on such work has been suggested for many years now. The First Plan itself, about fourteen years ago, suggested such measures in order both to reduce unemployment and to raise yields per acre in agriculture. Yet little has been achieved on this front. In a sense, the greatest shortage in countries like India is of suitable men or, rather, suitable organization. Organizational difficulties which hinder systematic unemployment relief also hinder any bold attempt to find productive employment opportunities on a mass scale.

There is also a great deal of seasonal unemployment in rural India. It has been estimated that 24 per cent of agricultural labourers get work for less than ten days in a month. As more and more jobs become available in either industry or rural public works (of the kind advocated above), at wage rates higher than the partly employed get in agriculture, there will be increasing movement of such people away from agriculture. But the alternative employment will have to possess some degree of permanency to attract large numbers of these people away from their traditional homes and occupations.

7. Conclusion

Our conclusion can be brief. The performance of the Indian economy so far gives ground more for concern than for satisfaction. There is hope, but only if the whole texture of operations can be changed. Economic development in India is clearly not a matter of just increasing national output per head. That is how it is measured, and that will also be its most obvious outcome. But the means to that objective are truly multifarious. The country needs a cultural revolution, an agrarian revolution, and an industrial revolution. They must all come quickly if the pace of economic development is to be faster than it has been so far.

Perhaps rapid economic development in a narrow sense may yet come if only an industrial revolution and an agrarian revolution take place. But if the aim is, in the words of the Third Plan, 'to provide the masses of the Indian people with the opportunity to lead a good life', then a cultural revolution is necessary. And, indeed, it is necessary even for economic development in the narrow sense, because it is clear that the agrarian revolution in India cannot come about until the mental outlook of a great number of farmers has sufficiently changed for them to experiment readily and persistently with new methods and new exertions.

Though there is a small go-ahead élite, largely in the cities, the vast majority of the Indian people both in towns and villages act and apparently think about everything the way they might have done centuries ago. Education—in schools, in colleges, in adult classes and through other means—has failed in India. Among the most important things needed is a great emphasis on learning at all levels.

Another great problem in India today is that of efficient administration. From the very top to the lowest level, there is need for greater enthusiasm and speed. Both the individuals and the system are at fault; but perhaps the basic fault lies with the system which is so designed that every decision takes more time than it should. There is far too much paper work. Consequently, the time-lags between initiating an idea and the moment when things begin to be delivered are long and frustrating. Plenty of good ideas are available, but the implementation remains sluggish. Some of the trouble about administration is no doubt due to the federal character of the constitution: different state governments pull in different directions on important economic matters, and even if enough enthusiasm about some scheme has been generated at the centre, it does not always get properly communicated to the largely autonomous corresponding ministries in the states. If economic transformation is to move at a rapid rate in India, then along with the changes mentioned above a fundamental reform of the system of administration is also required.

CHAPTER V

The Economic Development of Ghana

by WALTER BIRMINGHAM

Tropical Africa is a part of the world which can be classed generally as of low income and sparse population, although some countries are much better off than others and the population varies in density from one or two people per square mile in the Sahara desert to over 300 people per square mile in Eastern Nigeria. Ghana is the wealthiest of the tropical African countries but she has a low income per head in comparison with the rich countries of the world and her density of population is still sparse though rising rapidly.

Census-taking in tropical Africa is notoriously difficult. Nigeria's serious political crisis of 1963 was due to the fact that the Federal constitution provides for parliamentary representation based on the population. In consequence the results of the 1962 Census fell under suspicion and were never officially divulged. The census had to be taken again at great extra cost and with elaborate precautions against miscounting, only to produce figures which were still not acceptable to all the policital parties with their strong regional attachments. The second count was officially accepted by the Nigerian Federal Government but since the figures imply an annual rate of increase in the population of $5\frac{1}{2}$ per cent per annum, some demographers are sceptical of its accuracy. Ghana is fortunate in that it has no federal system to provide an incentive for distorting the results. The Ghana Census taken in 1960 was meticulously planned and executed with expert assistance from the United Nations. It was followed by a survey designed amongst other things to check against mistakes in enumeration. There seems little doubt that the official figure of 6,726,800 is a substantially accurate aggregate of the total population in that year and the Government Statistician's estimate of the current rate of population increase as 2·6 per cent per annum is probably close to the truth. With an area of 92,100 square miles, Ghana in 1960 had a population density of 73 per square mile.

Ghana enjoys and suffers from an equatorial climate; her coast to the south is $4\frac{1}{2}°$ north of the equator and her sub-Sahara border 420 miles inland is at latitude $11° 10'$ north. The country nowhere stretches more than 300 miles from east to west and it is virtually centred on the meridian of Greenwich with the capital, Accra, 3,000 miles due south of London. Equatorial temperatures remain monotonously close to 80°F with little variation either daily or seasonally. In Accra the temperature rarely falls below 70°F or rises above 95°F. Further north there is a slightly greater range but nowhere is it extreme. The rainfall, however, shows much greater variation despite the small area of the country, and this is reflected in the natural vegetation. In the south-east is an area of coastal savannah and in the south-west equatorial rain-forest. The forest spreads right across to the east of the country inland of the coastal savannah, and then thins out gradually to become savannah again in the northern half of the country.

Ghana has no highlands of any significance; her highest hills do not reach 3,000 feet. Her only important river is the Volta which approaches the country in the north-west and forms the border between Ghana and the Ivory Coast until it crosses the country from west to east and then flows south to the sea at Ada. Its economic importance has in the past lain in the water it provides for riverine communities and in its fisheries. The Volta has never been intensively used for transport; rather is it notable as a major barrier to communications, since it was first bridged only in the 1950's and until then four ferries had to carry all the traffic from north to south of a country which is notorious for its internal movement of both merchandise and people. Its economic value has been transformed by the Volta Project which, by damming the river some 70 miles from its mouth, has created a major source of hydro-electric power. When fully developed some 730,000 kilowatts of installed capacity will be available. The inland lake behind the dam, 3,000 square miles in area, has great potentialities for fisheries, for cheap transport, and for irrigation. The Volta Project has for long been the dramatic focus for the development plans of Ghana although it would be quite false to conclude that everything has depended on it. The dam was completed in 1964, the lake will be filled by 1965, and the hydro-electricity will be operating the aluminium smelters by 1966; but the economic development of the country has gone on apace without any contribution until now from the Project.

Development planning dates back to the distinguished governorship of Sir Gordon Guggisberg after the first world war when Ghana was still the Gold Coast Colony. His ten-year plan for the decade of the 1920's was designed primarily to provide the infrastructure for future economic development. Railways in the cocoa and forest belt, the harbour at Takoradi, new roads, hospitals and schools were all opened, and of the many surveys undertaken one was of the possibility of a hydro-electric scheme for the River Volta.

The world depression and the second world war effectively inhibited much development during the 1930's and 1940's but in 1951 the Colonial Government adopted another ten-year plan. This was little more than the sum of all the projects which government departments had in their files or thought up in response to a circular asking them for their plans. There was little conscious co-ordination and less regard for the potentialities of the economy. The expressed intention was to give priority to economic and productive services, although only 17 per cent of the planned expenditure of £74 million was allocated to such projects. Communications were to take 35 per cent of the planned expenditure, social services 33 per cent and administration 15 per cent. Thus infrastructure was again stressed and in the event Ghana developed her infrastructure far beyond her capacity to use it in those years, but this meant that she had a solid foundation on which to build the achievements of her later development plans.

The strength of the Gold Coast economy at this time is clearly illustrated by the proposed sources of finance for the ten-year plan of 1951. Increases in the export duty on cocoa were to provide £27 million, surpluses on the annual budget were to give £13 million, existing assets were to cover £8 million, grants from the British Colonial Development and Welfare Fund were relied on for £3 million and £23 million had to be found from loans—only 30 per cent of the total of £74 million.

The years immediately following the second world war were years of intense political activity in the colonies. The Gold Coast was already advanced in its constitutional development and in 1951 the first election for a fully responsible government was held. Dr Nkrumah's Convention People's Party came to power and one of the first decisions of the new African administration was to accelerate the ten-year development plan to complete it in five.

After securing independent self-government in 1957 the Ghana Government announced that this plan had been substantially completed, a two-year consolidation period was allowed and preparations were made for an ambitious Second Development Plan with (Sir) Arthur Lewis as economic adviser to the Government to father it. This was launched in 1959 with a maximum programme of capital investment of the order of £350 million which can be compared with the gross domestic product for the country of £383 million in 1958. Such an ambitious programme was probably announced because aspirations have, for political reasons, to be expansive, but a more realistic programme for immediate implementation selected certain projects and limited the proposed capital expenditure to £226 million. The details are perhaps of no great importance because the plan was abandoned within two years and preparations began for a new Seven-Year Development Plan, imbued with many socialist principles and utilizing the latest techniques of comprehensive national economic planning. Although no reasons were given for this decision, it can be noted that it followed hard on the visit of President Nkrumah and some of his senior advisers to the Soviet Union in 1961.

This decision marked a radical change in the approach to economic planning in Ghana. It is worthwhile therefore to examine at this stage the weaknesses of the old 'colonial' planning and to attempt some assessment of its achievements.

Planning of the colonial pattern which prevailed until 1960, when Ghana abandoned its colonial constitution and became a republic, was essentially the method of the shopping-list. Government departments were asked what items they wanted on the list with estimates of cost, and the 'plan' consisted of the aggregate of these items. If the total cost was thought by the co-ordinating department to be too large then some items would be struck off. Once the shopping list was approved, departments would go ahead with any projects they could effectively implement or they would expand their departmental empires and charge the development funds allocated to them. Fulfilment of these plans was rarely assessed by reference to precisely defined physical objectives. When the expenditure on the 1951 Development Plan for Ghana had reached a sum approximating to the planned total, as it had by 1957, then the plan was regarded as substantially completed in spite of the fact that it had proposed the establishment of many industries such as textiles and cement and institutions such as a medical school, none of which had come into being. Yet the introduction to the *Second Development Plan, 1959–64* summed up the first development plan of 1951 in this way: 'The Plan achieved its object in laying the framework on which economic development can now be built.'

Plans of this type were never made by reference to the structure of the economy. The effect on the national product was not estimated, the allocation of existing or potential resources was not planned in detail and a comprehensive view of the country's financial resources and its balance of payments was lacking. There were grave deficiencies in this type of planning but to be realistic one must recognize that, were such a macro-economic framework an essential pre-requisite to any plan, then no plan could have been produced because the statistical basis was quite inadequate.

An examination in detail of Ghana's Second Development Plan of 1959 reveals quite clearly that no comprehensive view of the economy had been taken. There is no estimate of the population or the expected increase during the period, nor of the manpower resources likely to be available, no consideration of how to achieve and maintain full employment, no assessment of nutritional levels and the means to their improvement, no computation of the gross national product and how the development plan might affect it, no attempt to estimate the productivity of capital in the different uses proposed in the Plan.

'An assessment of our development requirement during the next five years has been made and, in addition to £100 millions to develop the country's hydro-electric potential, £243 millions is required for general development', according to the *Second Development Plan 1959–64* (page 1), but 'it is appreciated that the task set is a formidable one . . .' and so 'the Government has decided therefore to select from the Plan a number of projects upon which it will embark immediately but to which it will add as opportunity occurs of increasing the financial resources available either internally or by borrowing'. The 'summary of projects for immediate implementation' involved a financial expenditure of £126 million (page 2).

Here we see a significant appreciation of the need to assess priorities but there is no indication of what criteria were used. It is said that 'the plan now presented provides for increased emphasis on the development of Agriculture and Industry' (page 3) and this was true by comparison with the earlier plan, if financial allocations are a guide. In the first plan only £7,616,000 was allowed for agriculture whereas the Second Plan allocated £24,668,000 to it. And industry and trade were allowed £25,331,000 in the Second Plan compared with only £5,548,000 in the first.

The programme for agriculture under the Second Development Plan had 'six main targets' as 'top priorities'. These were:

(1) To raise the yields of the cocoa industry.
(2) To establish large acreages in rubber and bananas in the wet south-west.
(3) To establish the foundations of the cattle industry.
(4) To raise the yield of cereals in the Northern Region.
(5) To bring the Volta flood plain under irrigation.
(6) To study and promote the use of fertilizers.

By 1964, the first item was the only one in which any substantial progress had been made. As with so many underdeveloped countries, the agricultural revolution is recognized as an urgent necessity yet change is extraordinarily difficult to bring about within the conservative social structure of Ghana's agrarian sector. The negligible progress towards the agricultural objectives in the earlier years of

TABLE 5.1

Expenditure on the Gross Domestic Product, 1955–1962

(a) AT 1960 PRICES

	1955	1956	1957	1958	1959	1960	1961	1962
							£ million	
Private consumption	278	282	298	288	317	339	364	335
Government consumption	37	38	40	40	42	48	53	60
Fixed capital formation	60	60	58	58	81	96	99	92
Changes in stocks	—	+5	−6	−1	+10	+11	−14	−6
Exports	86	95	107	94	109	123	137	151
Imports	−106	−104	−109	−97	−126	−148	−163	−140
Expenditure on gross domestic product	355	376	388	382	433	469	476	492

(b) AT CURRENT PRICES

	1955	1956	1957	1958	1959	1960	1961	1962
							£ million	
Private consumption	252	262	291	279	317	339	393	405
Government consumption	26	30	33	35	39	48	55	63
Fixed capital formation	52	56	56	55	75	96	104	96
Changes in stocks	—	+5	−6	−1	+10	+11	−14	−6
Exports	101	91	96	110	120	123	122	121
Imports	−97	−99	−107	−95	−126	−148	−163	−144
Expenditure on gross domestic product	334	345	363	383	435	469	497	535

Sources: Miss D. Walters, *Report on the National Accounts of Ghana 1955–61* (typescript 1962, available in the Central Bureau of Statistics, Accra).

Birmingham, Neustadt and Omaboe (ed.), *A Study of Contemporary Ghana: Vol. One, The Economy of Ghana* (London, 1965).

Central Bureau of Statistics, *Economic Survey 1962* (Accra, 1963).

the Second Plan perhaps explains to some extent why the Plan was abandoned and a new one modelled on the Soviet pattern adopted.

The industrial programme of the Second Plan demonstrates a similar divorce between aspirations and an assessment of what the resources of the country could encompass. The chapter on industry opens with the sentence: 'Specially high priority will be given within the next few years to promoting the establishment of not less than 600 factories of varying size producing a range of over 100

TABLE 5.2

Origin of the Gross Domestic Product, 1955–1961
At 1960 Prices

						£ million	
	1955	1956	1957	1958	1959	1960	1961
Cocoa	44	53	50	42	63	75	71
Other agriculture	119	125	127	132	140	142	148
Forestry	16	18	21	22	26	26	25
Mining	16	17	22	21	21	21	20
Manufacturing	3	4	6	7	8	9	11
Other recorded private industries	58	62	64	69	73	75	79
Rent, personal and household services	32	35	37	39	41	43	46
Government enterprises and public corporations	5	6	6	6	8	9	10
General government	18	19	20	20	22	24	26
Residual item	44	37	35	24	31	45	40
Gross domestic product	355	376	388	382	433	469	476

Source: Birmingham and others, *op. cit.*

different products' (page 16). Between 1959 when the plan commenced and 1964 when it was due to be completed, fewer than 150 new industrial establishments were actually opened. Thus fulfilment of the programme was short even of 25 per cent.

By 1961, when it was decided to commence work on the preparation of a fully comprehensive development plan, the statistical prerequisites were rapidly being assembled. The census of population taken in 1960 was only one of the many sources of statistics which were being developed under the vigorous young Ghanaian Government Statistician. From these it is possible to give a fairly comprehensive picture of the Ghanaian economy.

The gross domestic product of Ghana, computed at 1960 prices,

M

was £355 million in 1955. By 1960 it had risen to £469 million, an increase of 32 per cent in the five year period and a compound rate of growth of 5·7 per cent per annum. This was an impressive achievement and compares not unfavourably with the growth rates of the British and European economies during the same period. (These figures are taken from the national expenditure account which is set out in detail in Table 5.1.)

TABLE 5.3

The Labour Force, 1960

INDUSTRIAL CLASSIFICATION

Industry	Employment		
	Male	*Female*	*Total*
	Number in thousands		per cent of employed
Agriculture, forestry, hunting and fishing	1,003	576	1,579	62
Mining and quarrying	46	3	48	2
Manufacturing	136	99	235	9
Construction	87	3	89	3
Electricity, gas, water and sanitation	14	—	14	1
Commerce	96	276	372	15
Transport, storage and communication	68	1	68	3
Services	124	31	155	6
	1,573	988	2,561	100
				per cent of adults
Total employed	1,573	988	2,561	68·6
Unemployed	109	55	164	4·4
Home-makers	11	677	688	18·4
Others	196	123	319	8·6
Total adults (aged 15 and over)	1,885	1,846	3,730	100

Source: *Advance Report*, 1960 Census.

Ghana is the world's largest producer of cocoa and hers is often called a cocoa economy but in fact this crop is merely the most important item in an agricultural output which, with forestry, is responsible for over half of the national product. As with all under-developed countries agriculture is Ghana's major economic activity. In 1960 cocoa contributed 16 per cent of the national product, other agriculture 30 per cent and forestry 6 per cent. Despite her rapid economic development during the preceding years manufacturing contributed less than 2 per cent in 1960; the significance of this is only appreciated when it is known that manufacturing output rose from 0·8 per cent of the national product in 1955 to 1·9 per cent in 1960. (Table 5.2 shows the origin of the gross domestic product.)

Ghana has a youthful population with 45 per cent of her people under the age of fifteen. In consequence the labour force of the country is comparatively small with all that this implies for growth and planning. The cost of education is unduly high; each productive worker has to carry relatively more passengers, and capital formation is made more difficult. The full employment of school leavers presents annually a problem which strains the capacity of the labour market to grow sufficiently quickly to absorb the whole supply.

Some offset to the burden of youth on the economy is given by the high proportion of women who are economically active in Ghana. Of the adult female population, 62 per cent are in the labour force— a much higher proportion than in many countries. Most of the women work on the land or are traders, with three in every four either employers or self-employed but a rapidly growing number are finding employment in manufacturing and services, since there are tradition- ally no barriers to the education of women, to their mixing in society or to the kinds of work they may do. Although only 40 per cent of the total population is in the labour force, 73 per cent of the adult population is in it thanks to the large part taken by women.

The industrial classification of the labour force, showing 62 per cent of employment in agriculture, with commerce absorbing 15 per cent and manufacturing taking up only 9 per cent, stresses one im- portant characteristic of any underdeveloped economy—the great dependence on agriculture. By contrast, fully developed economies, even though agriculture remains an important industry, rarely retain more than 15 per cent of the labour force in this sector; industry and commerce predominate, activities of high productivity which support high standards of living. But another characteristic which reflects the same basic fact is the unskilled quality of most labour in underdeveloped countries. This is most clearly displayed in the occupational classification of the labour force.

To call the majority of workers in Ghana 'unskilled' is to use that term in the special sense associated with modern industrial tech- niques. The traditional occupations, such as tanning, fishing and petty trading, require a high degree of skill of a sort, but proficiency in these occupations is not related either to literacy or to mechanical operations. It provides no basis for the activities of a modern high- productivity economy, which require literate mechanical skills applied in a framework of industrial discipline which would be intolerable in traditional occupations. In this sense the Ghanaian labour force is still overwhelmingly unskilled.

Another characteristic of Ghanaian labour which distinguishes it, with some underdeveloped countries, from the developed ones, is the extent of migration which prevails. In Britain the movement of workers from North to South has attracted a great deal of attention but the vast mass of British labour is highly immobile both geo-

TABLE 5.4

The Labour Force, 1960

OCCUPATIONAL CLASSIFICATION

Occupation	Employment		
	Male	Female	Total
	Number in thousands		Per cent
Professional and technical	48	12	60	2·3
Administrative, executive and managerial	13	0·4	13	0·5
Clerical	40	3·0	43	1·7
Sales workers	68	279	346	13·5
Farmers, fishermen, hunters and loggers	988	574	1,562	61·0
Miners and quarrymen	32	1·9	34	1·3
Transport and communication	51	1·2	52	2·0
Craftsmen, production process workers and labourers not elsewhere specified	294	101	396	15·6
Service, sport and recreation	39	16	55	2·1
All occupations	1,573	988	2,561	100

Source: *Advance Report*, 1960 Census.

graphically and occupationally in comparison with a country such as Ghana. The 1960 Census enquired into migration in the employed labour force and found that only 43 per cent of men and 53 per cent of women were non-migrants.

In the past it was thought that migrant labour was predominantly unskilled labour moving from the arid or over-populated areas of the former French West Africa or Northern Ghana to the mines and farms of Ashanti and Southern Ghana. Large numbers of men certainly moved into these regions and Ghana was regarded in the surrounding territories as El Dorado, because of the wages which could be earned in its fabulous gold mines by men whose only alternative was a meagre subsistence from the family farm, harried by recurrent demands from the authorities to pay 'l'impôt' in hard cash. The mines all reported high labour turnover suggesting that the migration is possibly seasonal to find work during the northern dry season when there is nothing to do on the farms, or alternatively motivated by the need to earn cash to pay taxes for the family and buy them trade goods which even a 'subsistence' economy does not do without.

Migrant labour was meeting a demand for labour in mines and on farms which the local population would not or could not supply. It allowed for the development of new industries such as gold-mining and cocoa growing yet because this labour was still rooted in the

TABLE 5.5

Migration of Labour
Migrants in the Employed Labour Force, 1960

| | Male | | Female | |
	Thousands	Per cent	Thousands	Per cent
International	276	17	67	7
Long-distance internal	292	19	112	11
Short-distance internal	326	21	288	29
Non-migrants	679	43	521	53
Total employed	1,573	100	988	100

Source: *Advance Report*, 1960 Census.

distant traditional homelands there was a limit set to the degree of skill which could be acquired. Different members of the family would do their stint in the mines to earn cash but did not settle. This pattern kept labour turnover high and the degree of acquired skill low.

Such a view of the phenomenon seems only to have had limited validity. The census shows migration to be of much greater significance and more widespread occurrence. The analysis of industries employing migrants shows proportionately fewer migrants engaged in agriculture than non-migrants and also indicates that not only mining but the other modern sectors such as manufacturing and construction draw heavily on migrants. These workers are presumably those most willing to adapt themselves to changed conditions and therefore most likely to acquire new skills and techniques. If the migrant workers settle down in their new locations and occupations they hold great potentialities for the future economic growth of the economy. The rapid urbanization now occurring in Ghana suggests that the migrants are willing to settle permanently in new places and jobs, indeed want to abandon the traditional life for the attractions of town and city. This adds to the growth potential but imposes on planners the difficult task of absorbing the migrant labour rather more rapidly perhaps than the achieved growth rate has hitherto allowed.

That this is likely to be a problem in Ghana as it is in many countries in the early stages of their economic awakening is indicated by the extent of unemployment discovered by the 1960 Census. The number of adults on the Census day who had not worked at any time during the previous month, who had no fixed job and who were looking actively for work was 164,000 of whom 110,000 were men and 54,000 were women. These were $6\frac{1}{2}$ per cent of the male labour force and 5 per cent of the female labour force, but if one looks to the labour force under the age of thirty who were unemployed, the situation seems much more serious. As many as 12 per cent of men and 9 per cent of women under thirty were unemployed. And if those seeking work are regarded as part of the wage-labour force into which they should be absorbed, then 19 per cent of the men and 60 per cent of the women are unemployed.

Such figures can, however, be misleading. If they are taken to indicate that at present wage-rates there are plenty of men and women willing to enter the labour market and that growth of the economy is not inhibited by a shortage of potential workers they can be accepted. But the demand is for workers with some kind of skill applicable to modern processes. Before the potential labour force can be used effectively in high productivity occupations a large investment of time and capital is required in suitable education and training. This has been planned for the future and the present situation simply means that the past planning has been inadequate to satisfy the aspirations of all those who know something of what a modern industrial economy has to offer and would like to enjoy it. The men and women who had not worked during the month preceding the Census were not likely all to be 'unemployed' in the sense that industrialized countries have unemployed workers. They would be maintained by other members of their extended families and there might be plenty for them to do in the nature of subsistence employment if they were willing to do it. But they would prefer to be regarded as actively looking for work even though there was little or no hope of finding a job that would satisfy their aspirations.

This raises a serious question of economic policy for development. Should wages be kept as low as possible in order to encourage labour-intensive production and absorb the maximum number of people into wage employment? Or should a minimum wage be enforced to provide at least adequate nutrition, itself a prerequisite for high productivity, and a reasonable standard of living? If the latter policy is adopted wage employment can grow only as fast as jobs can be created which have a productivity high enough to meet these minimum standards. Other workers have to remain self-employed, many of them in the subsistence sector at low income levels, until economic growth in high-productivity sectors can absorb them.

In countries such as India, where there is a serious land shortage in the subsistence sector, maximum wage-employment seems to be the right policy. But in Ghana, sparsely populated, with no undue pressures on the land available to the subsistence sector, there is much to be said for leaving the population undisturbed in the traditional economy until the modernizing sectors can absorb them. Such a policy is bound to create differentials in real standards of living which will attract more people who want paid jobs than there are jobs available. Thus the apparent level of voluntary unemployment, measured by the numbers seeking paid work, will be high although the numbers with nothing to do may be comparatively small.

In Ghana, legislation providing for a national minimum wage of 6s. 6d. per day was passed in 1960 for everyone except farm workers and a few other minor categories. This looked like a policy of high wages since it meant a rise of at least one shilling a day on the prevailing rate for unskilled workers and certainly its immediate impact was to increase the number of registered unemployed and to determine the marginal gold mines to close down (although in fact they did not because the government bought them up and continued to operate them).

Unfortunately such a high-wage policy can only be effective if inflationary pressures can be kept in check. If high wages genuinely reflect high productivity and inhibit wage-employment in low-productivity jobs, then inflation should not run with high wages. But a substantial part of all wage employment is in the public sector and here employment does not depend on productivity. Moreover market prices are often fixed by rings—in Ghana the market mammies—who fully understand how to secure for their wares whatever cash is available in the consumers' pockets. When wages rise, prices will neatly rise by sufficient to transfer the extra income to the mammies with no increase in supplies. The attack on poverty has to be made on the supply side and it is only when an increase in the supply of food is organized that prices can be held stable while wages rise.

The balance of wage increases and money prices leaving the real standard of living unchanged is illustrated by an examination of the real wages of unskilled labourers in Accra. A series of cost-of-living indices has been computed which can be related to give a price index right back to 1939 and the daily wage rates are also known for this whole period. From these a real-wage index has been constructed.

Wage increases have meant an immediate increase in standards of living each time they have occurred, but the advantage has been short-

TABLE 5.6

Index of Real-Wages of the Unskilled Labourer in Accra, 1939–1962

Date	Daily Wage Rate	Index of Money Wage	Cost of living Index	Index of Real Wage
May 1939	1s. 6d.	100	100	100
December 1941	1s. 10d.	122	151	81
November 1945	1s. 10d.	122	186	66
November 1946	2s. 1d.	139	198	70
November 1947	2s. 9d.	183	212	86
December 1948	2s. 9d.	183	227	81
September 1949	3s. 2d.	211	243	87
December 1951	3s. 3d.	217	333	65
December 1952	4s. 6d.	300	326	92
December 1955	4s. 6d.	300	344	87
April 1956	5s. 2d.	344	351	98
December 1957	5s. 2d.	344	351	98
December 1958	5s. 6d.	367	354	104
December 1959	5s. 6d.	367	364	101
July 1960	6s. 6d.	433	364	119
December 1962	6s. 6d.	433	426	102

Note: Of the dates for which information is available, those have been selected which show most clearly the changes in the different series.

lived except when the increase in wages has been to enable the standard of living to recover from a serious deterioration due to such circumstances as the war-time shortages of the 1940's and the cocoa boom of the 1950's. The unskilled labourer's standard of living was virtually the same in 1962 as it had been in 1939. Perhaps the correct conclusion to draw is that when workers are on subsistence wages inflation cannot depress their wages for long. But another apparent conclusion is that when economic growth occurs, as it undoubtedly has during this period, the unskilled labourer cannot hope to share in the gain—it all goes to the other factors of production and to the workers whose skills are at a premium. The third conclusion is one already drawn, that improved standards for the unskilled worker have to be planned for in the supply of those consumer goods which are the basic items in his standard of living.

Ghana now has a wealth of statistics about the population and the labour force and these are invaluable for planning. But to know something of the capital stock and its productivity is equally important. The statistics relating to capital are sparse and estimates have to be made which are inevitably open to serious criticism. Nevertheless some attempt has been made to arrive at a figure for the capital stock of the country and of the capital-output ratios.

One serious difficulty in assessing the capital stock of the economy is created by the importance of cocoa, a tree crop in the agricultural sector. Obviously there has been intense capital formation on the cocoa farms to enable Ghana to produce something like 40 per cent of the world's cocoa. But how to arrive at its worth is an exercise bristling with difficulties. A discussion of these would be inappropriate here but the results are included in the figures used.

TABLE 5.7
Capital Stock and Capital-Output Ratios, 1955–1961

AT 1960 PRICES

Year	Capital Stock	Gross Domestic Product	Average Capital-Output Ratio
	£ million	£ million	
1955	779	355	2·2
1956	844	376	2·2
1957	885	388	2·3
1958	940	382	2·5
1959	1,015	433	2·3
1960	1,164	469	2·5
1961	1,296	476	2·7

Source: Birmingham and others, *op. cit.*

The capital stock of Ghana was worth £1,164 million in 1960, of which £567 million was the value of works and buildings ('construction') and £361 million the capital in the cocoa industry.

By comparing the capital stock with the gross domestic product a capital-output ratio is obtained which indicates the productivity of capital in the whole economy. Since this is an average it does not, of course, show what any additional capital in some specific use would add to the national product, nor can any causative relationship be assumed. But it does give a rough indication of the present performances of the economy, and in the absence of more detailed micro-economic knowledge of capital-output relationships it can be assumed that such average ratios would not change dramatically with the growth of the economy and an increase in its capital endowment. In a growing economy it is likely that the marginal capital-output ratio is less favourable than the average capital-output ratio. As capital in the economy increases it should be expected that the most productive uses will be exploited first and so the ratio should become less and less favourable unless there are significant changes in the state of knowledge and innovation. The macro-economic average capital-output ratio for the Ghana economy is estimated to have changed from 2·2 in 1955 to 2·7 in 1961 and this conforms to expectations.

Statistics of capital formation are much more reliable than the estimates of capital stock. They show that the proportion of the gross domestic product devoted to fixed capital formation rose from 15 per cent in 1955 to 21 per cent in 1961. In that year out of a gross domestic product of £497 million, fixed capital formation took £104 million of which about one-half was financed by the deficit in the balance of payments current account. This is a remarkably high rate and indicates that great pressure is being put upon the economy by the government to secure a rapid rate of economic growth. Inevitably a price has to be paid in the rapid depletion of the country's overseas balances, in heavy taxes to restrain consumption and in price-increases for many commodities.

The external trade of Ghana on the export side can be easily summarized. In 1951, exports of cocoa, minerals and timber accounted for 96 per cent of the whole. In 1961 these items still accounted for 95 per cent. Cocoa during the decade has fallen from 68 per cent to 61 per cent, timber has risen from 5 to 13 per cent and the three important minerals, gold, diamonds and manganese, have fallen from 23 per cent to 21 per cent. These figures mask the fact that the physical volume of cocoa exported almost doubled during the period but the fall in the price of cocoa resulted in earnings from cocoa falling off relatively to the other exports.

Every development plan since the days of Guggisberg has stressed the need for diversification of exports. With the full operation of the Volta Project and its associated aluminium smelters there is some hope that before long another major product will be added to the list. The Seven-Year Development Plan also allows for growing exports of manufactures but it is likely that cocoa, minerals and timber will remain the basis of Ghana's external earning capacity for a long time to come.

Imports of great variety, mainly manufactures, enter Ghana and their volume and value rise year by year. In 1960, 50 per cent of all imports were consumer goods and capital equipment accounted for 22 per cent, again emphasizing the rapid rate of capital formation in the economy. Since the balance of payments is critical to a country's capacity to achieve economic growth it is worth looking back over Ghana's external accounts for several years. The value of imports and exports can be reduced to the balance of visible trade and from this must be subtracted the invisible items and transfer payments which Ghana, in common with most underdeveloped countries, has

TABLE 5.8

The Balance of Payments Current Account, 1950–1962

£ million

Year	Balance of Visible Trade	Invisible Items and Transfers	Balance on Current Account
1950	+31	−11	+20
1951	+35	−15	+19
1952	+25	−14	+11
1953	+21	−16	+5
1954	+54	−13	+41
1955	+17	−15	+2
1956	+3	−16	−13
1957	+4	−19	−14
1958	+29	−18	+11
1959	+6	−17	−11
1960	−3	−31	−34
1961	−19	−34	−53
1962	+3	−32	−28

Sources: *Economic Surveys* and *1962 Statistical Year Book*, Central Bureau of Statistics, Accra.

to make for shipping and banking services, the service of overseas capital and so on.

From 1950 to 1955 cocoa prices were high, government expenditure was modest, capital formation was still small, and consumption was kept in check by substantial export duties on cocoa which at one time were taking for reserves well over half of the cocoa earnings. The large favourable balances of those years encouraged a somewhat extravagant attitude towards the country's overseas balances— imports were allowed to rise with little regard to the economic advantage of conserving reserves for a distant future. After 1955 the balance of visible trade was in most years much smaller and even severely adverse in 1961. Thus the balance on current account, after meeting invisible items, was consistently adverse from 1956 onwards except in 1958.

By 1961, the government was convinced that drastic action had to be taken. Taxes were increased and import controls imposed with the result that a favourable balance of visible trade was restored in 1962.

The effect of the growing deficits on Ghana's overseas reserves was to reduce the total held in 1955 of £208 million to only £72 million in 1962 and this included the reserve held to back the currency circulation, so that the financing of development from then on had to rely either on internal earnings or grants and loans from abroad. Nothing more could be taken from accumulated reserves.

Ghana shares the experience of other underdeveloped countries so far as her terms of trade are concerned. She imports mainly manufactured items, the prices of which have rarely fallen, and usually risen during the past decade whereas her exports, mainly of primary products, have a long-term tendency to decline. The early years after the second world war were favourable to Ghana's cocoa, particularly since the rapidly growing markets for chocolate enabled the government monopoly held by the Cocoa Marketing Board to shift the bargains made with chocolate manufacturers powerfully in favour of the sellers. Pre-war prices, negotiated by a small group of manufacturers with a large number of peasant growers, left all the bargaining strength with the buyers, whereas in the post-war years they were met by the counteracting strength of a single seller controlling over one-third of the world supply. Thus the London price of cocoa, which in 1938 averaged £25 per ton, was £208 in 1950 and £467 in 1954, although by 1962, with the volume of production double what it was in 1954, the price was down to £170 per ton. The effect of these circumstances can be seen in the improvement of the export price-index up to 1954 when the price of cocoa reached its all-time peak. This dominated the terms of trade which moved substantially in favour of Ghana up to that year. After that, with the decline in cocoa prices the terms of trade deteriorated to such an extent that by 1962 she would have had to export 98 per cent more by volume in order to earn as much as she did in 1954. In fact in 1962 she exported 89 per cent more by volume to earn 5 per cent less than she did in 1954.

However disadvantageous it is for Ghana that the demand for her major product is virtually of unitary elasticity, it has to be recognized that this is a stabilizing influence on the economy in that reductions in the volume of the cocoa crop due to adverse weather and other conditions are compensated by higher prices. Moreover it is perhaps worth noting that when output is large and prices fall the factorial terms of trade are not deteriorating since the increased crops are secured by high productivity from a constant factor endowment.

With the wealth of economic information accruing from the 1960 census and the statistical breakthrough at that period, and with many trained economists available as a result of the government's intensive drive from its first assumption of power to produce graduates from its own university, Ghana was ready in 1961 to undertake full-scale planning of its economic development, using the latest techniques. This was not, however, to be a managerial revolution. Objectives were to be defined by the political leaders and the experts were to advise how they were to be achieved.

In July 1962, the Congress of the Convention People's Party, the ruling party since 1950 when responsible government under an

TABLE 5.9
The Terms of Trade, 1948–1962
1954 = 100

| Year | Price Indices | | Terms |
	Imports	Exports	of Trade*
1948	92	53	175
1950	93	59	158
1952	117	74	158
1954	100	100	100
1956	101	68	149
1958	101	90	112
1960	107	70	153
1962	103	52	198

* Import price-index as a percentage of export price-index.
Source: *1962 Statistical Year Book.*

African leader was secured, issued its 'Programme of Work and Happiness' and this became the political directive for the preparation of the Seven-Year Development Plan which was eventually inaugurated in April 1964. The declared purpose of the Plan is to build up the economic strength of Ghana in order to forward four principal objectives: the independence and unity of Africa, the preservation of world peace, socialism in Ghana, and the welfare of her people through the elimination of poverty and ignorance and the control of disease.

These ends might themselves inhibit or encourage Ghana's economic growth but planning has to recognize that growth is not an end in itself. Economic objectives are only acceptable in so far as they enable scarce resources to make their maximum contribution to the objectives decided by the political policy-makers. That the President is an advocate of pan-Africanism, and a leader of the neutralist bloc in world affairs, who in 1956 wrote, 'Today I am a non-denominational Christian and a Marxist socialist and I have not found any contradiction between the two', is a fact of the utmost significance to any plan for the economic development of Ghana.

The Plan aims to increase the gross national product by $5\frac{1}{2}$ per cent per annum over the seven years 1964 to 1970. Since the population is estimated to be increasing at the rate of $2 \cdot 6$ per cent per annum, the increase per head in the national income is planned to be slightly less than 3 per cent per annum. This is hardly likely to satisfy the aspirations of many of the people of Ghana since they are now aware of their country's leading role in Africa and everyone looks to rapidly rising standards of living as the mark of successful leadership. But to aim at a higher rate would be unrealistic and the planners recognize this. The performance of the economy during the six years 1955–60 gave a growth rate of $5 \cdot 7$ per cent per annum. To plan for much less would be over-cautious but to plan for much more would be inviting serious internal tensions which might jeopardize the attainment of any development at all. If the Plan is fulfilled the gross domestic product will increase from £545 million in 1962 to £796 million, at 1962 prices, in 1970.

Investment required by the Plan over the seven-year period amounts to £1,016 million including depreciation. The allocation to the various sectors is as follows:

	Per cent
Agriculture	17
Industry	20
Mining	4
Transport	6
Housing	8
Infrastructure	11
Social services	13
Other	7
Depreciation	14
	100

To arrive at an estimate of how much new capital will be required to achieve the proposed growth, a capital-output ratio of $3 \cdot 5$ has been used. The macro-economic average ratio of the period 1955–60 was about $2 \cdot 5$ and the marginal ratio was slightly better than $3 \cdot 5$, so that the planners can here also be given credit for not being unduly optimistic. At a ratio of $3 \cdot 5$ the increment in the gross domestic product would be 28½ per cent of the increment in capital. To meet a growth rate of 5½ per cent would require 19 per cent of the gross domestic product to be devoted to capital formation and this is incorporated in the Plan. It can be compared with the 21 per cent of the gross domestic product devoted to fixed capital formation in 1961.

Internal sources of finance are expected to meet two-thirds of the capital requirements and the other third, to come from abroad, relies on £227 million from grants and loans to the government and £100 million as private investment.

The balance between the public and private sectors is indicated by the distribution of net investment. Of the total of £876 million, the state sector is to have £333 million (38 per cent), the private sector £274 million (31 per cent), and joint enterprises £269 million (31 per cent). Thus Ghana, with all its socialist ideology, recognizes that a mixed economy is the only practical policy while it is so heavily dependent on the goodwill of the rest of the world, in which the likely sources of the vast amounts of capital it requires are the wealthy countries with mixed economies strongly oriented to respect for private enterprise capital.

The balance of payments assumed in the Plan is inevitably adverse since heavy imports of capital equipment will be required, but careful computations have been made of what expansion can be expected in the export industries and what can be done by way of import substitute industries to damp down the propensity to import. A summary of the conclusions reached is provided by the following figures:

TABLE 5.10
Development Plan: Balance of Payments, 1970

Exports		Imports	
		£ million	
Cocoa	100	Consumer goods	80
Timber	32	Capital equipment	58
Gold	14	Producer goods	67
Diamonds	11	Services and miscellaneous	26
Aluminium	14		
Other	24		
	195		231

Perhaps the most impressive aspect of these figures is the acceptance by the planners of the continued dependence upon exports of cocoa, minerals and timber. Even after a further decade of economic development the proportion of exports provided by these items is expected to be 90 per cent.

One of the subsidiary but crucial economic objectives of the Plan is to provide full employment for a labour force which is expected to grow by 20 per cent during the seven years. In any case the efficient use of resources demands a policy of full employment but Ghana's rate of population growth is so rapid that the maintenance of full employment is one of the objectives most likely not to be achieved. In 1963 the employed labour force was 2,504,000. By 1970 it should be 2,997,000. Agriculture in 1963 employed 60 per cent of the total and this will be reduced by 1970 to 54 per cent, although the absolute numbers in this industry will be greater. High-level and middle-level occupations which in 1963 engaged 20 per cent will expand to 26 per cent of the larger total.

Throughout the Plan, objectives are stated in physical terms and this is one of the most important aspects making for realism in any programme for economic development since it makes possible effective criticism, discussion and testing of performance. The production targets are a good example of how these processes work. In the draft plan submitted to a group of international economists, the production of cereals was shown as increasing during the seven years by 58 per cent but after criticism and discussion the final projections for the gross domestic product allowed only 28 per cent. Similarly, the increase to be derived from industry, construction and power was reduced from 135 per cent to 53 per cent.

Although nutritional standards are much higher in Ghana than in many underdeveloped countries, they are still far from adequate and a high priority is given to their improvement, both for humanitarian reasons and because good nutrition is a prerequisite for higher labour productivity. Calorific intake in 1962 was estimated to be 1,800 calories per person per day and protein intake 40 grammes. One objective of the Plan is to raise these to 2,700 calories and 70 grammes of protein per person per day. The modification of the agricultural targets no doubt means that these nutritional objectives have already been deferred to some date beyond 1970 and one has to recognize that this is probably another example of realistic planning in the knowledge that this is the most conservative sector of the economy and the one most difficult to develop rapidly.

Private consumption is often regarded as the ultimate purpose of all development plans since it sums up the dividends to the ordinary citizen. The Plan allows for an increase at constant prices from £405 million in 1962 to £543 million in 1970, an expansion of

35 per cent or 4·1 per cent per annum. Since the population is increasing by 2·6 per cent per annum this allows only an increase of 1·5 per cent annually per person, a very modest improvement in the standard of living during the plan period when capital formation is also making heavy demands on resources.

A critical aspect of private consumption from the planners' point of view is the demand it makes on imports. In the Plan imports for private consumption are allowed to increase by only 26 per cent (3·5 per cent per annum) from £91 million to £115 million. But the concern for adequate nutrition appears in the allowance for food imports to increase by 50 per cent from £26 million to £39 million whereas imports of manufactures are restricted to an increase of only 16 per cent, from £65 million to £76 million.

The final word on Ghana's economic development can perhaps be on the compatibility of her political objectives and her economic aspirations.

The independence and unity of Africa are objectives for which Ghana has already made large sacrifices of scarce resources at a time she could ill afford them from her domestic requirements. Moreover her opposition to associate status for herself or any African nation with the European Economic Community, thereby renouncing the certainty of favourable tariff arrangements and a generous inflow of capital, is probably a major short-term disadvantage. But in the long run the prospect of a large, even a continental, African Common Market with a population approaching 500 million by the end of the century and its industrial revolution still in the future is something which cannot be dismissed as an insignificant alternative especially since the fear lurks perpetually in Africa that association with Europe means a dependent economy of primary producers always getting the worst of the bargain with its industrialized partners.

The preservation of world peace by the policy of neutralism or even by the holding of the balance of power between East and West is likely to discourage the flow of capital from both contenders for spheres of influence in Africa but more especially from the West which has until now been both more able and more willing to lend its support. Ghana is loth to recognize this but perhaps is willing consciously to sacrifice expediency to principle. What she does clearly recognize is that military commitments are 'not development' and that they can be a heavy drain on the current budget. Here is the clearest incompatibility between political objectives and economic aspirations. If she must support the military struggle against colonialism and racialism, then the price she has to pay is without question a

N

slowing down of her development and a failure to meet the economic objectives of the Seven-Year Plan.

Ghana's attachment to socialism is much less likely to be an impediment because she has clearly defined the scope for foreign private enterprise in her mixed economy, she has given and observed reasonable undertakings to respect the rights of foreign capitalists, and she has made generous concessions to attract foreign capital.

Ghana's concept of a welfare state, with its emphasis on social services of a high order, implies a preference for projects in education, health, housing and security which, though ultimately highly productive, are long-term investments. This inevitably limits her ability to encompass short-term projects with dividends to be enjoyed in the near future by a population with a strong positive time-preference and expectations which must frighten any statesman. Education is a creator of aspirations unlimited by any appreciation of hard economic realities and it takes far more time to realize the higher productivity of better education than it does to create the demand for it. Here is an incompatibility which can never be avoided and every statesman in a developing nation has to accept it as one of the discomforts of his destiny.

CHAPTER VI

The Economic Development of Sierra Leone

by HOWARD REES

1. *The Economy*

Sierra Leone is a small West African state about the size of the
Irish Republic (nearly 28,000 square miles in area). With a population
of 2·2 million, it is, according to available statistics,[1] the third most
densely populated country in mainland Africa. Until self-government
in the late 1950's, the country consisted of a small coastal area
administered as a Crown Colony, and a British Protectorate. Under
self-government they became a single political unit and in 1961
Sierra Leone became politically independent. In this chapter we shall
first of all examine in some detail the nature and extent of economic
change between the end of the Second World War and the attainment of independence. After that we shall consider some of the
problems associated with economic development and the extent to
which the 1962–1971 Development Plan recognizes and overcomes
them.

Little is known as yet about the size and composition of the
national income but rough estimates of the gross domestic product
have been made. The United Nations estimate for 1958 was approximately £23 per head whilst a special correspondent of *The Times* has
estimated per capita income as £35 in an unspecified year.[2]

---

[1] Population statistics for underdeveloped countries are often unreliable. In
Sierra Leone's case the average rate of growth of the population between mid-
1958 and mid-1961 was given in the United Nations Demographic Yearbook for
1962 as 2·7 per cent—one of the highest in Africa. In the 1963 Yearbook however, the growth rate between mid-1958 and mid-1962 was estimated to be 0·5
per cent—one of the lowest rates in the whole world, indicating perhaps the
lowest rate of natural increase, since there is no significant emigration from
Sierra Leone.

[2] The United Nations estimate was published in its *Yearbook of National
Accounts Statistics* and *The Times* estimate was contained in an article entitled
'Tensions persist in Sierra Leone' in the issue of May 6, 1964.

Except for the Creoles, whose forefathers founded the Colony, the population is organized along tribal lines. There are thirteen tribes, but the majority of the population belong to the two largest— the Mende and the Temne. Under tribalism, the social and linguistic groupings and differing loyalties have militated against the rise of nationalism. Political independence has failed to change very much the lives of the majority, who have apparently shown little active interest in it. The consequent absence of a feeling of national purpose and destiny, reinforced by peasant conservatism, has bedevilled the efforts of those seeking to develop rapidly the country's economy.

The basic occupation of tribesmen and some Creoles is agriculture. Many farmers, however, supplement their incomes by fishing and other non-agricultural occupations. Along the northern and north-eastern borderlands some nomadic and semi-nomadic herdsmen live, but the rest of the agricultural population—the great majority— are cultivators.

The country is in the wet tropical belt. Its rainfall, which is both very heavy and highly seasonal, is lightest in the extreme north-east where 79 inches is the average for the decade ending with 1960 and heaviest on the west coast with an annual average of very nearly 180 inches. Much of this rain is precipitated in the three months from mid-July, although the rainy season lasts from April or May for about six months altogether. During the rest of the year rainfall is rare and too light to benefit plant life.

The rainy season starts with squalls. The strong winds remove some of the dry top soil which has been uncovered and loosened in preparation for sowing; and the heavy rain showers which follow the winds can cause serious soil loss on sloping ground, the seriousness being accentuated by the shallowness of the top-soil in the first place. These weather conditions—the sudden storms when the ground is parched and stripped of vegetation in preparation for planting, the dryness of the soil in the dry season which makes it, for the most part, useless for cultivation without irrigation at that time of the year, and its saturation during the rainy season—combine to hamper progress in agriculture and to depress levels of output.

During the dry season, there is little agricultural activity, apart from preparing clearings for the coming season's crops. The pace of activity becomes more leisurely and production takes the form mainly of building, repair and maintenance of dwellings, granaries, fences and the like; collecting wild fruit (especially the fruit of the oil palm which grows in profusion over a large area and occurs in some measure almost everywhere in Sierra Leone), and other forest products, some hunting and handicrafts; and a good deal of casual wage employment in the towns and elsewhere.

Agriculture, mining and services between them generate virtually the whole of the national product. Sierra Leone has not suffered to the same extent as some underdeveloped countries from undue concentration of production on a narrow range of products. In agriculture, there is a variety of subsistence crops, surpluses of which are marketed, the principal ones being rice, cassava and palm oil. There are also a number of export crops, chief of which are palm kernels (a by-product of palm oil production), cocoa, coffee, ginger and piassava. Sierra Leone is one of the two major producers of the last-named, the other being Brazil. Only three minerals have been important in recent years. These are diamonds, iron ore and chromite. Mining and export of chromite ceased in 1963 but arrangements were then already in progress to start mining and exporting bauxite and rutile, an ore of titanium.

The economic pattern today is not fundamentally different from that which obtained before the last war. Agriculture is still the major occupation, employing probably 80 per cent or more of adults. Their dependence on agriculture for a livelihood, however, has been much reduced by the greater scope for supplementing agricultural incomes with earnings in non-agricultural employment in the dry season.

Service industries, especially trade and public services, are still the other major employer of labour—manufacturing having failed to develop. The scale and scope of trade is roughly divided along racial lines; the Europeans tend to operate on the largest scale as importers, exporters and wholesalers, and retailers of their imports. The Levantines are next in importance, being mainly small and medium size shop and storekeepers and wholesalers, on a smaller scale than the Europeans. They are also intermediaries in agricultural produce trade, though retailing of local agricultural and horticultural produce and fish is reserved for Africans. Africans are a numerical majority in trade but on the lowest levels—as small shopkeepers, stall-holders, hawkers and employees of traders of foreign origin.

The major change in trade since the war has been a decline in the importance of private exporters brought about both by the decline in the relative importance of agricultural as compared with mineral exports and by the Sierra Leone Produce Marketing Board taking over the function of exporting cocoa, oilseeds and later coffee and ginger. The pattern of external trade has changed little in respect of the broad categories of goods imported and exported. Exports are almost entirely composed of primary products or products which have undergone a little simple processing, whilst imports are mainly manufactures. Sierra Leone is a typical underdeveloped country in this respect, with its economy based on traditional agriculture and possessing a small modern sector which is highly localized in a few towns and mining areas.

Despite the failure to industrialize or to modernize the economy in other directions, real incomes have risen rapidly, as Table 6.1 indicates, and the increase has been widely distributed. Undoubtedly economic policy has had some effect, but the most rapid changes followed events which were outside the control of the public authorities. The first such event was the 1939–45 war itself which, by causing

TABLE 6.1

SOME INDICATORS OF CHANGES IN REAL INCOMES, 1950–1961

	1950	1955	1961
1. Footwear imports (thousands of pairs)	276	734	2,257
2. Index of volume of food imports, excluding rice (1950 = 100)	100	362	564
3. Index of relative wage change compared with change in cost of model diet for an unskilled labourer in Freetown (1950 = 100)	100	132*	177
4. Coins and notes in circulation at December 31st (£ million)	2·2	9·9	14·4†
5. Heavy commercial vehicles licensed	367	2,126	3,664†

* 1957 figure.
† 1960 figure.

large numbers of young men to be uprooted and subjected to a strange environment in which some were trained in skills useful to them in civilian employment, fitted them better psychologically and vocationally for urban life. As well as swelling the supply of skilled and disciplined wage labour, the effect of their war-time experience made many others who returned to agriculture less ready to accept tribal discipline. The weakening of tribal discipline continued in the ensuing period until in 1955 and 1956 it culminated in a widespread rebellion against the chiefs.

The war brought improvements in communications when the first road link between Freetown and the Protectorate was made. Previously it had only been possible to reach the Protectorate from Freetown by bush-path, railway or water. The road link had not been made because of the competition which road transport would offer to the heavily-subsidized Sierra Leone Railway.

The rapid growth of road traffic after the war resulted in a much more mobile rural population than previously, which, coupled with the new experiences of many young men during the war, provided a better climate for development. Tribal control has been weakened and there has been a considerable growth in the volume and range of imports transported to the provinces. The flow of seasonal work-seekers into Freetown and elsewhere from the countryside has grown, and seasonal wage work has, since the war, become a part of the established way of life of peasant cultivators in the less remote areas. The growth of road traffic has in turn provided a reason for road improvement and extension of road mileage. In 1946 there were about 1,800 miles of road altogether. By 1961 there were 3,800 miles, a number of ferries had been replaced by bridges, and 210 miles of road between Freetown and Bo, the provincial capital, had been bitumenized.

The Korean War marked the start of the second phase in the improvement of real incomes. Its outbreak gave rise to an international stock-piling panic which resulted in the creation of artificial shortages of raw materials and foodstuffs. Prices rose rapidly, whilst the prices of manufactures in the industrialized countries were at that time little affected. The greatly improved terms of trade for Sierra Leone gave a substantial boost to real incomes, since the economy is heavily dependent on international trade, whilst the attractive prices paid over the next few years for agricultural exports accelerated the growth of cash-cropping in suitable areas.

In the early 1950's, inflated cash incomes were devoted mainly to the purchase of imported consumers' goods. Imported foods supplemented, or were substituted for, domestic produce; and alcohol, cloth and clothing imports were greatly increased. Imports of certain building materials rose appreciably but most of the increase was absorbed in consumption. The effect of the high marginal propensity to import was to damp down the inflationary pressure on prices of domestic produce, and hence to accentuate the monetary advantages of cultivating cash crops for export in preference to surpluses of subsistence foods for the domestic market.

The third phase started in 1955 when export prices were beginning to slump. At that time illicit diamond mining and dealing, which had first been sufficiently serious to attract the attention of the authorities in 1951, had become out of control, and law and order in the diamond areas could no longer be preserved. Substantial fortunes were gained by some illicit miners who spent them rapidly and conspicuously to acquire elevated status in the eyes of their fellows. The effects of the greatly increased value of diamond production were thus quickly spread to others and there was a rapid rise in wage rates both to restore the level of real incomes in the face of the inflation of prices of local produce and some imports, and to provide a counter-attraction to would-be diamond miners.

Table 6.2 shows the changes in volume of some main imports compared with 1950. It shows that the volume of imports in these commodity groups had all increased by the end of the produce boom —especially food, drink and tobacco. At the height of the diamond boom in 1957 there were further increases in these three groups, and in textiles and building materials; and between 1957 and 1962, when diamond mining had become more stabilized and many former miners had returned to agriculture, only food and vehicle imports increased. Nevertheless the level of imports of all the commodities included in the index (even of cigarettes which by 1962 were being produced locally) remained substantially higher than in 1950.

TABLE 6.2

VOLUME INDICES OF SELECTED IMPORTS, 1955–1962 (1950 = 100)

Commodity Group	1955	1957	1962
Foodstuffs	597	778	954
Alcoholic beverages	448	599	204
Cigarettes	278	404	127
Textiles and clothing	172	233	231
Motor vehicles, bicycles and tyres	148	151	329
Building materials	337	547	450

The increase in real incomes was not primarily the result of increased production except in diamond mining, but the rapid growth of government revenue which was concomitant with it, led to a greater volume of investment in infrastructural development. This and the changes in mental attitudes, tastes and appetites for manufactures have provided more favourable conditions for later expansion of the national product.

Table 6.3 illustrates the development of the infrastructure by taking the three key years which were also used in Table 6.1. These are the years immediately preceding the full impact of the Korean War, the diamond boom and Independence. Thus the change from one period to the next provides some indication of developments which have taken place in the intervals between each of these events.

Little has yet been said about public policy with regard to development. It has not been passive, though the insistence upon retaining a *laissez-faire* political framework has limited the scope for, and effect of, positive economic planning of resource development and allocation, so that piecemeal policies have resulted. The strength of peasant conservatism, the quality and quantity of human resources, and the limited funds available for public investment, together with the insecure state of law and order, have been such that the initiation of rapid or fundamental changes by the government has not been contemplated; it has been thought necessary to await changes in the social and economic climate before radical changes could be considered.

TABLE 6.3

SOME INDICATORS OF INFRA-STRUCTURAL GROWTH, 1950–1961

	1950	1955	1960/61
Electricity generated (million kwh)	5·9	12·0	36·8
Towns with public electricity service	2	8	14*
Mileage of roads	2,075	2,963	3,770
Education (numbers of pupils):			
Primary	34,520	69,276	86,244
Secondary	3,041	5,904	7,512
Teacher training	⎱214	604	629
Technical and vocational	⎰	1,322	1,185
Public capital and development expenditure (£ thousands)	887	2,012	1,068
Average employment in building and construction†	8,567‡	8,279	11,428

* Relates to year 1959/60.

† In firms employing more than five.

‡ December figure. The average, which is probably somewhat lower, is not available.

2. The Major Changes in Agriculture

Agriculture is at the hub of economic development. It is ultimately from the agricultural population that additional labour for other sectors is drawn, and it is important that this should be done without jeopardizing domestic production of foodstuffs or, initially,agricultural exports. In other words, economic development means, among other things, increasing agricultural labour productivity. In some areas the availability and quality of land are the bottlenecks, and labour drawn into other occupations from these areas may well, though not necessarily, entail a larger overall increase in labour productivity than if labour is drawn from other areas. But increased labour productivity alone is not sufficient; the total food supply must increase more rapidly than the population grows if standards of nutrition are to be improved. The loss of agricultural labour needs to be limited by this consideration, as otherwise imports of foodstuffs will increase and locally produced foods will tend to become more expensive.

With very few exceptions, agriculture is organized on a small-scale, peasant basis. There is no wage labour and land is not a sale-able commodity except in and around Freetown. This immobility of labour within the agricultural sector, and the non-transferability of land (except in some places, temporarily as security for a loan) inhibit the development of modern, large-scale farming. It is the climatic conditions, however, which provide the major obstacle to the introduction of modern techniques. To understand this, it is necessary to understand the rationale of the traditional techniques.

The system of agriculture universally adopted in the uplands is called the bush-fallow system. Land is brought into cultivation for two or three years and then left fallow—usually for eight to ten years—until it has recovered its fertility. If the period under cultivation were extended, there would be a dramatic fall in the yield and the recuperation period might have to be lengthened. The technique adopted is to clear a patch of bush, where the state of vegetation indicates that its fertility is sufficient for cultivation, by hacking down non-economic trees and undergrowth, and burning the debris on the spot, thereby destroying seeds and any vegetation left standing. Trees are felled to within three or four feet of the ground but the stumps are not removed. Economic trees like oil palms are not felled.

About the start of the rainy season the soil is lightly hoed, the object being to loosen the soil just sufficiently for planting whilst disturbing the roots as little as possible. These roots serve to bind the shallow humus together or form pockets to contain it so that soil loss when the rains break is minimized. The retention of roots and stumps also helps to conserve the soil later, when the cultivated crops have been harvested, by providing rapid soil cover. If the trees and stumps were removed, and the soil disturbed more by deep digging, soil loss would be more severe and fertility would decline more rapidly. In addition, since the greater part of the uplands is periodically cultivated, the supply of wild food crops would disappear. So far, no fully effective way of eliminating the fallow period has been discovered, and the complete removal of wild vegetation would not only shorten the cultivable period, but would also necessitate a longer recovery period. All in all, therefore, crop yields would be much lower, and the chances of crop failure would be much increased.

Clearly under these climatic and soil conditions mechanical cultivation requiring the complete removal of tree stumps and roots would not be appropriate and there is as yet no efficient substitute for the labour-extravagant manual methods which make use of only a small proportion of the total cultivable area each year. Chemical fertilizers are sometimes helpful in extending the period of cultivation but large amounts may be needed to offset losses through leaching. In any case, they cannot replace, but only supplement, humus in the soil.

Official policy to increase land utilization and peasant incomes, and at the same time reduce the effects of soil erosion on the steeper slopes, was directed during the 1950's towards encouraging the greater use of tree crops—particularly cocoa and oil palm. To offset the reduction in rice output which would result, and to cater for increased consumption, swamp rice cultivation was actively encouraged.

There are about 1½ million acres of swamp, that is, 8 per cent of the total land area. Of these, the mangrove and riverine grassland swamps are revitalized by annual inundations which deposit silt washed down from higher ground. This is sufficient to maintain their fertility under continuous cultivation. Unfortunately much mangrove swamp, being subjected also to tidal flooding, is too saline for rice growing without the slow process of empoldering. The cultivable swamps are capable of yielding 1,600–2,000 pounds of rice per acre and sometimes more, and are thus superior to the best-favoured upland areas both in respect of yields and because no fallow and clearance of brush are required once the land is cultivated.

Before the turn of the century there seems to have been very little swamp cultivation, probably because there was generally sufficient well-drained land to support the population and because swamp farmers were regarded as being socially inferior to the upland farmers. The movement to cultivate the swamps started in the mangrove areas—especially in the north-west. The cultivators were not local people, who were not short of well-drained land, but people from further south and east who were apparently driven to migrate by land shortage.

In the 1950's the Department of Agriculture used its tractors to open up grassland swamp for cultivation. It handed over the new areas to district councils who leased them to farmers in one-acre plots. This pattern of local authority ownership and leasing is a post-war feature which started in 1946 when inland swamps were cleared and let to nearby upland farmers. The system has the advantage over private ownership that transfer of land is easier to effect.

Although the riverine grasslands were on the whole as fertile as the mangrove areas and were much easier and quicker to bring into cultivation, they were comparatively neglected. Thus only 3,400 acres out of 63,000 acres of fertile black alluvium around the lower reaches of the Waanje, Sewa and Jong Rivers in the south, were cultivated in 1950. Despite official encouragement, the proportion of grassland swamp under cultivation remains small and progress is slow. The major reason seems to be the slow growth in demand for swampland. This is probably due largely to the replacement of dry-farmed rice by perennial crops on upland farms during the export boom and the diamond rush when the export boom was subsiding. The increased incomes resulting directly and indirectly from these events have mitigated the shortage of land caused by population growth and declining fertility under annual crops, and hence also the demand for additional land.

The grassland and some of the mangrove swamps are firm enough to be cultivated mechanically. In these and in suitable inland swamps the Department of Agriculture has provided ploughing, harrowing, and seed-harrowing services on contract to individual farmers. The service has proved popular and has probably encouraged farmers to cultivate the swamps. In the latter half of the 1950's the fast-growing co-operative movement formed unions of producers' marketing societies to extend ploughing and harrowing facilities and release some of the Department's equipment for opening up new land. The demand for ploughing services declined, however, when advance payments of part of the ploughing fee were required in 1958 and the whole of it in 1959, and although demand grew again, in 1961 it was still well below the 1957 level.

Advance fees were required because of mounting bad debts. The non-repayment of loans and advances has been a common experience of the public authorities since the war, and it has inevitably limited the extent to which loans can be made to farmers and others. Yet, apart from the co-operative movement and traders who are often in a much stronger position to exact repayment, there are few channels open to private individuals to obtain loans for projects which would contribute to the overall economic development of the country.

The success of the official policy of encouraging cocoa-planting in place of rice, especially on the steeper slopes, is demonstrated by the rapid growth in the volume of cocoa exports. In 1946, about 570 tons of cocoa were exported. Exports increased to 1,600 in 1950 and then fluctuated between 1,600 and 2,000 tons until 1956 when nearly 3,000 tons were exported. By 1962 exports had reached 4,700 tons.

In addition, the rapid rise of cocoa prices after the outbreak of the Korean War made cocoa a more lucrative crop than either palm oil or upland rice, the sale of which was officially discouraged at that period. Consequently the demand for cocoa seedlings in the Mende

Uplands—the principal producing area of rice for the domestic market and a substantial producer of oil palm products—rose sharply and after a lag of about three to five years this was translated into an increase in cocoa production. At the same time, the amount of upland rice cultivated was reduced.

Another crop grown alongside cocoa in the Mende uplands has been coffee. The official policy regarding this crop has been a passive one of meeting the demand for coffee seedlings but not encouraging its cultivation. However, even without official encouragement production grew rapidly; just how rapidly is not known, because domestic coffee consumption increased with the growth of private affluence than followed the outbreak of the Korean War and the effects of diamond mining, but recorded exports which in 1946 had been about 140 tons rose to 350 tons by 1950, to 3,000 tons by 1956 and to 5,000 tons by 1960.

The factors operating in this case were similar to those which influenced farmers to cultivate cocoa, except that there was no propaganda, and in the second half of the 1950's it came to be realized that coffee is not nearly so selective a crop as cocoa; most well-drained areas are suitable for its cultivation. Consequently, in contrast to cocoa, expansion of coffee production resulted from the spread of cultivation over a wide area as well as increased cultivation in the original producing areas around the centre of the country.

The fruit of the oil palm is one of the most important of the country's vegetable products. Its flesh is rich in palm oil which, with rice, constitutes the basis of the national diet. Palm oil is also used in the manufacture of margarine, cooking fat and soap. The kernel is also rich in oil, though this is less valuable than palm oil. Palm kernel oil is not extracted in Sierra Leone, but kernels are the major vegetable export. Formerly palm oil was exported too, but in more recent years Sierra Leone has had to import oil for domestic use. Probably the growth of the population and improvements in nutrition are partly to blame but there is little doubt that production declined in the 1950's and early 1960's.

Since the formation of the Sierra Leone Produce Marketing Board in 1949, the development of the oil palm industry has become an important part of agricultural policy. The scheme to popularize oil palm cultivation and develop the industry was financed out of Sierra Leone's share of the surplus built up by the West African Produce Control Board during and after the war, which was transferred to its successor in Sierra Leone, the Produce Marketing Board. The funds were spent in a variety of ways: on research; to finance the purchase, propagation and free distribution of improved varieties of palm;

for education and propaganda relating to oil palm cultivation; to provide fruit-processing facilities and to effect infrastructural improvements in the major producing areas.

The object of cultivating oil palms when there was a surfeit of wild palms in many parts of the country was to increase output and hence peasant incomes and exports. The superiority of the cultivated varieties lies in their greater oil/kernal ratio, their lower percentage of waste, and their early maturing which enables fruit to be collected without the necessity of tree-climbing so that the amount of fruit harvested does not depend, as it does in harvesting wild fruit, on the availability of young men to climb the palms. Thus oil palm production need no longer compete for labour with dry-seasons wage employment in the towns and the rest of the agricultural labour force can be more fully employed.

Despite the prospects of appreciably higher incomes, peasant farmers have been apathetic towards oil palm cultivation. They have accepted and planted oil palm seedlings, but since they do not value them highly, they have neglected them and a large proportion, probably the majority, have died. The poor siting of many of the survivors, and competition from weeds, have delayed maturity and reduced yields. The failure to induce farmers to replace wild palm with palm groves and group plantations stems partly from ignorance of the merits, but in a large measure it is due to conservatism—the persistence of mental attitudes more appropriate to the earlier subsistence economy.

Wild palms are regarded as a gift from God and there are sufficient of them over much of the country to provide not only the farmers' own requirements of palm oil, but also as much more as they choose or are able to produce for sale. The fact that by cultivating oil palms a higher level of production could be achieved with less effort and less dependence on the supply of young men is either not appreciated or, equally probably, farmers are content, having provided themselves with an adequate food supply and money income to maintain a satisfactory living standard, to take their leisure or attend to other matters.

In the 1950's a number of small oil mills were set up in the dense palm belts to process the fruit of wild palms until such time as farmers could be induced to set up plantations and groves around the mills. It was hoped that they would both stimulate interest in oil palm cultivation and provide a starting point for industrialization. They did neither, and due to miscalculations of the extraction rate and of the length of the full-capacity working period, the mills never covered their operating costs.

Apparently it was thought that since similar mills had been successful in Nigeria, even taking account of the inferiority of the Sierra Leone varieties compared with the Nigerian, they could be made a commercial proposition in Sierra Leone. It was not appreciated that tribal precept commonly forbids palm fruit collection before the cultivated crops are harvested—another hangover from the earlier subsistence economy. Harvesting of cultivated crops finishes usually in the New Year and cultivation begins again with the start of the rainy season in April or May. The mills' experience has been that although they planned to operate for nine months of each year, they have been able to purchase worthwhile quantities of fruit for at most four months but often only for one or two months, during which the amount offered has been excessive. The rapid deterioration of fruit awaiting processing adds to their losses because the quality of the oil is poor.

To make things worse, the farmers' own valuation of their labour in processing the fruit by hand is low and the price expected for the fruit is not very different from that obtainable for the oil and kernals. The low valuation of their labour arises because palm oil extraction is a task performed by the womenfolk in a period when there is no great pressure on them to perform other tasks and the opportunity-cost of their labour is low. The stones are sun-dried and stored for cracking at the height of the rainy season after the annual crops have been sown and when there is little else that can be done, so kernel extraction is a task for the whole family. Again the labour opportunity-cost is negligible and the valuation of leisure may well be negative.

The main function of the Marketing Board is to purchase agricultural produce through its appointed agents. The Board is non-profit-making, many middlemen are circumvented and buying expenses are kept low. Surpluses gained on a rising market are used to maintain producers' prices when the market slumps. Commodity prices are liable to large and frequent changes and by eliminating intra-seasonal price changes and smoothing inter-seasonal changes it was hoped that the greater security offered would reduce the frequency and extent of crop-switching and in conditions of greater stability agricultural production would rise. Thus producers would make a two-fold gain in incomes—a gain because a larger proportion of export proceeds on average would acrrue to them and a further gain arising from increasing output. To achieve these aims, it was necessary for the Board to have a statutory monopoly of export of the crops with which it was concerned.

Relative prices and the kinds of crops cultivated appear to be closely associated. Farmers tend to switch to crops which are expected to be most lucrative in the following season. Presumably plans for planting tree crops are also governed partly by expectations based upon experience in the recent past. It is therefore necessary that the Board has an effective monopoly over the purchase and sale of all crop alternatives, otherwise over periods when the Board's prices are relatively unfavourable there will be a tendency to concentrate more on other crops. Thus the Board's power to control prices of the crops in which it deals can be limited by outside competition unless pricing policy includes offering relatively favourable prices at all times compared with those for alternative crops. This pricing policy does, in fact, appear to have been adopted by the Board, though its wording is ambiguous. Such a policy is not, however, entirely consistent with one of price stabilization which also forms part of the Board's pricing policy.

The Board's experience with coffee exports gives a good illustration of the difficulties of controlling producers' prices and stabilizing production. When the Marketing Board was formed in 1949, it took over from the West African Produce Control Board the marketing of oil seeds, coffee and cocoa. World prices for coffee were rising at that time, and those offered by the Board were relatively low, perhaps because of inaccurate forecasting of the season's prices, or perhaps intentionally to acquire quickly a workable price stabilization fund. When coffee prices started to rise still more rapidly at the outbreak of the Korean War, the Board's prices lagged badly and producers withheld supplies or traders refused to sell to the Board. There is some evidence of coffee being left unharvested whilst farmers concentrated on more rewarding crops, but most of the crop in 1951, 1952 and 1953 seems to have been sold privately and smuggled into French Guinea. Other crops do not seem to have been similarly affected, presumably because sufficiently large competing markets did not exist. When statutory marketing of coffee was relinquished in 1953 the effect was instantaneous; coffee exports through legal channels rose from less than $1\frac{1}{4}$ tons in 1952 to over 1,000 tons in 1953. This was more than three times the previous post-war peak in 1950. In the following year exports totalled 2,400 tons and by 1960 exports had reached 5,000 tons. In 1961, the Board reassumed the monopoly of purchase of coffee for export and once again exports fell dramatically to 2,400 tons in 1962 from 4,900 tons in 1961—and once more there was evidence of smuggling.

When coffee was freely marketed and cocoa was not, exports of coffee rose far faster than those of cocoa. This may have been in part because the freely-marketed crop offered better prices, but cocoa purchases were subsidized for a number of years when, even if an alternative market existed, effective competition for the cocoa crop was unlikely.[1]

There was also a decline in sales to the Board of oil seeds which, on the inadequate evidence available, appears to be explained either by the presence of another market or, more probably, by the substitution of other crops with relatively more favourable prices. By including coffee and ginger in the list of statutorily-marketed crops in 1961 the Board came much nearer to having a complete coverage of export crops; only piassava and kola nuts, among the important export crops, are outside the Board's control. It is still necessary, however, to control traffic across the country's borders more effectively. Moreover, for pricing policy to be fully effective, all agricultural produce, whether destined for internal markets or not, needs to be sold through the Board, or complementary organizations. Whether this solution would be politically acceptable is doubtful, but if it were, a powerful weapon would be added to the armoury of the economic planners. At the moment, however, the Board is not regarded primarily as a tool of the economic planners but as an agent of the producers, albeit that their interests seem at times to have been submerged.

Some other notable changes in agriculture since the war have been a scheme to settle nomadic herdsmen, the spread of co-operation, and the changed attitude towards plantation agriculture. To deal with the first, the scheme, known as the Cattle Owner Development Scheme, was aimed at preventing overgrazing and consequent soil erosion, making fuller use of the land, and providing a steady supply of better quality cattle to the meat markets. To this end, land for letting to pastoral farmers was enclosed and a water supply provided for each enclosure. Progress has been slow but the sceheme has been moderately successful and a few farmers, as well as improving their pasture, grow arable crops, and seem to have settled well. The scale of the enterprise is small, however, and in 1960 there were only 109 holdings out of which 86 were occupied. Instruction in animal management, and breed improvement is undertaken by the Animal Husbandry Station established at Musaia.

Co-operation is a post-war phenomenon in Sierra Leone, and one which has considerable potentialities as an organ of economic development. It was not unknown before the war but the few societies which operated functioned without knowledge of co-operative principles or organization. A Department of Co-operation

---

[1] In those years when the subsidy was small the evasion of the 7½ per cent export duty might have made competition with the Board worthwhile. There is, however, no evidence of any smuggling.

O

was formed in 1949, and the co-operative movement spread rapidly and is now firmly established. There are two main types of society: the producers' marketing society and the credit and thrift society. The difference between them is in emphasis rather than in function. Broadly speaking the membership of the producers' marketing societies comprises the heads of farming families, who sell their crops on behalf of the whole family through the co-operatives and who borrow and save on the family's behalf. The credit and thrift societies are much more the preserve of the small man—usually a member of a farming family, who has privately-produced crops to dispose of in much smaller quantities than the jointly-produced ones which are more often disposed of through the producers' marketing societies. He places private savings at the disposal of the co-operative and borrows from them for private reasons rather than for general improvements to the farm.

Co-operation started in the south-west but spread rapidly in the south and rather more slowly elsewhere. It extended to fishermen and more recently to cattle owners and diamond miners. Its value in economic development lies in several directions. In the first place, it fills a need for rural credit. Banks are unwilling to make unsecured loans to farmers who own very little that is saleable and whose reputation for prompt repayment is not of the best. Money-lenders and traders will make loans on security of crops or land.[1] The effective rate of interest charged by money-lenders and traders is extremely high and this discourages productive investment. Borrowing from them is therefore confined to cases of distress or profligacy.

Small loans have been made by public bodies for such purposes as cocoa planting, mangrove clearing, and the purchase of mechanical nut-crackers; and subsidies have been given to farmers under the Marketing Board's policy of price stabilization and by the government for fertilizers, ploughing fees and planting materials. The gaps left in agricultural investment finance and personal loans are filled by the co-operatives which examine schemes with great care and impose stiff repayment terms.

The strength of the co-operative movement lies in the fact that it makes use of the already familiar philosophy of co-operation instead of competition, but introduces fresh ideas like thrift, the circumvention of middlemen to increase money incomes, greater efficiency in production, and financial independence within this acceptable framework. It has been instrumental in removing some of the apathy of the

[1] They can never 'own' the land but they may enjoy its usufruct, for a specified period, or indefinitely until the loan is repaid. Land pledging does not appear to be very widespread, however.

population towards economic change and its importance in this respect is likely to continue to grow.

Post-war agricultural policies have all stopped short of using direct measures to change agricultural organization. Non-traditional crops and new techniques have been introduced but the concentration on subsistence production, the system of land tenure, and the use of the family as the labour unit have been little changed by colonial rule. In part this is because peasant attitudes in these matters are difficult to change, but it is also because British colonial policy in Sierra Leone has been consciously conservative and evolutionary.

The policy was a wise one so far as agriculture was concerned, for to remove its traditional base would be to destroy the nucleus of a social security system which costs nothing to operate and reduces wastage of human resources. Peasant agriculture has the great merit that it is flexible and is able to operate with quite wide variations in factor proportions. Using well-tried methods of cultivation, it is able to ensure that the basic needs of the cultivators will be met whilst at the same time it is able to absorb redundant labour from other industries or release unskilled labour for non-agricultural work quite rapidly and without serious disruption of agricultural production. The result is that the rate of involuntary unemployment is very low.

Yet the system is not without serious drawbacks for economic development. Per capita investment is extremely small, and techniques are highly labour-intensive with the result that labour productivity is low. Further, the high priority given to subsistence production results both in the diversion of the major part of the available resources to that end and in a low degree of specialization of crops. Since production for the market uses only those resources surplus to subsistence needs, the opportunities for increasing productivity by the growth of specialization are severely limited. Surplus resources are devoted to whichever uses seem most attractive— to non-agricultural employment, to the production of crops for the market, or to leisure. Since survival is ensured, risks can be taken in deploying surplus agricultural resources. This may well be the major reason why peasant farmers in Sierra Leone are highly responsive to changes in relative prices and will readily and rapidly switch crops, or refuse to harvest crops the yield or price of which is considered too low, in preference for other activities. Thus between 1950 and 1958 there was a 50 per cent increase in agricultural exports (excluding palm kernels) a partly lagged response to the large rise in export prices between 1950 and 1954—whilst rice and palm oil production for home consumption declined.

It would not be true to say that a choice exists between social security, in the form of the traditional institutions, and economic development, for without the security offered by peasant agriculture, unemployment would probably be greater. It is unlikely that a small country like Sierra Leone can afford for some time a comprehensive social security system and if traditional agriculture were to disappear the unemployed would still have to seek financial assistance and hospitality from their kinsfolk. The result would be that the latter's savings, or capital if any, would be dissipated and human resources would be less fully used. But this would not mean that an impasse had been reached. Quite apart from evolutionary changes in agriculture, the proposals in 1959 (repeated in the 1962–71 Ten-Year Plan) to try to interest Sierra Leoneans and others in starting plantations, offers a start to more radical changes which need deprive few people initially of a chance to cultivate the land if they should so choose. At the same time, because the whole of the product will be marketed, because the most efficient specialized production methods known are likely to be used, and because there is scope for experiment which peasant agriculture does not provide, yields are likely to be larger and of better quality, and the impact on the market will be disproportionately large in terms of the labour employed.

3. Mining

A wide variety of economically useful minerals is known to occur in Sierra Leone but few of them on a scale which it has yet been thought worthwhile to exploit. Consequently mining has been restricted to diamonds, iron ore and chromite, together with small amounts of platinum and small and widespread gold deposits. Mineral extraction provided employment for more than 30,000 people in 1962. At the height of the diamond boom in 1956 and 1957, probably well over twice that number were employed during peak periods. Minerals worth more than £16,500,000 are recorded as having been produced in 1962, and one must add to this an uknown but probably substantial quantity of illicitly marketed diamonds. If we omit the latter, output per head is valued at over £500 compared with an estimated £30–40 per adult worker in agriculture. Nearly £1,750,000 was paid in wages and salaries and more than £1,250,000 was paid to alluvial miners for their stones so that the annual average personal income was about £100. To assess the overall direct effects of mining we should also have to take account of direct government revenue from mining of £2,250,000 and local purchases and services valued at over £2,000,000.

The structure of the mining industry has been mainly monopolistic. Gold and platinum mining were exceptions, but these never reached very large proportions. In the 1950's the monopoly of diamond mining by the Sierra Leone Selection Trust was broken through wholesale illicit mining by local inhabitants and Guinea nationals. For the rest, the Sierra Leone Development Company have been the sole miners of iron ore (though a Liberian-based American company has recently been prospecting in eastern Sierra Leone), and Sierra Leone Chrome Mines of chromite. Similarly, mineral prospecting for bauxite, columbite, rutile and oil have been undertaken by single organizations. Except for the Selection Trust there does not appear to have been any deliberate attempt to monopolize production, but rather to ensure a sufficiently large scale of production, having regard to high costs and the considerable economies which can be effected by large-scale operations, to ensure that the enterprise is worthwhile. Because of the small size of the country and the relatively large area covered by some concessions, competitors tend to be precluded.

It would probably have been worthwhile to exploit more minerals had the state of economic development been more advanced, because it would then have been easier to assay deposits, and operating and transport costs would have been lower. Experienced managerial staff and well-qualified technical personnel have mostly to be imported at salaries higher than they could earn in their own countries; and there are costs associated with their employment which would not have to be met in industrialized countries. There is no locally-produced oil or mining equipment as yet, and the costs of shipping them to Sierra Leone inflate their prices. Similarly, since there is no metallurgical industry, minerals have to be shipped abroad so that the net return is further reduced.

The infrastructure is inadequate and mining companies have had to provide the requisite social overhead capital. The Selection Trust had to construct ninety miles of road, the Development Company had to construct a railway and a port with specialized loading equipment, and both had to build what amounted to small towns to house their employees, with apprentice training schools to train future workers. They had to generate their own electricity, provide hospital facilities, water supplies and the other essentials of urban life. This is a good example of the state of underdevelopment impeding further development.

The mining industry also provides examples of the inter-relationships between economic development and the preservation of law and order. The effect of a breakdown of law and order was to stimulate development and not, as is more usual, to impede it. The examples relate to the small gold boom of the 1940's and the much larger diamond boom of the 1950's. The gold rush set the precedent and pattern for the diamond rush, and the modification of mineral policy which expediency dictated turned out to be more effective in providing a stimulus for development than the previous policy.

The small gold rush of the 1940's occurred when new deposits of alluvial gold were discovered and there was a movement of many unlicensed miners to the area. Illicit mining could not be stopped, so an alluvial gold mining scheme was introduced to control it. Areas where illicit digging had taken place were demarcated as alluvial gold mining areas and mining was legalized on payment of a small licence fee and with a further condition that henceforth all gold mined should be sold through the official channels. In point of fact, whilst law and order were restored, illegal sales of gold to the goldsmiths were not prevented. Probably most of the gold produced was sold to them because they offered better prices.

The attention of the authorities was first drawn in 1951 to the incidence of illegal diamond mining on the Selection Trust workings at night-time. This followed a season when rice crops were very poor and the tribe mainly involved—the Konos—were mainly subsistence farmers lacking the means to supplement their food crops by purchasing rice. About the same time there was a large influx from French Guinea of more sophisticated Madingoes, who appear to have taken the leading part in illicit mining and diamond smuggling. The movement spread rapidly in succeeding years and it attracted men from most parts of Sierra Leone. They became bolder and at one stage employed troops to fight rearguard actions with the police whilst the miners, sometimes in groups of several hundreds, escaped. Tactics were frequently changed and police action was ineffective because of the large numbers involved, the opposition of the local population, the large area covered, and the remoteness of many of the diggings.

A scheme closely modelled on the alluvial gold mining scheme was introduced in 1955 and strong action was taken to repatriate the large numbers of Guinea nationals whose political power over the local people constituted a threat to the preservation of law. With diamond mining legalized it was easier to control the remaining miners but, as with gold, unofficial sales were not easily curbed. The introduction of the scheme enabled miners to sell their diamonds to the Diamond Corporation of Sierra Leone (and later to the newly-formed Government Diamond Office), without fear of arrest, and in 1956 the value of their exports was £1,600,000. In the following year 'alluvial' diamonds sold through official channels were valued at more than £5 million. The value of diamonds sold through illegal channels and smuggled out of the country probably far exceeded this. It was officially estimated that some £10–£15 million worth were smuggled out of the country annually in 1956, 1957 and 1958, after which the extent of smuggling was apparently reduced but never eliminated.

The most obvious outcome of the breaking up of the Selection Trust's monopoly was the large increase in diamond production. This was reflected in the legal exports shown in Table 6.4.

TABLE 6.4

DIAMOND PRODUCTION: LEGAL EXPORTS
1956–1962 (£ million)

Source	1956	1957	1958	1959	1960	1961	1962
Alluvial scheme	1·6	5·0	4·8	4·0	12·1	11·5	7·11
Selection Trust	1·8	1·4	2·4	2·9	4·4	4·4	—*

Source: Annual Trade Reports.

* Selection Trust production for 1962 was over 600,000 carats. They were sold to the Government Diamond Office at the end of 1962 and exported in 1963. At 1960 and 1961 average values, the output for 1962 would be worth £3·8 million.

The other obvious effects were on the national revenue and on the money incomes of many people not engaged in diamond mining. In 1950, ordinary revenue amounted to £2·9 million. By 1961 it had risen to £12·2 million. The increase was due in a large measure to the effects of alluvial diamond mining. About £700,000 was collected in licence fees and export duties from alluvial diamond mining scheme activities, but since a large proportion of miners' incomes are spent on imported goods, the gain in revenue from customs duties on these imports and income tax on commercial businesses dealing in them,[1] must be taken into consideration as well, of course, as revenue arising from the expansion of other incomes as an indirect result of the increase in mining incomes. The latter include new incomes in the mining areas derived from the provision of food and shelter and other services and from the collection of rent on diamond claims.

The large increase in ordinary revenue did not, however, bring about a commensurate increase in public capital expenditure. Central government capital expenditure in 1960–61 was only £1 million compared with £860,000 in 1950. The difference between the two

[1] No income tax was levied on sellers of local produce because of the small scale of these selling activities and the practical problems associated with assessment and collection.

may well have been accounted for by the substantial increase in labour costs arising out of the diamond boom and the growth of trade union power. Capital expenditure, however, fluctuates considerably from year to year and changes over the period are not sufficiently indicated by looking only at the two end years. The highest capital expenditure between the two years was in 1954 when it reached £2·2 million. This was only before any large diamond production other than by the Selection Trust. High produce prices much more than illicit diamond mining probably provided the wherewithal and the incentive. The increase in ordinary expenditure on the infrastructure—public works, electricity, medical services, education, transport and the like—was more significant. Between 1950 and 1960–61 it increased from £670,000 to £5,300,000. When increases in labour and material costs are taken into account this still involves a considerable growth.

Alluvial mining has, however, led to much waste of resources, since unsystematic digging and the crude methods of diamond extraction employed are aimed only at short-run profit maximization. The Selection Trust and the Ministry of Lands, Mines and Labour have recently introduced schemes and measures to improve the standard of mining with considerable success.

Little need be said specifically about the other minerals except that in both the other major mining concerns, as in the Selection Trust, mechanization has increased and hence production per man has grown since the war. Mineral exploitation provides a ready source of income for economic development because overseas investors are generally more interested in schemes where the principal outlets lie in world markets rather than in production for a small and not very buoyant domestic market.

4. Manufacturing and Services

It is impossible to state the number of people employed in the service industries because the degree of specialization of occupations is low and many perform services as well as producing goods. For instance, farmers, urban housewives and children commonly engage in trade, moneylenders are also engaged in other occupations, porters and labourers may be farmers during the rainy season and follow the service trade in the dry season.

The predominance of services over manufacturing industry is indicative of the primitive state of economic development. The shortage of money capital, arising from the general low level of incomes and from social attitudes to wealth and savings, results in uneconomically high borrowing rates and economizing on available finance by minimizing the amount tied up in fixed capital. Furthermore, widespread illiteracy and the somewhat sketchy education of the majority of the literate are less of a bar to minor success in commerce than in industry where, because the scale of the enterprise is usually larger, and a greater degree of managerial ability is called for, and because technical skills and technological knowledge are required to a greater degree, all but a small proportion of the population are excluded. There is no organized market where funds available for investment may be obtained fairly cheaply when required. The result is that ability to initiate manufacturing enterprises and to finance them have to be coupled, and some who possess the necessary entrepreneurial and technical qualities are excluded.

With the increase in real incomes, growing sophistication of tastes, and changing attitudes, the demand for manufactures is rising, but this has led to a growth of imports rather than to the stimulation and growth of the manufacturing sector. It is noteworthy that larger manufacturing businesses have nearly all been initiated by the government or expatriates, and since the size of the domestic market for most products is relatively small, Sierra Leone has not provided an attractive prospect for foreign entrepreneurs compared with larger and more virile economies.

Secondary industry takes the form mainly of handicrafts like cloth weaving and basket making, simple processing like palm oil and kernel extraction, or the manufacture of articles by methods in which the capital-output ratio is low like saw-milling, furniture manufacture, soap making, and plastics moulding. Most industries can be classified into two groups: those in which transport costs are sufficiently high to make effective competition with imports possible, such as furniture making, baking and mineral water bottling; and those in which the element of personal service is important like bespoke tailoring, building, and milling customers' rice.

The sector is small compared with agriculture and services both as regards the size of the labour force and in terms of its contribution to the national product. At the end of the war in 1945 it was believed that the country was ripe for industrialization and a small grant was made out of Colonial Development and Welfare funds to provide finance for small businesses. It was thought that larger-scale production would grow once entrepreneurial experience had been gained and the pool of experienced managerial and technically-skilled labour had grown under the stimulus of the expansion of industry. The scheme, however, was unsuccessful. Few individuals put forward any business proposals and the majority of proposals were in any case considered to be unworkable or outside the scope of the Development of Industries Fund. Nearly all who were given loans failed in their enterprises and the Fund, instead of snowballing as repayments and interest payments on loans were made, was depleted through bad debts.

In a developing country where most entrepreneurs are inexperienced, markets are not well-established, a reasonably regular source of raw materials is difficult to ensure, and labour is often inefficient and unreliable, the business mortality rate is high. This is true of the whole of tropical Africa, and the high failure rate in Sierra Leone was not exceptional. This is one of the reasons for the reluctance of commercial banks to lend money to finance the setting up of businesses.

Another important reason for the high incidence of business failure, is the code of kinship obligations which leads to the depletion of business profits and private savings through the calls of needy relatives. The possibility of investment and reinvestment is thus reduced, and the ability to accumulate depreciation funds to replace fixed capital is jeopardized, so that most African businesses in Sierra Leone are small and many are obviously under-capitalized. One gains the impression that indigenous businessmen lack the initiative and drive of their European and Asian counterparts, and that they tend to be less acquisitive and more cautious. The social code which tends to prevent the rewards for enterprise from being enjoyed by the entrepreneur may be the major reason for this, and may provide the key to the explanation of the decline of African participation in commerce in this century.

5. *Prospects and Problems*

This section is devoted to examining the framework and major proposals of the 1962–1971 Development Plan and considering some of the problems of planning and development which are brought to light.

This is the third development plan and it is more ambitious and imaginative than either of its predecessors. In framing it, however, the authors suffered from the same serious handicap in not having available much information which could have helped them, and consequently the Plan is vague on a number of issues. They did not know, for instance, the size, structure, distribution and rate of change of the population and the national income. Nor did they have more than the sketchiest statistics, where they had any at all, on the size and structure of the labour force, crop acreages and production, and land use. On the balance of payments they had one crude estimate. One of the early tasks which the Plan proposes is to make good some of the deficiencies in statistical and other information by establishing two research institutes, conducting a series of censuses and surveys, and widening the range of regularly-collected statistics.

The Plan starts with the assumption that there will be a growth in agricultural and mining efficiency which will cause part of the labour force to become redundant. Industrialization will then be needed to provide employment for this labour. In order to make industrialization possible, public investment will have to be greatly increased— especially in transport and communications, water and power supplies, education, housing and health and welfare services. The demand for imported capital goods will be much higher than formerly, so agriculture and the new manufacturing industries should produce import-replacing goods in order to allow as much as possible of the export earnings to be used to purchase capital goods. Agricultural exports should also be increased. In fact it is envisaged that agriculture will bear the major part of the burden of development in the early years, and in order to stimulate trade with capital-supply countries with which trade had been non-existent or unimportant, the range of agricultural products for export will need to be widened and exchange controls to be relaxed. In order to provide a better climate for investment there are to be fiscal reforms including reductions in import duties, tax concessions to new investors and an extension and tightening of corporate and personal income tax collection. The civil service will be reinforced by recruitment and training to carry the Plan through efficiently, and the maintenance of law and order strengthened.

The development of primary production, manufacturing industry and commerce is to be left mainly to private enterprise but foreign domination is to be prevented and, where it already exists, removed. This means that foreign investment in the purchase and export of such agricultural produce as is not subject to the Marketing Board monopoly, import retailing, fishing, motor transport, and manufacturing industries in which capital and skill requirements are not beyond local resources is not to be encouraged.

Larger-scale industrial enterprises and those where technical and other requirements are beyond local resources, and mining and plantation agriculture, are to be the major fields of investment for foreigners, but they are not to be allowed to dominate them. This is to be prevented by semi-nationalization, the partial take-over of capital and control of selected firms by the state. Ultimately Sierra

Leoneans should be able to own shares in these concerns and participate in their management.

In order to help finance development, it is proposed to establish a central bank to take over the duties formerly performed by the West African Currency Board and the commercial banks, to use the marketing board surpluses, to form a co-operative bank, and to institute savings campaigns to mobilize private savings. The possibility of the formation of indigenous commercial banks, mortgage and loan companies and insurance companies is also mentioned.

The cost to the State of implementing the Plan is estimated at an average of £30½ million for the first five years, and considerably less for the second five years. This is made up of £20 million capital expenditure, and the rest to cover recurrent expenditure—presumably relating only to the commitments entailed in the Plan. For the five years immediately preceding the Plan, average recurrent expenditure was £11½ million, and total recurrent expenditure is likely to be appreciably greater in the first quinquennium than the £10½ million quoted in the Plan. With ordinary revenue expanding at more than 13 per cent per year from 1956 to 1961, average capital expenditure was only £2 million. For the first five years of the Plan it is assumed that ordinary revenue will increase at the rate of only 5 per cent. Obviously therefore, the financing of the Plan will have to depend very much upon external finance.

There is no evidence, except possibly in the assumption about the size of the school age population in 1975, that population changes have been taken into account. The planners were wise not to base plans on the mid-year estimates, which are so unreliable as to be valueless for the purpose of estimating the growth rate, but there is little doubt both that the population is growing, and that its rate of growth will become greater year by year. The crude birth rate is undoubtedly very high and so is the crude death rate, but whilst there are no obvious reasons for expecting the former to decline for a long time (in fact the increasing use of antiobiotics to treat the prevalent venereal diseases may well lead to a higher birth rate), there is every chance that death rates will be reduced if medical and health services are improved. Migration is small and need not be taken into account. Thus a higher population growth rate than that obtaining when the Plan was formulated might reasonably be expected before the end of the decade.

The greatest reduction of the mortality rate is likely to be among the very young, of whom it is believed an exceptionally large proportion fail to survive the age of weaning. Such a reduction would lead to a change in the age structure of the population in favour of

THE ECONOMIC DEVELOPMENT OF SIERRA LEONE 221

the younger age groups. At the same time the educational programme has as its target universal education by 1980. This means that by the end of the planning period the availability of juvenile labour in agriculture will be much reduced and, coupled with the larger numbers of surviving children per adult worker, it means that the proportion of dependents will increase and output per worker will have to be raised merely to keep living standards from declining.

The Plan requires an expansion of agricultural output such that the volume of exports will be increased, whilst at the same time raw materials will be required on an increasing scale, if the attempt at industrialization is at all successful, and agricultural imports must be replaced as far as possible by domestic produce. At the same time the level of production of foodstuffs already being supplied to the home market must not decline. If population growth is taken into consideration, the requirements for home consumption are that food output per head of the total population (not merely per farm worker) must be held level, whilst the output of other crops must be increased merely to pay for the increase in imports demanded by the growing population as well as to provide foreign exchange for increased capital imports. It would apparently not be an over-estimate to say that not only production of the foodstuffs already supplied to the domestic market, but other agricultural production as well must expand at least as fast as the population. Therefore, unless the proportion of agriculturalists in the population is held constant, output per agricultural worker will need to be increased to maintain nutritional standards and cater for the same per capita import requirements of consumption goods. This is apart from the increases which the Plan requires. But a relative decline in the agricultural population, when the population is expanding, may not also be an absolute decline, in which case the existence of diminishing returns in agriculture may still lead to a decline in output per worker unless techniques, crops, organization and labour efficiency can be improved sufficiently to offset it.

The Development Plan lists a number of ways in which agriculture may be improved, among which are widespread use of mechanical aids and plantation agriculture. Both are labour-saving techniques and it may be with these in mind that the planners have anticipated labour redundancies. They could certainly raise the level of output per worker, and possibly the absolute level of output, but it is by no means certain that other techniques which are not predominently labour-saving could not effect a larger increase. For instance, irrigation and flood control could increase land utilzation (and labour utilization) and intensive methods associated with the use of fertilizers would increase labour requirements, as would more thorough weeding and pest control which would increase the size of the harvest.

Unless it becomes possible to keep output of the various types of crop abreast of population growth, either the provisions of the Development Plan will need to be modified or all labour which can make a positive contribution to agricultural output will have to be retained without regard to the relationship between the value of its output and its earnings in available alternative occupations. In modern agriculture the retention of all labour with a positive marginal product is only possible if the enterprise is non-profit-making, that is, if it is a co-operative or publicly-owned. Otherwise the approximate relationship between marginal output and the wage level governs employment, and labour whose marginal product is positive but is valued below the prevailing wage level, becomes redundant. Traditional agriculture, on the other hand, has no such restriction since it is in effect a partnership of all the participants, and not a profit-making form of enterprise. It has the further advantage over modern agriculture that because the techniques customarily used are far more labour-intensive than is usual in the latter, it is possible to vary the technical coefficients to a much greater degree.

Three aspects of cost associated with alternative techniques also need to be considered. These are average production costs, initial costs associated with changes, and import costs. It may well be that production costs are appreciably less under peasant agriculture than under more modern forms if labour is valued at its opportunity-cost, because capital requirements are very small and labour opportunity-costs are low, especially for female labour which is much used in traditional agriculture. Where capital formation is on other grounds justified, investment in very long-lived capital, such as irrigation schemes, or less long-lived investment, such as plantations, may be preferable from the viewpoint of production costs to short-lived capital used in mechanization and artificial fertilizers.

Initial costs are important because capital funds are bound to be scarce in the early years of the planning period, and they have to be allocated in such a manner as to try to optimize their allocation according to some criterion—perhaps to maximize the average rate of growth of the national income within the planning period, or to minimize the period elapsing before economic independence is attained. Initial costs are not important when the funds are allocated from overseas specifically for a particular project or purpose, but where public revenue or private borrowing is concerned, economies in agricultural investment will make more projects within the sector, or greater investment in other sectors, possible. From this viewpoint, investment in fertilizers would be preferable to investment in irrigation schemes, unless the latter were undertaken largely with voluntary labour. The balance of advantage is reinforced by the fact that the cost-recovery period for fertilizers would be small compared with that for an irrigation scheme, and the effect upon the national income of a given outlay would tend to be much more rapid if it were used to purchase and distribute fertilizers.

Since the demands upon overseas earnings are likely in any case to be heavy, those schemes which have the highest import requirements in relation to the increase in production effected need to be allotted the lowest priority unless they are directly financed from overseas, and schemes which use domestic resources are to be encouraged. This means that irrigation schemes and plantations, for instance, are preferable to mechanization and fertilizers from this particular viewpoint.

It is obviously impossible to be dogmatic regarding the choice of techniques and the distribution of investment without much detailed information on costs and yields. Such information is not at present available but in the absence of such information the wisest course would seem to be to concentrate initially on increasing peasant production whilst restricting larger-scale more highly capital-intensive modern agriculture to the sparsely-populated and previously uncultivated areas. In this way land and labour resources would be most fully used. Avoidance of the widespread mechanization which the Plan advocates should enable considerable economies to be made in the use of investible funds and at the same time reduce the pressure on imports. Voluntary labour for irrigation schemes and other structural work aimed at land improvement and reclamation should be used as much as possible. This arrangement would also have the advantage of making use of cheap and abundant labour resources, instead of expensive and scarce capital, until such time as capital funds are less scarce, employment vacancies in the other sectors are increasing more rapidly, and training and education fit a new generation better both for modern agriculture and for other employment. This opinion is reinforced by the belief that the natural increase in urban population, coupled with those who are forced to leave agriculture because living standards are depressed by over-population, and those who voluntarily leave agriculture, are likely to meet all or most of the demand for year-round employees during the planning period. The last category includes most of those whose education has extended beyond two or three years in a primary school; their numbers are increasing quite rapidly. These are likely to form the nucleus of a skilled labour force if industrialization becomes a reality.

If changes in agriculture are not rapid enough, there is a danger of over-cultivation spreading as the population increases and of a larger number suffering from declining living standards. It is to these rather than to labour displaced by labour-saving devices that the planners should look for a supply of non-seasonal unskilled labour. To begin with, the demand for unskilled labour is likely to be small in the rainy season, when the scope for outdoor work is very limited, and very much greater in the dry season. Moreover, the dry season demand is likely to increase as schemes for developing the infra-structure get under way. Except from 1955 to 1957, when at the height of the diamond boom there was a wholesale migration of male farmers from some areas to the diamond workings, there has in the past been no difficulty in obtaining unskilled seasonal labour. Male labour's marginal productivity in agriculture is probably at or near to zero and the loss of part of the labour force has probably not made a great difference to agricultural output in relation to the number of men who have temporarily left the industry in recent years. It is likely that increased demands in the future can also be met without seriously hazarding agricultural output. This seasonal labour, together with the non-seasonal labour which may be expected to rise from sources mentioned above, may well provide as much labour as manufacturing industry and other non-agricultural activities are capable of absorbing. Then the necessity to plan the permanent removal of labour from agriculture by introducing labour-saving techniques, and the problem of how best to do this whilst creating the minimum reduction in agricultural output do not arise.

It is planned that the rate of growth of education, upon which economic development depends so much, will be restricted, both because primary school education is to be phased with employment opportunities and because a low upper limit to the pupil-teacher ratio is to be imposed. The programme for primary education is based upon the supposition that there will be a primary school age population of 470,000 in 1975 and that the annual rate of output of teachers will have reached 460. This rate of output may well be over-optimistic in view of the small numbers of school-leavers adequately qualified for teacher-training who are likely to become available in the next few years, and because employment opportunities, particu-larly for males, outside the field of education will increase if develop-ment proceeds according to plan. Even if this rate is achieved, how-ever, universal primary education will only be possible by 1975 if the average class size is about 40. This is unacceptable, for reasons not stated in the Plan, and a target size of 30 is mentioned, though for the first five years of the Plan an upper limit of 36, which is approximately the 1961 ratio, is to be accepted. This means postponing the advent of universal primary education until 1980 at least.

Similarly, although the shortage of people with a secondary school education has proved a serious handicap in the past and will clearly continue to be so for many years, the upper limit on class size in secondary schools is to be 30. Hence the number of people qualified for higher education is reduced and so is the number eligible for teacher-training, the civil service, and management training. The justification for these low maximum ratios is an insistence on quality rather than quantity, which the country as yet can ill afford. Not only would larger classes be instrumental in providing a more adequate supply of skilled, managerial and professional labour, thus easing one of the major bottlenecks in economic development, but it would make fuller use of the scarce educational resources and at the same time reduce the cost to the public purse. This is because there is as yet no free education in Sierra Leone, so that the greater the number of pupils per class, the greater the contribution from private sources to the cost of education. Instead, teachers salaries are to be raised to bring them into line with the civil service, class sizes are to be reduced, and the goal by 1980 is free education for all, which the country may well only be able to afford at the expense of other aspects of economic development. In so far as the shortage of classroom space is a factor limiting the rate of increase in the number of school places and the size of classes, it would probably be worthwhile to erect simple open-sided classrooms at low cost and even to hold some classes out-of-doors.

The need for an expanding manufacturing sector is much more than to provide additional employment for redundant primary producers, although its capacity to do this is not so limited as in modern agriculture. The expansion of secondary industry can increase economic stability and provide a better basis for, and a faster rate of, self-sustained growth.

Since Sierra Leone is a minor producer of all crops other than piassava, the size of Sierra Leone exports has little effect upon world prices. Thus the change in the supply component of prices bears little relationship to changes in the volume of Sierra Leone's exports. On the demand side, too, Sierra Leone, as a minor importer of manufactures exerts little effect. Thus commodity price fluctuations are virtually unrelated to changes in Sierra Leonean exports and therefore to agricultural output. Moreover, the relationship between controllable inputs and outputs is much more capricious in agriculture than in manufacturing processes. The combination of variations in crop yields and export prices serves to make the incomes of far-

P

mers, produce buyers, and exporters very unstable; and the effect of the price stabilization policy of the Marketing Board, whilst it helps to stabilize producers' proceeds, has only a very limited effect in this direction. The unpredictability of cash incomes reinforces producers' reluctance to give up the security which subsistence production affords for the very uncertain prospect of a higher total income. Consequently major changes in crops and techniques are held up.

Changes in the level of cash incomes from mining and agriculture are reflected in the demand for imported consumers' goods and hence in trading profits. And since up to the present the major part of ordinary revenue has been derived from import and export duties, public revenue is also liable to unpredictable changes which cause difficulties in national budgeting and make for caution in planning capital expenditure.

If a larger proportion of productive resources were employed in manufacturing, the degree of instability could be reduced; a greater proportion of agricultural output could be directed to the home market where prices could be either controlled or at least reflect to some degree changes in output, thus exerting a stabilizing effect on farmers' and traders' incomes. Direct taxation of manufacturing profits and employers' incomes is more feasible and less costly than attempting to tax farm incomes directly, and with a reduced dependence on international trade, changes in the terms of trade would be of less importance.

The larger domestic market for food crops which would result if a higher proportion of the population was dependent for a livelihood on non-agricultural employment, coupled with a much greater internal demand for agricultural raw materials, would increase the stability of farm incomes and would probably make the break with subsistence production easier. Once available resources cease to be concentrated on subsistence production, the way is open for larger strides in increasing agricultural output and raising substantially the level of farm incomes. In addition, the relative stability of prices in the manufacturing sector would contribute towards reducing fluctuations in the size of the domestic product, whilst at the same time allowing a greater choice of occupations and using more fully the abilities of the population.

Even if changes in agriculture enable substantial numbers of people to take up non-agricultural employment, it is unlikely that the manufacturing sector will grow very quickly. The principal difficulty lies in the small size of the population, and the level and distribution of income. A certain amount of industrialization is clearly possible so long as the domestic demand is sufficient to justify setting up factories, but in many industries the output necessary to secure economies of scale is in excess of local demand; adequate tax concessions, subsidies and tariff protection can make smaller-scale, higher-cost production practicable. Since the country is not well-known to overseas investors, and market prospects cannot be easily assessed, there may be difficulty too in competing with better-known countries for overseas investment in smaller projects. In any case, the small size of the population, which is unlikely to reach 4 million within twenty years, limits the scope of sales in the domestic market; the danger exists of firms failing to survive because technological change has been such as to increase the scale of production at which a firm becomes competitive beyond the level to which the domestic market can be expanded.

A country as small and poor as Sierra Leone is likely to experience difficulties, too, in attracting overseas funds for public investment in competition with larger, more politically-important countries and those which, by virtue of their size, have greater scope for mounting impressive development programmes—particularly since the cost per head of the population served by the improvements normally diminishes as the size of that population increases. This is also a problem, when local finance of development schemes is considered because the cost to each taxpayer tends to be greater the smaller the population, and the scope for internal finance of development schemes is therefore more limited than in larger populations with a similar average taxable capacity. Consequently it is the small country which has the greater need of external financial aid for public development projects.

From the foregoing discussion the question arises as to whether the country is too small to be economically viable. Much depends upon the adaptability of agriculture, but there are too many other factors to make a definite answer possible. What can be said is that Sierra Leone is surrounded by countries with populations of a similar magnitude, the problems of which are not dissimilar from Sierra Leone's. The prospect of achieving self-sustained growth would be considerably enhanced for all of them if they could contrive to form themselves into an economic union, thus increasing rapidly the size of the domestic market and possibly economizing on development expenditure by co-ordinating their plans. Such a union may be as loose as a customs union or it may entail political federation. In either case larger-scale enterprises would be justified and more effective use could be made of the available resources.

CHAPTER VII

New Zealand's Economic Development

by J. W. WILLIAMS

New Zealand is often referred to as an exception to two propositions which are commonly made about development. The first is that countries with national incomes composed largely of agricultural products are poorer than industrial countries, and the second, that in the process of development, the relative importance of agriculture declines. With a gross national product of about £600 per head, New Zealand is one of the wealthier countries of the world. We may ask to what extent it is dependent on agriculture and how far is the existing degree of dependence only a temporary phase of development which will later give place to industrialization and perhaps a greater degree of self-sufficiency? We may also enquire whether there are any special circumstances which may account for the present position and finally, what disadvantages are involved in a high degree of specialization.

The proportion of the population engaged in farming, while high for a wealthy country, is only 14 per cent, but this figure, in fact, does not convey an accurate impression of the numbers actually concerned. The typical New Zealand farmer is very much a specialist and many things which in other countries are done as part of normal farm work are, in New Zealand, carried out by contractors. Shearing, for example, is almost invariably a job for teams of specialists; fertilizer is spread by aircraft; butter and cheese are made in factories; sheep and cattle are killed, dressed and frozen in freezing works. Most farms are of moderate size and are worked by the owner with perhaps some help from his family but with little employment of permanent labour. Many of the commercial activities of the country are concerned with the selling of farm produce and the finance of farms, with much of the transport system organized to carry farm produce to market. Table 7.1 provides what is probably the best picture of the situation.

The values shown are at the farm gate or factory door and are net of inputs from other industries except that some farm inputs such as fertilizers have not been excluded. The value of commodity production in 1961 was only 65 per cent of net national product; while a good proportion of non-commodity production consists of consumer services—retail shops, education, government administration—of the rest, it is likely that farming absorbs more than half. As a rough estimate we could say that agriculture and other primary production accounts for nearly half of the national income.

What then are the circumstances which have made specialization in agriculture particularly successful? In terms of comparative advantages, New Zealand's position can be explained as one of a high ratio of land to labour and of specialized capital to labour. New Zealand is a country moderate in size, with a population of 2½ million and with a land area of 103,000 square miles, of which about

TABLE 7.1

Value of Commodity Production, 1961

	£ million	Percentage of total
Farming (including processing)	352	47
Mining, fishing, forests	51	7
Manufacturing and power	265	35
Building and miscellaneous	81	11
	749	100

Source: *Official Year Book.*

two-thirds is suitable for cultivation with existing techniques. The land is not particularly fertile by European standards and the productivity of the most intensively farmed areas has been built up and is maintained by heavy applications of fertilizers. Farming is predominantly the grazing of sheep and cattle, although the country is self-sufficient in most food crops. The climate provides particular advantages in terms of adequate, evenly distributed rainfall with mild winters, while scientific methods of farming such as the development of pasture grasses, stock breeding, soil analysis and farm management are widely applied and have resulted in a high level of efficiency. Furthermore, there are two agricultural colleges of university standard and most of their graduates are practising farmers. All these factors have made New Zealand the lowest cost producer of dairy products in the world, the lowest-cost producer of mutton and lamb and one of the lowest-cost producers of wool. Although it was the comparative advantage of abundant land which led to agricultural specialization, New Zealand now has an absolute advantage in particular kinds of agriculture with the price of land not very different from what it is in Europe.

New Zealand is not well endowed with natural resources other than land. Forests once covered the country but a great deal has been either cut out or burnt for cultivation. The climate is favourable for forest growth and pines which have been introduced and cultivated in plantations have done remarkably well, forming the basis of a growing wood-pulp and paper industry and some export of timber. Forests still cover nearly a quarter of the land area but less than one quarter are 'merchantable' by present standards. Mineral resources, especially metallic ores, are limited in extent and not conveniently concentrated for exploitation, while there is enough coal for the small local consumption. Iron ore occurs in very substantial amounts in iron bearing sands, but only recently have the various attempts to recover the ore from the sand met with any success. As the result of recent experiments a suitable process appears to have been discovered and plans for an iron and steel industry are now being formulated. No worthwhile deposits of oil have been found. Hydro-electric power provides by far the most important source of energy, with a large proportion of the available sources in the North Island already in use, but there are still large reserves of power in the South Island. Finally, an aluminium plant using this hydro-electric power and bauxite from Northern Australia has been planned.

Although New Zealand has not the basic natural resources for large scale industry and much of its capital is specialized in the production, transport and marketing of primary products, a good deal of small scale industrial development has taken place. The growth of this may be traced to a distinct historical pattern resulting from the colonization by Europeans (starting in the 1840's) of this near empty land.[1]

Most settlers during the first twenty years came with some sort of sponsorship, and Wakefield's colonization scheme was based on the concept of more or less self-sufficient communities which would reproduce English life with proprietors, farmers, farm labourers and craftsmen. Things did not quite work out like this, but the concept did provide a degree of balance in the economy. Isolation from England, and in the earlier years of the small settlements from one

[1] The Maoris who occupied New Zealand at that time lived mainly by hunting and fishing and had reached a high level of material culture in the use of stone, wood and fibres. They were quick to pick up European methods and grow new crops, wheat, maize and potatoes. There were, however, only a few of them—estimates range from 140,000 to 200,000—and though a 'dual economy' existed for a while before 1840, after about 1870 they were absorbed into the economy of the settlers except in a few isolated areas.

another, led to the development of skills in repair and maintenance of machinery and in the fabrication of new parts and an early establishment of localized industries—flour mills, saw-mills, brick-works and so forth. The technical skills then acquired laid the foundation for the small-scale industry of later years. Today 200,000 people are engaged in manufacturing which has grown at about the same pace as the rest of the economy. Most industry is on a small scale, partly because of the small overall market and partly because

TABLE 7.2

National Income, Overseas Trade and Capital Formation
1954–1961

	£ million				1958 = 100	
	(1)	(2)	(3)	(4)	(5)	(6)
	National income at current factor cost	*Current receipts from rest of world*	*Current payments to rest of world*	*Net domestic capital formation*	*Wholesale prices*	*Consumer prices*
1954	802	266	305	186	92	88
1955	844	295	327	180	93	91
1956	887	309	326	168	96	94
1957	936	309	358	190	97	96
1958	902	297	320	185	100	100
1959	1,039	348	305	180	102	104
1960	1,115	327	383	227	102	105
1961	1,146	327	377	216	102	106

Sources: United Nations, *Yearbook of National Accounts Statistics 1962*, pp. 184–186.
 United Nations, *Statistical Yearbook 1962*.
Note: The time-basis is the fiscal year beginning April 1st for columns (1)–(4).

of the high costs of transport within New Zealand. A very wide range of products is turned out and only about 15 per cent of imports are now in the form of finished consumers' goods. A good many consumers' goods produced in New Zealand are, however, made from imported components and do not contain a large proportion of local added value. The 1952–53 inter-industry study of the New Zealand economy gives a figure of £25·25 for the import content of every £100 of final output of manufacturing industry. The proportion would be higher today but not markedly so. When we allow for the fact that many of the larger industries use little in the way of imports it is apparent that those which do so have a rather low ratio of added value to import content.

Such specialization with New Zealand's factor endowments, which in earlier years were built up with the aid of overseas borrowing, especially from Britain, has provided the picture of recent growth as shown in Table 7.2. National income has grown in monetary terms by some 43 per cent between 1954 and 1961, while wholesale prices have risen by 11 per cent and consumer goods prices by 20 per cent; current receipts from the rest of the world (principally for merchandise exports) and current payments to the rest of the world (principally for merchandise imports) have each expanded by about a quarter. A more detailed breakdown of merchandise trade is provided in Table 7.4 to show the nature and degree of this specialization.

That the division of labour depends on the extent of the market is a well established proposition in economics. The only New Zealand exports which have a world market are wool and timber, other exports being linked to specialization for the British market. For sales of butter, cheese and meat New Zealand has depended mainly on this market, which is the largest one for imported meat in the world and the only substantial market for lamb. The number of large meat exporters is limited as shown by Table 7.3.

TABLE 7.3
Principal Exporters of Meat, 1963

	Beef and Veal Thousand tons	Lamb and Mutton Thousand tons
Argentina	502	36
Australia	276	81
New Zealand	121	357

Practically all butter and cheese is sold on the British market, although some is re-exported as also is a small proportion of lamb and mutton. Before 1939, about 95 per cent of meat exports went to Britain and between 1939 and 1954 almost the whole went to her under bulk purchase agreements. Since 1954, however, markets have been developed elsewhere and, in 1963, 46 per cent of sales were outside Britain. The meat diverted to other markets has been chiefly beef and veal. In the same year, 94 per cent of the lamb went to Britain. Small sales of lamb were made in the United States and Canada. Britain took about one-third of mutton exports; more than one half went to Japan and the rest to North America.

There are obvious prospects for the expansion of meat exports to the developing countries especially in the East. New Zealand already supplies three-quarters of Japan's imports of meat, but the total quantity is small. The principal difficulty of these countries is the ability to pay for meat imports and reliance for increasing sales has to be placed on rising standards of living. Promotion of sales of lamb to North America has had some success and New Zealand is the main overseas supplier. Even so, exports to North America in 1963 amounted to less than 11,000 tons out of a total of 357,000 tons. In the developed countries, it is restrictions on trade which are the biggest barrier to expansion of the market. In America, the restriction on beef is potential rather than actual, but it is evident that any considerable expansion of New Zealand's sales would be likely

TABLE 7.4

Composition of New Zealand Overseas Trade, 1957–1960

£ MILLION AT CURRENT PRICES

	1957	1958	1959	1960
Exports:				
Total	273	246	290	299
(a) Food	141	141	167	162
including (i) *Meat*	*71*	*79*	*77*	*81*
(ii) *Dairy Products*	*64*	*55*	*84*	*74*
(b) Crude materials	124	96	111	125
including—*Wool*	*106*	*80*	*90*	*102*
Imports:				
Total	263	253	205	252
(a) Manufactures	108	105	85	106
(b) Machinery	75	71	55	72
(c) Raw materials, Fuels, Oils, Chemicals	51	51	45	53

Source: United Nations, *World Trade Yearbook 1961.*

to lead to restrictions. As is well known the policies of the countries of the European Economic Community are based on a rigid system of protection for agriculture. British subsidies affect the market and hence the price of lamb in Britain; limitation of imports is being discussed. New Zealand, along with other primary producing countries, feels that trade libaralization policies such as those advocated by the signatories of the General Agreement on Tariffs and Trade (GATT) have stopped short of agricultural exports. Whatever may be the merits or demerits of her own restrictionist policies over imports, New Zealand does not deserve criticism from countries which have protectionist agricultural policies.

Dairy products now suffer competition from less efficient home producers in export markets, and actual and potential competition from surpluses arising from high support prices in Europe. Butter consumption per head in Britain is considerably lower today than it was before the war. This is probably a reflection of the rise in average income in Britain, for butter, as a complementary good to bread, shares with it the status of an inferior good, while at the same time its use both as a spread and for cooking has been affected by the great improvement in margarine and other fats.

Wool has stood up to post-war changes in incomes and consumption habits better than anything. The threat from man-made fibres appears to be much less serious than it looked like being. Prices have been high and rising and have induced a switch to sheep on many New Zealand farms.

The disadvantages which New Zealand has met as a specialist producer of food are, first the fact that production was adapted primarily to the British market which has now ceased to expand and secondly, that butter and frozen meat are luxuries which most of the world cannot afford.[1] In the long run one would expect that an efficient food producer would be in a very strong position in a world in which population is growing fast and in which a large proportion of the present population are now badly fed. There are in the world today agricultural surpluses in the sense that food producing countries would like to sell more than countries who need more food are prepared to purchase. It is wrong to describe this situation as 'poverty in the midst of plenty'. One must keep in mind the magnitudes involved. All meat which New Zealand could possibly produce would, if distributed evenly among the hungry peoples of the world make a welcome addition to their diet, but it would not go far in satisfying their needs. In 1963, for example, Australia and New Zealand together exported 4,024 million pounds of meat. This would have meant $1\frac{1}{3}$ pounds of meat a year for each inhabitant in the world, and remembering that this is mainly on a carcass basis, it would have meant $1\frac{1}{3}$ pounds of, say, rather fat and bony chops.

A number of developing countries could pay for meat and butter if they wished to use foreign exchange earnings for the purpose, but they usually prefer to use them for the purchase of capital goods. In the medium to short-run period fresh markets for New Zealand's exports are going to be difficult to find. In the long run, unless protective agricultural policies in Europe and America are reversed, New Zealand's future is closely tied up with the growth and prosperity of the newly developing countries as their markets widen for protein foodstuffs.

[1] Note the slow expansion of export receipts as compared with national income as shown in Table 7.2.

Hence the prospects of export-led growth for New Zealand look very cloudy in the next fifteen years, and insofar as growth based on the domestic market takes place, this is likely to run into balance of payments troubles as rising imports associated with domestic growth outstrip rather stagnant exports. Thorough planning would not alter the harsh economic realities, but it might make for more consistent solutions. Yet, what measure of control and state interference would be acceptable in this free enterprise society which also has had paternalist 'welfare' state legislation for many years?

The average New Zealander is well educated, resourceful, adaptable, able to acquire new skills rapidly and very mobile. He lacks some traditional skills and attitudes which are common in industrially advanced countries. New Zealand still has some of the characteristics of a 'pioneer' economy and New Zealanders retain some of the pioneer virtues such as self reliance, a willingness to tackle anything new, freedom from the handicaps of traditional ways of doing things and ingenuity in 'make do and mend'. These virtues are overlaid by the ideal of security typified by the welfare state. Curiously enough this characteristic also derives from pioneer days. The early settlers were not adventurous, but usually people of middle-class descent who were hoping to build up a new and secure life under conditions which were more favourable than they found at home. From the first they were accustomed to look to the settlement companies for guidance and later the provincial and central governments were regarded as instruments which they could use to obtain whatever economic benefits were available from state action. Today, if anything goes wrong, from floods and earthquakes to falling overseas prices, the general assumption is that the government should 'do something about it'. This was the basis of 'socialism without doctrines' of the nineteenth and early twentieth centuries.

The welfare state was, however, the work of the first Labour government which took office at the end of 1935. The depression was a tremendous blow to New Zealand. Export income fell from £56 million in 1928 to £35 million in 1931 and was not back to the 1928 figures until 1936. Unemployment rose from 3,400 registered unemployed in 1928 to a peak of 80,000 (about 16 per cent of the labour force) in 1933.

The watch words of the government were 'insulation' and 'security'. By this time the depression was nearly over, although recovery had been slow and incomplete. Government measures were therefore not designed to pull the economy out of a depression, but to try to ensure that the secondary effects should not occur again. Marketing of dairy products was taken over by the state. A guaranteed price (that is a fixed buying price) which would give the farmer a 'reasonable standard of life' was paid. The marketing of meat was taken over by a producers' board with government support and encouragement. Control of the foreign exchanges, including sterling, was put in the hands of the central bank and control of imports by licensing was introduced, primarily to protect the balance of payments. A thorough-going welfare state was set up internally with a national health service, universal pension without means test, children's allowances and other benefits. Control of prices introduced during the war was continued afterwards in a less widespread form.

The welfare state is now universally accepted as the basis of the economy in New Zealand and is not now a political issue. State and producers' board marketing of dairy produce and meat is not seriously challenged.

Import and exchange control (including transactions within the sterling area) have only occasionally been relaxed. Any relaxation has produced such heavy pressures on the exchange that control has had to be re-imposed in order to prevent sterling reserves from falling to very low levels.

An important characteristic of New Zealand society is a high degree of egalitarianism. There are few poor people and no very rich. What is more striking, however, is the narrow range of incomes among the middle class and the similarity of their way of life. This situation is partly due to legislation—high income tax and extensive social security benefits—but the legislation reflects a strong sense of the justice of equality. Along with this feeling, however, is what is perhaps a less desirable one and not conducive to economic progress and growth, that no one should be hurt by any economic change. In particular no one must suffer from unemployment.

A remarkable achievement of the post-war period has been the reduction of unemployment almost to vanishing point. The numbers of registered unemployed have only once exceeded an average of 1,000 in any year since 1952 and seasonal variations are quite small. These figures are in relation to a labour force of 800,000 to 900,000. The number of registrations certainly underestimates the extent of unemployed when the level of employment is high as most people changing jobs and young people not yet in their first job do not register. Nevertheless, unemployment has been at a very low level, however measured. Maintenance of employment at this level is now expected as a permanent feature of the economic situation and any government which allowed the unemployment rate to rise to as high as 1 per cent of the labour force would certainly be defeated in the next election.

The maintenance of such a low rate of unemployment does, however, mean a constant pressure of demand on supply. To maintain literal full employment we need 'overfull' employment, that is a permanent 'shortage of labour' with unfilled vacancies considerably in excess of unemployment. This 'economic miracle' has been achieved without excessive inflation and without heavy pressure on wages. Retail prices approximately doubled between 1945 and 1963 and in this period import prices increased by 75 per cent while export prices rather more than doubled. Award wages in real terms, on the base 1954 = 1,000, were 912 in 1946 and 1,005 at the end of 1963. Actual wages paid have tended to run ahead of award wages to a greater extent in recent years than in earlier ones, but the gap has not greatly widened.

Pressure of demand on supply occurs with full employment, not only with respect to internal resources, but also with respect to overseas funds. This is particularly so when local manufacture has a high import content. Exchange and import control can prevent exchange reserves from disappearing, but there is always political pressure to have import licences maintained or increased. As a reduction in imports can threaten unemployment in particular industries it is very difficult for a government to resist this pressure. It is possible that the excess of demand over the supply of foreign exchange would be less if the New Zealand pound were devalued. The usual argument against devaluation is that it would give temporary relief only as, under New Zealand conditions, wages and prices would quickly adjust themselves to new levels and excess demand would appear again. On the other hand devaluation would increase the gross return to farming and, depending on the elasticity of supply, this might encourage the production of further export goods which would relieve the overall position. The extent of the net return to farming would, of course, depend on the extent to which internal costs rose as the result of devaluation and the extent to which farmers were effected by higher internal costs. As farmers employ little labour and are not much affected directly by the cost of imported materials a higher net cash return might be available for a considerable time. Farmers would, of course, be affected as consumers by higher costs, but there would be a squeeze on land rents, or what is the New Zealand equivalent, interest on mortgages in real terms, at any rate in the short run.

It is probable that a free exchange rate would be more appropriate to New Zealand conditions. A fluctuating rate is likely to have a smaller effect on wage claims and it is possible that some of the economic rents now enjoyed by holders of import licences would be squeezed. Although New Zealand is now—since 1962—a member of the International Monetary Fund and to that extent is committed to fixed exchange rates, there is a strong body of opinion which opposes membership and if the advantages of a free exchange market were generally appreciated there would be no strong opposition to withdrawal unless welfare state policies led to persistent depreciation. As New Zealand is a price taker for her exports the level of exchange is of no significance to her customers. Exporters to New Zealand would, of course, be affected by flexible exchange rates, but if followed by a considerable relaxation of import and exchange control, they would probably be better off.

The effects of import licensing on economic development has probably been, on balance, unfavourable. It has been used as a method of protecting industry and an attempt has been made to favour those industries which have a high ratio of added value to imported materials and components. To a large extent, however, import licensing is based—as it must be—on 'past performance'. It would conceivably be possible to make the issue of a licence conditional on the attainment of some target of improvement in productivity or reduction in cost but, politically and administratively, it would be impossible. When licences are issued on a 'past performance' basis and when there is an excess demand for imports, the possession of an import licence practically guarantees a profit which the possessor has only to stay in business to enjoy. He has a valuable asset from which he can earn a rent and, if after the claims of the state and of established firms are met there are few funds available, there is not much risk from the competition of new firms. Although the effect of this system cannot easily be measured, it seems unlikely to encourage economic growth or improvements in productivity.

The growth of productivity has in fact been slow and New Zealand is well down in the international 'league tables' of recent years. The growth of net output per labour hour in manufacturing over the last decade has been 2·4 per cent per year. There has been a very wide range of productivity growth rates in particular industries. It is difficult to see from the data available any obvious relationships between slow or rapid growth and factors which might be thought likely to affect growth. Figures are not available for individual firms and industry figures hide the variations which may exist between firms. There is some evidence to suggest that firms which are subsidiaries of large overseas firms or which have acquired overseas technical advice and management methods have done best. The typically small New Zealand family firm has probably a slow rate of productivity growth. A number of the old-established localized industries show a decline in productivity.

Although slow productivity growth does not imply a low level of productivity it is likely that the two things are related. Manufacturing in New Zealand has had tariff protection for many years and protection through import control since before the war. The tariff wall does not, at first sight, appear very high, but in relation to added value it is in many cases of the order of 100 per cent to 200 per cent or more. Thus a tariff of 10 per cent on gross value becomes one of 100 per cent on added value if there is no tax on components for a product assembled in New Zealand and where added value is only 10 per cent of gross value.

To sum up the present economic situation of New Zealand, we may say that it is a country which by specialization according to comparative advantages and the good fortune to have had suitable markets available has done very well for itself. With the tariff of protection and import and exchange control a substantial structure of small scale industry has been built up. The basis of the economic philosophy of the country is the welfare state. There is no hesitation in using state powers for particular ends, but the economy is essentially a private enterprise one. Private enterprise has, however, been able to lead a quiet life and as well as receiving protection from the state, has protected itself by agreements on prices, markets and trade practices. Much of the 'enterprise' of recent years has been that of foreign firms who have established branches or subsidiaries in New Zealand.

The growth of the European Economic Community and the possibility that Britain might become a member has shown that the old pattern of specialization and the existing pattern of trade might not prevail in the future. There have been two reactions to this possibility. The first has been to look for an expansion of manufacturing at almost any cost so as to reduce dependence on imports. This is the original 'insulation' argument. Attempts to expand overseas markets for manufactured goods have also been made. New Zealand has a small trade in manufactured goods with the Pacific and exports a little machinery, mainly relating to agriculture, to other countries but total exports of manufactured goods amount to less than 3 per cent of all exports and even these have a considerable import content. The other reaction has been to look for new markets abroad and to encourage the exports of wool, paper and wood-pulp which appear to have an assured and even expanding market abroad.

It may be possible, of course, to develop both agriculture and industry. The question is how far the expansion of one is at the expense of the other. New Zealand farms are land-intensive, giving a high output per man, but a relatively low output per acre. A good deal of capital is used in the form of meat freezing works, butter and cheese factories, wool stores and transport, including ships to take the products to market. It seems likely that a large increase in capital used in agriculture would make it more difficult to invest industrial accumulations of capital in farming, but probably quite a lot has moved the other way in the form of profits on the sale of land being invested in industry. Land values have been moving steadily upwards since settlement began and land is freely bought and sold. There is, however, some evidence to suggest that farming capital in New Zealand is under-utilized and that an expansion of output of the order of 50 per cent could take place without a great deal of extra capital formation.

There seems little doubt that any substantial expansion of output would require at least a proportionate expansion of labour. There is little under-employment at present in agriculture and more intensive farming would require more labour. It would probably also be necessary to pay higher wages and to provide better housing, schools and other amenities. In all these things country workers are worse off than those in towns.

It appears then, that unless the overall rate of capital formation is increased, or the proportion taken by the state is reduced, there must be some choice between the expansion of farming and the expansion of industry at least in the long run. On the institutional side there appears to be room for large-scale farming by public companies which could raise capital funds from the public and make use of the best technical methods. There does not appear, however, to be any lack of people wishing to farm if one may judge from the prices paid for farming land. On current values a return of only 4 per cent seems to be sufficient to lead individuals to buy more land, a figure which would hardly attract funds into industry. There is the possibility, however, that a judgement of the position on the basis of land values is deceptive. Most land is bought by one farmer from another and provided the amount of finance grows in proportion land values can be at a high level without the fundamental profit position being affected.

One result of a search for new markets has been a revival of interest in the possibilities of a customs union with Australia. New Zealand buys from Australia about three times as much as she sells to Australia. The main imports are manufactured goods, steel, and motor-cars and the main exports are timber, wood-pulp and paper.

The principal advantage for New Zealand would be the opportunity to sell more butter. Although Australia is a butter exporter, costs of production on the average Australian farm are a good deal higher than they are in New Zealand. Production for export is maintained only by charging a higher price in the domestic market. New Zealand would benefit either from sales in the Australian market or by displacing Australian exports in the British market. In return Australia would have access to the New Zealand market for manufactured goods. There would, in consequence, no doubt be some displacement of New Zealand industries, but it might well take the form of larger factories established perhaps as branches of Australian firms displacing a number of small ones. New Zealand has some small but efficient light engineering industries which might well be most efficiently used in supplying components for motor vehicles and other industrial products in Australia rather than, as at present, being used to assemble imported components in New Zealand. As is usual in these circumstances agricultural commodities are the difficult ones and it appears unlikely that Australia will be prepared to sacrifice its less efficient dairy farmers in the interests of a customs union.

New Zealand has never had a full scale development plan but there is now some discussion on the feasibility of such a plan. It would, of course, be a 'target' plan as there is little likelihood of any change from a basically free enterprise economy despite the willingness to interfere for particular reasons. The initial element of such a plan would be some estimate of a feasible rate of growth depending on productivity growth and population growth and an assessment of how the import content of this rate of growth could be met, whether by increased exports or further import replacement or more use of local resources or more efficient use of imported materials. As suggested earlier the difficult period might be the next ten to twenty years. After that the basically strong position of New Zealand as a low cost food producer should enable her to maintain, or surpass, a standard of living as good as her present one. The growth of population will, in time, provide a larger internal market for industry and for the output of her farms and to that extent reduce her dependence on external trade.

The answer to a question asked at the beginning of this chapter appears to be in the affirmative. The present high degree of dependence on agriculture appears to be a temporary phase of development although exports of agricultural products are likely to be still of major importance in the next ten or twenty years at least. The rather slow, but steady growth of manufacturing is likely to expand

Q

at an accelerating pace if only because of a decline in the comparative advantage of agriculture. As agricultural production is basically land-intensive the proportion of the population engaged is likely to fall in the long run and employment will have to be found in industry and service occupations for most of the population. The long run prospects for agriculture, especially the production of meat, are good provided the world can in future afford to use land to produce meat. Agriculture is likely to keep up the national income to a high level even if manufacturing in the end displaces it from its predominant role in the country's economy. New Zealand is rapidly moving away from dependence on a single market. She must now look for sales to a wide range of countries. In doing so she will be moving much more into a world economy. Her interests will run parallel with those of most underdeveloped countries and she may expect to benefit from their growth. On the other hand, with a population growth of $2\frac{1}{2}$ per cent per annum, New Zealand's resources will have to be devoted to an increasing extent to providing for her own needs. This poses a dilemma. For a considerable time to come the internal market will be too small to make efficient manufacturing possible. Industries will for a long time still be largely dependent on imports of materials and components. To make these imports possible exports must expand in proportion to the growth in population and as a greater population will consume more meat, dairy produce and wool, to meet these two demands agricultural production must expand at an even faster rate. This may mean that some capital will have to be used for agricultural expansion rather than going to industry, but if industry cannot expand then either more manufactured goods will have to be imported or New Zealanders will have to reduce their own consumption of potential export goods. Probably both will happen. New Zealand is in effect, at an awkward stage of development. Although adjustments will have to be made at a much higher level of income her position is not so very different in principle from a country such as India which is also faced with the problem of at the same time increasing exports, expanding industry and feeding an increasing population.

In summary then, New Zealand provides an example of a high income 'export' economy with poor immediate prospects of achieving substantial economic growth because of limitations in the size of the markets confronting it. On the one hand, little growth in demand for its agricultural and pastoral exports can be expected from its traditional markets, so that it must wait on the success of growth plans elsewhere in the world for any sustained growth in demand for its own exports to emerge. On the other hand, the markets for its industrial products (largely domestic) are so small that available economies of scale have not been fully realized, thus putting its manufactured products at a cost disadvantage in unprotected third markets and discouraging further industrial expansion. Overall state planning, if acceptable politically, might help to remedy this by taking bigger risks than the private entrepreneur dare to break this vicious circle, but would perhaps do little to solve successfully the problems posed by the current awkward stage of her economic development except for imposing consistency of plans; 'target' or 'indicative' planning would contribute even less. New Zealand also provides an illustration of the importance of human capital and traditions in raising real income per head to a very high level on what is only moderately fertile land. For a near-empty land was peopled by British stock, already well-versed in farming techniques and mechanical skills, well-educated, with easy access to the London capital market, and not inhibited in their attitudes to growth by political, religious, or social dogmas.

CONCLUSION

We have now made a survey of the theoretical aspects of economic growth and have examined both the actual attainments and the plans made by a selection of rich and poor countries in their pursuit of greater wealth. What can be learned from all this?

The most obvious, and perhaps the most important, conclusion we have to draw is that economic growth is far too important an objective in itself to be left to the decentralized decisions of a large number of economic subjects operating through the complex of markets which we describe as a system of free enterprise. There is no evidence that the desire of a society for certain social ends will be attained by each individual in that society pursuing his own self-interest, however enlightened that self-interest might be. There is no guarantee, or even great expectation, that the socially desired rate of economic growth, level of employment, or pattern of production will be secured unless quite positive action is taken by the state to attain them.

In coming to such a conclusion we recognize that value judgements on what is socially desirable have to be identified before any economic policy can be determined and we realize too that value elements are inextricably involved in what at first might appear to be purely economic alternatives. Self-sufficiency or industrialization might be objectives which give satisfaction in themselves quite apart from the economic ends they serve or prohibit; the choice of such policies is then an expression of social values and not merely an economic decision. The path taken by the economy is determined by decisions which are based on a complex of social values and economic expediency, and whatever may be the virtue of *laissez faire* in securing the maximum economic advantage, governmental intervention is essential if full weight is to be given to the social values.

But there are other grounds also for government intervention, or planning as we prefer to call it, which are purely economic, stemming from the failures of a capitalist economy to secure the maximum advantage from existing and potential resources. Fluctuations in economic activity, for instance, seem to be inevitable unless some form of government control of the economy is adopted. Such fluctuations can result in periods when there is no economic growth at all or even a fall in the real national product. Other phases of the cycle characterized by inflation can disrupt the price mechanism and allow serious mis-allocation of resources.

Another characteristic of free-enterprise is its failure to create an infrastructure adequate to support the optimum use of resources by the free enterprise system itself. Some governmental planning, to provide education, communications, adequate nutrition and welfare services generally to ensure an efficient labour force, is essential to any effective economic system.

Since social benefit is not always equated with private benefit there is here yet another ground for government action to ensure that the society as a whole, and not merely a limited group of private interests within it, is achieving the optimum. Failure to allow for external economies and diseconomies is not necessarily due to ignorance on the part of private entrepreneurs; it can be to their benefit, or at least not to their detriment, to ignore them, and their society is the loser. Moreover, there are powerful vested interests in the profit to be made from restriction and it is probably true that on the whole these are stronger than the vested interests which gain from rapid economic growth. If this is so it is necessary for the state to redress the balance by curbing the forces of restriction such as are displayed by some monopolistic private enterprises and in the labour market.

Saving and investment have been given a great deal of attention in this study, for they are critical determinants of economic growth. Here again we have seen that planning by the state is essential if the economy is to follow the optimum path of growth. Without planning of some kind there is virtually no hope that in a wealthy country such as Britain private investment decisions will take up the full flow of voluntary savings at all times. Even with planning it is difficult enough, and bad planning can make the situation worse. Moreover, when voluntary saving is inadequate to provide the investment necessary to the social optimum then more state intervention is imperative. Indeed, this latter situation is axiomatic for the poor countries. Their rate of voluntary saving is so low, and entrepreneural ability to create new investment so deficient, that in the absence of state intervention the most that one can hope for is that the growth of the national product will keep up with the increasing numbers of the population.

In sparsely peopled areas such as tropical Africa it is possible that the expanding population can move into the relatively empty areas where subsistence agriculture can maintain the existing standards so that income per head does not fall. But in the densely populated and poor areas of Asia, no such relief is possible. Already the land is fully cultivated to its primitive food-producing capacity. Labour has virtually a zero marginal productivity. Without irrigation there is no more land to be cultivated and without a social revolution no new methods can increase the output per head of the land already cultivated. Saving and investment by government action of some kind is the only way by which the constraint imposed by lack of capital can be relieved.

Unfortunately even such state action carried out with determination is most unlikely to meet the need for additional investment if the rate of economic growth is to be high enough to raise living standards at even a modest pace, let alone that which impatient Asians and Africans expect from their newly gained independence and the influence of the Western demonstration effect. Internal sources of capital in the poor countries might be made adequate if their governments were ruthless enough to keep a large proportion of the population below subsistence level for a long period. But such a solution, even though it has been an historical experience, cannot today be a consciously adopted policy. If adequate capital cannot be secured from a country's own economic surplus after meeting minimum subsistence requirements, then it has to be obtained from external sources. The rich countries find themselves having to provide the capital not only for their own growth but for that of the poor countries too.

The wealthy countries can possibly accept this as ultimately contributing to their own long-term growth for it is clear that trade and international specialization is growing more rapidly between the industrialized nations themselves than between the primary producers and the industrialized nations. Thus the industrialization of the poor countries and the consequent rise in their income per head should ultimately provide markets for the already rich countries, so contributing to their growth. But meanwhile the transfer of capital does put a strain upon the balances of payments, as we have seen from these studies of Britain, India and Ghana. A surge in imports inevitably accompanies a change of gear to faster growth and if capital transfers are being made at the same time by the rich countries, the strain on international reserves might well force the rich country both to slow down its growth and restrict its overseas loans and grants. Both India and Ghana, among the countries studied here, have development plans heavily dependent on overseas aid, yet the balance of payments crisis generated by the British move from a rate of growth of $2\frac{1}{2}$ per cent per annum to 4 per cent per annum has led the British Government to announce that the 1964 level of aid of some £180 million a year is the ceiling and that she cannot contemplate going beyond it.

The larger developing countries have for the most part now reached the stage in their planning when they can make comprehensive plans for the whole economy with considerable regard for balanced growth. The old method of the shopping list of projects, compiled from the programmes of the various government departments, has been abandoned and it is only the very small countries such as Sierra Leone which still have inadequate statistical material, and perhaps also administrative expertise, to make comprehensive plans.

Plans provide for internal consistency, anticipate constraints which might not otherwise have been foreseen, reduce uncertainty to a minimum, increase the numeracy of the estimates upon which action has to be taken, and guide the production lines to bring them as near as possible to the desired pattern. But a plan does not of itself guarantee growth. This is another important conclusion underlined by these studies.

Implementation of the plan is the crucial problem. For this to be effective it is possible that the first phase of many in the multiphase process has to be a re-orientation of social attitudes and a re-shaping of the social structure itself. The acceptance of state interference in the economic system, the willingness to pay taxes honourably, the reform of land tenure, the limitation of the obligations to the extended family, the release from social obligations to mark marriages, births and deaths by conspicuous consumption or to observe rigidly the customs of caste and class which inhibit the efficient functioning of the economy: these are some of the social changes pre-requisite to the implementation of many national economic plans. They are illustrated by the studies of the poorer nations rather than by the richer, because the latter have already taken off into self-sustaining growth, even though the rate is disappointingly low, and so must already have adapted their social attitudes and structures.

Following the social revolution, or simultaneous with it, there is the necessity for the administrative revolution. Most countries in the early stages of economic growth do not have administrations competent to create a structure within which an enterprise system and a price mechanism can work efficiently. Britain was no exception, but today it is countries like India which are faced with inefficient administration in an acute form. This is perhaps one way in which the small countries have an advantage over the larger ones: Ghana, for instance, has produced an efficient administration with little difficulty and in a very short time.

The major conclusion to be drawn especially from the study of rich economies such as that of Britain is probably not the crucial importance of imports and the balance of payments, for difficulties with the foreign trade sector of the economy are common to rich and poor alike. It is the danger the rich countries run that they will fail to recognize that regional stagnation is not incompatible with rapid economic growth of the economy as a whole. Unless the planners take particular account of the regional difficulties and plan for regional growth, there can be persistently high unemployment, declining industry, and continuing social deterioration in one part of the country, while another part, suffering from over-full employment, industrial congestion and serious housing shortage, yet sets a pace which makes the aggregate rate of growth for the whole country an apparently satisfactory one.

The contrast between Sierra Leone and New Zealand, each with a population of about $2\frac{1}{2}$ million, inevitably poses the question why some small economies are viable and have achieved high standards of living, while others have so far failed to rise much above subsistence level. Clearly New Zealand's success cannot be attributed to its being an empty land, for Sierra Leone has always been sparsely populated too. Much more probably, the difference can be attributed to the pioneering spirit, the ready acceptance of innovation, the skills in techniques of high productivity and the capital which the New Zealand settlers took with them to their empty lands. Moreover, New Zealand, from the beginning of its modern phase, has had both ready access to overseas capital markets and also institutions which could make the most of it. Sierra Leone illustrates the constraint imposed upon a small economy by a traditional society of rigid institutional framework, with its people lacking the endowments of British migrants born and brought up in an industrial society, and as yet having discovered no will to economize.

With all New Zealand's success in achieving a high per capita income, it is nevertheless clear from this study that the smallness of her home market impels her to look to overseas demand for her special products if she is to continue her economic growth. For Sierra Leone further growth is equally dependent on larger markets whether overseas or within the continent of Africa. In Ghana too, growth could be encouraged if she were able to become a part of a larger pan-African customs union or common market of some kind. The viability of the smaller emergent African states is probably as dependent on such a development as on any single other factor, for the access to new capital is greatly improved and the incentives to creating productive capacity strengthened when the demand for the country's products is more assured.

But here the experience of Britain and the study of her regional development becomes relevant once more. If some parts of Britain within this particular free trade area could remain backward in their development or become depressed after a period of prosperity, then we must expect that in African or Asian free trade areas some parts might remain backward or become depressed unless plans are made and deliberately implemented to ensure growth not only in aggregate but also in the individual countries and regions. The political complexities of such a policy are sufficient to discourage any expectation of a rapid advance in this direction. National solutions have still to be sought even though we hope for major advances in the emergence of some supra-national authorities which might implement planning on an international scale.

This, the need for international thinking and action, shall be the last conclusion to be drawn from these studies. Not only the rich nations but the poor ones also depend for their more rapid growth on major improvements in international co-operation. The serious deficiencies in international liquidity cry out for more effective planning of credit for rich and poor alike. World markets with more stable prices for the major primary products could reduce uncertainty for buyers and sellers and allow the poorer nations to make their plans for growth with some assurance that serious adverse movements in the terms of trade would not inhibit their implementation. The need for a much increased flow of capital from the industrialized nations to the developing nations has already been stressed. And finally we might add that if international agreement could relieve the nations of the burden of armaments, the consequent release of resources for the encouragement of economic growth would be a major contribution to the future of mankind.

APPENDIX

World Population Trends

by FREDA CONWAY

1. Introduction

The population of the world is now more than three thousand million persons and it has been estimated that this number will increase to six or seven thousand million by the end of the century. These are large numbers. Can the world support so many people? Will there be sufficient food and other material resources to meet their needs? Certainly this increase in the number of human beings will only be possible if the economies of many countries can be developed, to match their growth in population. And if it does come about, an increase of this size will in itself have important economic and social consequences for all the world.

The questions which are being asked today about the world population were being asked in England towards the end of the eighteenth century. At that time, the population of England[1] was less than 8 million, but it was increasing rapidly. Many of the people were living in poverty and it seemed reasonable to assume that if the population were to continue to increase at the same rate, poverty would become even more widespread and many would die of famine and disease. The theories concerning the dangers of over-population which were current at that time are generally associated with the name of Thomas Malthus. Of course, Malthus was proved wrong as far as England was concerned. Today the country supports six times as many people as there were in 1801 when the first English census was taken and they have a higher standard of living than Malthus could have imagined. But not all countries have been so fortunate.

The Malthusian theories proved relevant for Ireland. At the beginning of the nineteenth century, the Irish population was about half that of the English and it was growing at about the same rate. But food shortages and famines reduced the rate of increase of the Irish population, and after the potato famine of 1846 the population actually declined. Today the Irish[2] population is less than it was at the beginning of the last century and is now less than one-tenth that of England; for many years its population has been more or less stationary owing to continued migration from the country.

England was able to develop industries and expand her population, but Ireland did neither. This was partly because England had greater natural resources than her neighbour: she had the coal and iron needed

[1] All statistics quoted for England, relate to England and Wales taken together.
[2] Eire and Northern Ireland.

for the new industries, whereas Ireland lacked both these raw materials. The social and political conditions in England were also more favourable to new developments. England was Protestant and progressive whereas Ireland was largely Catholic and conservative. Ireland lacked an educated

Diagram 2. Annual Rates of Increase and Time Taken to Double Population

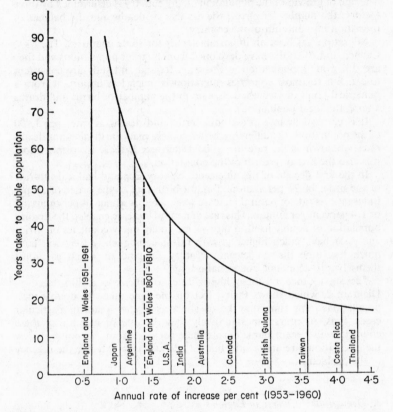

Source: UN Demographic Year Books.
Note: It is most unlikely that the rate of increase of these countries will remain stable for the time necessary to double their populations.

middle class which provided many of the industrial leaders for England. Also Ireland was to some extent exploited by absentee landlords in England, and this factor hindered industrial development, since the English landlords wished to maintain the rural character of the country.

Though it is useful to consider the experience of both England and Ireland the problems facing many countries today differ in important respects from those facing England and Ireland at the beginning of the nineteenth century. Of these differences, perhaps the most important is the rate at which population changes are taking place.

2. Rates and Change

The rate of growth of the population of any country is determined by three factors: the number of births, the number of deaths and the balance of migration into and out of the country.

Migration has been an important factor for some countries. The USA, Canada and Australia have developed from migrant populations and they are still gaining population in this way. Ireland and Italy are consistent losers. But for most countries migration is much less important from a numerical point of view than changes in the number of births and deaths among the local populations.

It is convenient to express both births and deaths as rates per 1,000 of the population: the difference between these crude birth-rates and death-rates is known as the rate of national increase. If there is no migration, it is also the rate of growth of the population.

In the first decade of the nineteenth century England had a death-rate of the order of 24 per thousand and a birth-rate of the order of 38 per thousand: its rate of natural increase was therefore about 14 per thousand or 1·4 per cent per annum. This rate of natural increase enabled the English population to double itself in fifty years. Today many countries of Africa and Asia have much higher growth rates; consequently they will have much less time than nineteenth century England in which to adjust themselves to economic and social change.

The significance of these higher rates of increase is illustrated in Diagram 2, which shows their effect on the time taken to double their populations: this time may be as short as twenty years in particular cases. It is, of course, most unlikely that the rate of increase of these countries will remain stable during these periods: from this point of view the calculations are unrealistic, but they do at least emphasize the urgency of the problem.

3. Demographic Change in England

Birth-rates and death-rates are influenced by two sets of factors: demographic factors such as the age-sex composition of the population, and social and economic factors such as urbanization and improved standards of living. These are long-term factors; wars, economic depressions and natural disasters produce short-term fluctuations which may be very large, but are of relatively less importance.

The way in which these various factors act can be illustrated by a brief account of English demographic history since 1801.

In 1801, the population of England was nearly 9 million and it has increased continuously since that date. The 1961 Census recorded a population of 46 million. But the rate of increase has varied considerably in this period: it was greater in the first half of the nineteenth century than in the second, greater in the last century than in this century.

These changes in the rate of growth were due to changes in both the birth-rate and the death-rate. In 1801, both rates were relatively high, about 38 and 24 per thousand respectively, and they remained fairly stable for the next forty years. By the end of the nineteenth century, however, both the birth-rate and the death-rate had declined, and this decline continued in the first three decades of this century. At the same time the difference between these rates has been reduced and in the 1930's the rate of natural increase reached its minimum—about 0·3 per cent per annum. The gap between the rates has widened slightly since then, mainly because of an increase in the birth-rate and the present rate of natural increase is about one half of 1 per cent per annum.

The fall in the death-rate during the nineteenth and early twentieth centuries was due to three factors, though they were not necessarily equally important. They were: improved sanitation, medicine and a generally rising standard of living. But this fall could not continue indefinitely. Changes in the rate of growth of a population naturally affect its age-structure and this in turn affects its rate of growth. By the 1930's, the population contained a fair proportion of older people and this accounted for a slight increase in the death-rate in that decade.

Population pyramids or profiles can be used to illustrate the age-composition of a population. They consist of a series of rectangles one above the other, whose lengths represent the number or proportion of persons in a particular age-group.

The population of England in the first half of the last century was a young population with a moderate rate of increase. Each age-group was more numerous than the next older group, partly because more children were born each year and partly because the relatively high death-rates reduced the number of survivors. The pyramid for 1841, the first year for which the age-distribution is known, suggests a triangle. Reductions in both the birth-rate and the death-rate tend to reduce the differences between numbers in adjacent age-groups. The pyramid for 1901 represents one stage in this development.

Although the birth-rate was falling during the years 1871–1901, the number of births continued to increase, but after 1905, the continued fall in the birth-rate meant a smaller number of births. The shape of the population pyramid changed again. The 1931 pyramid showed a bulge for the 20–30 age group, since the number of births was a maximum in the decade 1901–1911.

The increase in the birth-rate in the 1940's and 1950's produces a rather square effect for the pyramid of 1961.

It is more difficult to explain changes in birth-rates than changes in death-rates since they show greater year to year variations.

Wars and adverse economic conditions can have a greater effect on birth-rates than death-rates: both can cause people to postpone marrying and raising a family. In this century there have been two wars and serious unemployment: there have also been large fluctuations in the birth-rate. Some of the births postponed by war and unemployment were made up later when the war was over and economic conditions improved. For the study of long term trends it is, therefore, better to use a measure of family size than a measure of the births in a particular year or years.

Average family size is defined as the number of children born to couples who were married in a particular interval of time. Though it is a simple enough concept, it is not easy to measure. For the first half of the nineteenth century the necessary statistics are not available: and the ultimate size of family for recently married couples is not yet known.

The average number of children per family seems to have declined steadily from a little more than six (6·16) in 1861–69 to a little more than two (2·09) in 1930. The long term trend to a lower birth-rate which was characteristic of these years reflects this decline in family size, although the number of adults and consequently the number of families was increasing in this period.

The low birth-rates of the 1930's were only partly due to the decline in family size. The economic depression of the first few years of this decade caused many marriages to be postponed: also the sex-ratio amongst adults was conducive to relatively low marriage rates among women. Some of the births postponed in the 1930's were made up in the 1940's and contributed to the high birth-rates of the late 1940's, though these were also affected by war and economic prosperity. Economic prosperity has continued into the 1960's, the trend to younger marriages has also continued and the birth-rate is nearly as high now as it was at the beginning of the century. Since 1940, the average size of family has increased slightly: the trend to smaller families has been arrested and may even have been reversed.

Many social and economic factors encouraged the trend to smaller families in the seventy years before 1930. In the early years of the industrial revolution children became wage-earners at an early age. At that time a large family meant a larger family income. Also, since infant mortality was high, parents needed a large family if they were to ensure that some of their children would survive to care for them in their old age. But the Factory Acts which were passed in the middle of the nineteenth century restricted the employment of children. Compulsory education was introduced in 1876. Both of these changes increased the cost of bringing up a family. Rising standards of living and better facilities for education have further increased the cost of children in the twentieth century. In this century too, there have been many opportunities for women to obtain employment outside the home and most women find a job and a large family incompatible. As infant mortality fell, children had a better chance of living to be adults: fewer births were necessary to ensure survival of the family.

Industrialization has also meant urbanization, and in most countries urban birth-rates are lower than rural birth-rates. At the 1851 census 50 per cent of the English population was enumerated in urban areas and this proportion had risen to 80 per cent by the 1931 census.

In England as in most European countries, the birth-rate declined because people were limiting the size of their families in response to social and economic pressures and opportunities. Parents wanted smaller families.

4. *A Pattern of Demographic Development*

The demographic history of England has been similar to that of other Western European countries. Their study suggests a fairly simple pattern of demographic development. In the first stage, high death-rates are associated with high birth-rates, both of the order of say 40 per thousand. Both rates are subject to large annual variations, and the population can only increase slowly. In the second stage, birth-rates and death-rates decline, but death-rates usually decline more rapidly than birth-rates and the population increases rapidly. In the third stage birth-rates and death-rates stabilize at a much lower level, say around 15 or 12 per thousand. Again annual variations are important, and the rate of increase is slow.

For England, the second stage was begun before 1801: and the third stage was reached in the late 1920's.

Today the majority of countries are still in the first stage or the early part of the second stage. Even if they follow the European pattern they will experience large increases in population before stabilizing in the third stage. But the transition through the second stage is by no means automatic and the third stage may not be the final stage.

Ceylon is typical of many countries in the early part of the second stage. Within recent years its death-rate has been reduced considerably, but its birth-rate has shown little tendency to fall. The birth-rate is high, about 37 per thousand; the death-rate is low, about 10 per thousand: consequently the rate of natural increase is 2·7 per cent per annum—a rate which could involve doubling the population in about twenty-five years.

The only Asian country which has a birth-rate comparable with those of Western European countries is Japan. Today average family size in Japan is 2·5 children per married couple compared with 2·2 for England. Since, however, the population of Japan is much younger than that of England, her death-rate is low and her rate of natural increase about 1·0 per cent per annum, or half as much again as the English rate.

Though the fall in the Japanese birth-rate that has occurred since 1947 has been to some extent offset by the fall in the death-rate, the rate of natural increase has been halved since that year. Even so the total population of Japan is expected to increase from 89 million in 1955 to 116 million in 1975—an increase of 30 per cent in twenty years.

In England and other European countries birth-rates have risen in recent years. As explained in the last section some of the causes of these increases are temporary; nevertheless the trend to smaller families has been arrested. It is probably too soon to determine the effect of continued economic prosperity on the age of marriage and the effect of both on ultimate family size: it is, however, virtually certain that total population will continue to increase beyond the end of the present century.

For the world as a whole, birth-rates are not falling, and the population increase within the twenty year period, 1955–75, may well be as much as 40 per cent. For a few countries, the expected increases in population may be welcome, but many governments will be forced to consider policies of population control.

5. *Population Control*

There have been many occasions on which individual countries have attempted to control the growth of their populations. Various methods have been used or advocated. They include infanticide, abortion, steriliza-tion, contraception, abstinence and later marriage. Some of these methods must always be repugnant to civilized peoples. But even if scientific research can devise generally acceptable methods of family limitation, a policy of population control can only be successful in the long run, if social and economic conditions lead parents to prefer few children to many.

The trend to smaller families in England and other countries of Western Europe took place in a period during which the knowledge and use of contraceptives was much less widespread than it is today, when this trend is being reversed.

Within recent years, two important countries have succeeded in re-ducing their birth-rates to levels comparable with those current in Western Europe. They are Russia and Japan, and although their political systems are very different, their methods of population control have had several common features. Both countries used abortion as a major means of limiting the birth-rate in the first instance, but in both countries this practice is being abandoned.

Industrialization has involved the concentration of the population in towns, and provided work for women outside their homes. Standards of living have been rising, though the governments of both Russia and Japan have been able to limit the increases in consumption and to expand capital equipment. Both countries have developed educational systems: better educated people are needed for the new industries, but the provision of education adds to the cost of bringing up children, and parents then consider how many children they can afford.

In both countries the patterns of family life have changed and are chang-ing. In Japan the extended family system is giving way to the small family system in which the household consists of parents and children only. In Russia the collectivization of the farms, and the mass movements of population which occurred in the early years of the revolution disrupted family life, and made changes inevitable. Although the average size of family has declined and is declining in these countries, the number of families, like the number of young adults, is increasing and their total populations must be expected to continue to increase for the rest of the century, though not necessarily at their present rates.

Russia belongs to both Europe and Asia, and Japan is not typical of Asia. Nevertheless, their experience, like that of England a century earlier, is worth studying.

6. Geographical Distribution of Population

The expected growth of population will not affect all countries equally and consequently there will be some changes in the geographical distribution of the population. By the end of the century, Asia will contain a larger proportion and Europe a smaller proportion of the world's people than they do today. Latin America's population, though it is relatively small, is growing and is likely to grow more rapidly than that of the other continents.

TABLE A.1

ESTIMATED WORLD POPULATION, 1650–2000

| | | | | Millions | |
Continent	1650	1800	1900	1950	2000
Europe	100	187	401	574	947
North America	1	6	81	168	312
Latin America	12	19	63	163	592
Oceania	2	2	6	13	29
Africa	100	90	120	199	517
Asia	330	602	937	1,380	3,870
Total	545	906	1,608	2,497	6,267

Sources: Carr-Saunders, *World Population*. United Nations, *The Future Growth of World Population*, 1958.

Estimates of the population for continents at a number of dates are given in Table A.1. Those for the year 2000 are, of course, projections. They have been made by United Nations demographers, and are based on assumptions concerning future trends in birth-rates and death-rates which may or may not be realized.

In all these years Asia has contained more than half of the world's population, and it is interesting to note that the estimated proportion for the year 2000 is not very different from that of the estimated proportion for 1650 and is less than that for the year 1800.

7. Population and Economic Growth

If countries have plenty of unused resources, increases of population present no problem, and by providing both additional manpower and larger markets, population growth may be an aid to economic development. The USA and the Soviet Union appear to be in this position today. Both occupy large areas of fertile land, which were almost uninhabited

R

300 years ago and both have large and diverse fuel and mineral resources. Both are in some sense underdeveloped countries which can accommodate considerable increases in population. Density figures may be misleading, but it is worth noting that in 1950 North America and Russia had densities of only 8 persons per square kilometre compared with 28 for the world as a whole and 79 for Europe.

The favourable position of the Soviet Union and the USA can be contrasted with the obvious difficulties facing Asian countries such as Ceylon and India. These countries have developed from ancient civilizations: their populations have supported themselves for many centuries by the intensive cultivation of the land and today they are densely populated. In 1950 the population densities for Ceylon and India were 151 and 138 persons per square kilometre respectively, and a high proportion of their economically active population is engaged directly in agriculture. (See Table A.2.) Compared with Europe and North America, these countries have little manufacturing industry and their standard of living is low. It has been estimated that although Asia contained 53 per cent of the world population in 1955, it produced only 12 per cent of the world domestic product.[1] But these are countries which expect large increases in population in the near future.

TABLE A.2

ECONOMICALLY ACTIVE POPULATIONS, SELECTED COUNTRIES

Country	Year	As percentage total population	Percentage engaged in Agriculture	Manufacturing	Other
UK	1959	46	4	47	49
USA	1959	41	12	33	55
Japan	1959	49	36	25	39
India	1951	39	71	10	19
Ceylon	1953	37	53	12	35

Source: ILO, *Year Book of Manpower Statistics*.
Notes: Agriculture includes fishing and hunting. Manufacturing includes construction.

For such countries, the solution of their population problems must depend on a reduction in the rate of natural increase, an increased productivity through industrialization and an improved agriculture. These solutions are not independent: once these processes have been initiated they can help each other, but the present high rate of population growth in many countries adds to their economic difficulties.

Standards of living can only be raised if the gross national product is increasing faster than the population. Rates of natural increase of 2 per cent or more present serious difficulties for poor countries which need to add to their capital equipment as well as raise the level of consumption.

[1] Sir John Crawford: 'Problems of International Trade in Primary Products', *Progress*, 1, 1964.

On the other hand policies of family limitation or population control are more likely to be successful if standards of living are rising than if they are falling, since under such circumstances parents' desires to do well for their children encourage them to prefer a few children to many. Rapidly growing populations are generally young populations, with a relatively high proportion of children, and a relatively low proportion of persons of working age. In such populations, the number of dependents per worker tends to be high, and is a factor depressing the standard of living.

The proportion of the population engaged in economic activity depends on both the age-sex composition of the population and its economic and social organization. For the world as a whole it is estimated that 42 per cent of the population aged 15 or more are so engaged, but this proportion varies greatly between different regions. In Europe it is 45 per cent, in

TABLE A.3

AGE-DISTRIBUTION OF POPULATION, SELECTED COUNTRIES

Country	Year	Percentage of population in age-groups		
		Under 15	15–65	65 and over
England	1901	36	59	5
	1931	24	69	7
	1951	22	67	11
USA	1960	31	60	9
Japan	1950	35	60	5
	1959	30	64	6
India	1951	38	58	4
Ceylon	1955	41	57	2

Source: UN, *Demographic Year Book.*

South America 35 per cent. The rates for men and women follow different patterns; in Europe, 64 per cent of the males and 28 per cent of the females are economically active, but for Brazil the corresponding proportions are 91 and 15 and for Japan they are 85 and 50.

As populations increase, there is generally an increase in the number of both workers and dependents, but these two groups do not necessarily grow at the same rate. Population growth which is due mainly to a fall in mortality has little effect on the proportion of persons of working age. Such changes enable more children to survive infancy and reach adulthood, and more adults to live to an old age and become dependent. On the other hand a reduction in family size increases the proportion of persons of working age and this in turn can lead to a higher standard of living. England benefited from this aspect of demographic change in the early years of this century; the proportion of the population in the working age groups increased from 59 to 69 per cent in the years 1901 to 1931. At the present time Japan is benefiting in this same way.

For the world as a whole, and for many of the countries with the most serious population problems, current fertility and mortality rates are such

R*

that an increase in population is likely to reduce the proportion of persons of working age. The changing demographic situation cannot aid economic development in the near future.

8. *How Many People?*

There is no single answer to the question: how many people can the world support? This must depend on the standard and pattern of living which they are prepared to accept and their technical ability to make use of the world's resources. The size of a population is limited by its ability to satisfy its material needs: but some ways of satisfying these needs are more efficient than others, and the discoveries which enable man to make use of land and materials which were previously useless, also make it possible for more people to live in the world and enjoy a higher standard of living.

Man has lived on this planet for at least 200,000 years, but for most of this period his chief occupations were hunting and fishing. These require a great deal of space, and much of the earth's surface is too barren to support this type of life. It is very unlikely that the world could have supported a population of more than 10 million in this way.

The development of farming enabled men to live in communities, and the establishment of trade and commerce made possible the development of towns and cities. Precise information concerning the size of cities has only been available since governments have made regular censuses of population; nevertheless some information is available concerning the major towns in various centuries.

The towns of the ancient Greek civilization were relatively small: a few may have had 10,000 citizens but this would have been a large number. By the Middle Ages, a few towns had passed the 100,000 mark. Venice, Milan and Paris had grown to this size before the end of the thirteenth century, but even in 1600 only six of the European capital cities had achieved populations of this size. The Industrial Revolution made possible and necessary the development of more and larger cities. By 1830 the number of capital cities in the 100,000 class had increased to eighteen. In this century the major towns have become conurbations; in 1951 there were eight European cities with more than 1 million inhabitants. The population of London is now more than 8 million, but it is not the largest city in the world.

Today world population is more than 3,000 million: it has doubled itself in the last seventy years and may double itself again in the next thirty-five years. Though there is room for doubt concerning the likely rate of increase during the remaining years of this century, there can be no doubt whatever that unless there is some major catastrophe, world population will certainly increase very considerably.

What sort of a world will be required to house all these people? What sort of lives can they hope to lead? Certainly the accommodation of these extra millions presents serious social and economic problems. New or changed patterns of living will be needed in many countries, and the faster the rate of increase the less time there will be in which to make the necessary adjustments.

These problems are most serious for those countries where the chief difficulties today are poverty and limited resources and where populations are increasing rapidly. Many of the countries of Asia and South America come into this category. The reduction of poverty must involve improvements in agriculture, further industrialization and urbanization, better education and smaller families: but these remedies add up to a social revolution which these same countries may not yet desire and for which they may not yet be ready.

SELECTED READING LIST

AGARWALA, A. N. and SINGH, S. P. (eds.), *The Economics of Underdevelopment*, India, Oxford University Press, 1958.

BAUER, P. T., *West African Trade*, London, Routledge, 1963.

BENHAM, F., *Economic Aid to Underdeveloped Countries*, Oxford University Press, 1961.

COX-GEORGE, N. A., *Finance and Development in West Africa*, London, Dobson, 1961.

GHANA GOVERNMENT, *The Seven-year Development Plan 1963/4 to 1969/70*, 1964.

HIRSCHMAN, A. O., *The Strategy of Economic Development*, Yale University Press: Oxford University Press, 1958.

ISARD, W. and CUMBERLAND, J. H. (eds.), *Regional Economic Planning: Techniques of Analysis for Less Developed Areas*, Paris, Organisation for European Economic Co-operation, 1961.

LITTLE, I. M. D. and CLIFFORD, J., *International Aid*, London, Allen & Unwin, 1965.

LEWIS, J. P., *Quiet Crisis in India*, Washington, Brookings Institution, 1962.

LEWIS, W. A., *The Theory of Economic Growth*, London, Allen & Unwin, 1955.

MALENBAUM, W., *Prospects for Indian Development*, London, Allen & Unwin, 1962.

MATTHEWS, R. C. O., *The Trade Cycle*, London, Nisbet, 1959.

MEIER, G. M. and BALDWIN, R. E., *Economic Development*, New York and London, Wiley, 1957.

MYRDAL, G., *Economic Theory and Underdeveloped Regions*, London, Duckworth, 1957.

NEDC, *Growth of the United Kingdom to 1966*, 1963.
Export Trends, 1963.
Conditions Favourable to Faster Growth, 1963.
The Growth of the Economy, 1964.

NURKSE, R., *Problems of Capital Formation in Underdeveloped Countries*, Oxford, Blackwell, 1953.

POLITICAL and ECONOMIC PLANNING, 'The Location of Industry,' *Planning*, October 29, 1962.

PREST, A. R., *Public Finance in Underdeveloped Countries*, London, Weidenfeld & Nicolson, 1962.

REDDAWAY, W. B., *The Development of the Indian Economy*, London, Allen & Unwin, 1962.

ROSTOW, W. W., *The Stages of Economic Growth*, Cambridge University Press, 1960.

SIMKIN, C. G. F., *The Instability of a Dependent Economy*, Oxford University Press, 1951.

UNITED NATIONS, *Consequences and Determinants of Population Trends*, 1953.

WESTRATE, C., *Portrait of a Modern Mixed Economy: New Zealand*, Cambridge University Press, 1959.

WORSWICK, G. N. D. and ADY, P., *The British Economy in the 1950's*, Oxford University Press, 1962.

For thorough annotated lists of books and articles see:

HAZLEWOOD, A. (ed.), *The Economics of 'Underdeveloped' Areas*, Oxford University Press, 1959.

The Economics of Development, Oxford University Press, 1964.

INDEX

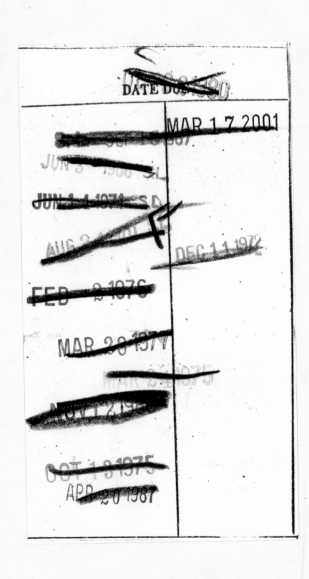